YOUNG PEOPLE IN R

Young People in Risk Society
The Restructuring of Youth Identities
and Transitions in Late Modernity

Edited by

MARK CIESLIK
University of Teesside, UK

GARY POLLOCK
Manchester Metropolitan University, UK

LONDON AND NEW YORK

First published 2002 by Ashgate Publishing

Reissued 2018 by Routledge
2 Park Square, Milton Park, Abingdon, Oxon OX14 4RN
711 Third Avenue, New York, NY 10017, USA

Routledge is an imprint of the Taylor & Francis Group, an informa business

Copyright © Mark Cieslik and Gary Pollock 2002

The editors have asserted their moral rights under the Copyright, Designs and Patents Act, 1988, to be identified as the editors of this work.

All rights reserved. No part of this book may be reprinted or reproduced or utilised in any form or by any electronic, mechanical, or other means, now known or hereafter invented, including photocopying and recording, or in any information storage or retrieval system, without permission in writing from the publishers.

Notice:
Product or corporate names may be trademarks or registered trademarks, and are used only for identification and explanation without intent to infringe.

Publisher's Note
The publisher has gone to great lengths to ensure the quality of this reprint but points out that some imperfections in the original copies may be apparent.

Disclaimer
The publisher has made every effort to trace copyright holders and welcomes correspondence from those they have been unable to contact.

A Library of Congress record exists under LC control number: 2001098446

ISBN 13: 978-1-138-73033-5 (hbk)
ISBN 13: 978-1-138-73028-1 (pbk)
ISBN 13: 978-1-315-18946-8 (ebk)

 Printed in the United Kingdom by Henry Ling Limited

Contents

List of Contributors   vi
Acknowledgements   ix

1. Introduction: Studying Young People in Late Modernity
   Mark Cieslik and Gary Pollock   1

2. Young Offenders, Risk and Personal Development Programmes
   Geoff Nichols   22

3. Young People and Illicit Drug Use in Postmodern Times?
   Tracy Shildrick   41

4. Victims of Risk? Young People and the Construction of Lifestyles
   Steven Miles   58

5. Global Clubcultures: Cultural Flows and Late Modern Dance Music Culture
   Ben Carrington and Brian Wilson   74

6. Research on Youth Transitions: Some Critical Interventions
   Tracey Skelton   100

7. New Deal or Raw Deal? Dilemmas and Paradoxes of State Interventions into the Youth Labour Market
   Barry Percy-Smith and Susan Weil   117

8. Domestic and Housing Transitions and the Negotiation of Intimacy
   Sue Heath   137

9. Ignoring the Past: Under-Employment and Risk in Late Modernity
   Gary Pollock   159

Index   176

List of Contributors

Ben Carrington teaches Sociology and Cultural Studies at the University of Brighton, England.

Mark Cieslik is a lecturer in Sociology at the University of Teesside. Mark has been researching young people since the early 1990s when he undertook doctoral research into young people, schooling and social exclusion. He is currently researching, amongst other things, the impact of recent education policy, in particular Education Action Zones as well as issues around lifelong learning. He is also convenor of the British Sociological Association Youth Study Group.

Sue Heath is a senior lecturer in Sociology at the University of Southampton. Her research interests focus on processes of transition to adulthood, with a specific interest in single young adults, household formation and forms of interdependent living. Recent publications include *Sociological Research Methods in Context* (Macmillan, 1999, with Fiona Devine) and articles in *Discourse: Studies in the Cultural Politics of Education*, the *British Journal of Sociology of Education* and the *Journal of Youth Studies*.

Steven Miles is a senior lecturer in Sociology at the University of Plymouth. His doctoral research explored patterns of consumption in young people. Since then he has been researching and publishing widely particularly around the areas of youth studies, social theory and consumption.

Geoff Nichols is a lecturer in the Leisure Management Unit, University of Sheffield. His main research interests are the evaluation of sports and outdoor activity programmes, especially those programmes which aim to reduce crime. Recent research based publications include papers in the journals, *Vista, Governance Local, Australian Journal of Outdoor Education, World Leisure and Recreation* and *Journal of Risk Research*.

Barry Percy-Smith is Research Fellow and Youth Research Co-ordinator at SOLAR (Social and Organizational Learning and Action Research), an interdisciplinary action research and development centre at University College Northampton, UK. His work involves collaborative action inquiry projects with young people, policy-makers and practitioners as research partners in organizational, programme and community contexts. He is currently working on projects with and for socially excluded and vulnerable young people around issues of education, training, guidance, homelessness, youth offending and neighbourhood renewal. His doctoral research examined young people's experiences of growing up in urban neighbourhoods – conducted as part of the UNESCO 'Growing Up In Cities' programme.

Gary Pollock is a lecturer in Sociology at Manchester Metropolitan University. Prior to this he worked at the University of Salford. He has undertaken survey research into youth labour markets and unemployment and has published several articles in this area. He is also currently exploring the youth transitions discourse in light of debates around late modernity and risk society.

Tracy Shildrick is a lecturer in Sociology and Youth Studies at the University of Teesside. She is presently completing her Doctoral research which explores youth cultural identification and the use of illicit drugs in the North East of England. She has recently published a number of articles based on this research.

Tracey Skelton is a lecturer in Geography at Loughborough University. She is the co-editor (with Gill Valentine) of *Cool Places: Cultural Geographies of Young People* (Routledge). She has conducted research with young women living in the Rhondda Valleys, South Wales. Her other key research area is the Caribbean and she is currently collaborating with colleagues at the University of the West Indies in order to conduct research with young people in the region.

Susan Weil is Professor of Social and Organizational Learning and Director of SOLAR, at University College Northampton, United Kingdom. Working predominantly in the health and education sectors her work focuses on the development of new forms of collaborative and action-oriented inquiry. She is currently working with NHS executives on whole systems change and capability development projects. She is formerly Higher Education Research Director at the Office of Public Management.

Brian Wilson is an assistant professor in the socio-managerial area in the School of Human Kinetics at the University of British Columbia, Canada. His research has focused on topics such as the rave subculture, youth culture in recreation/drop-in centres, media portrayals of race and gender, and audience reactions to these portrayals. His current work on alternative media and social movements includes a study of the 'anti-jock' Internet based youth movement.

Acknowledgements

This book is based on papers presented at seminars organized by the British Sociological Association Youth Study Group (for details see: www.britsoc.org.uk). This was re-established by Mark Cieslik, Andy Bennett and Steve Miles in 1999 as a forum for youth researchers to discuss the latest work in the field of youth studies. Each year the study group organizes one-day seminars as well as larger conferences and further publications based on these study group papers are forthcoming.

The editors wish to acknowledge the support of the BSA and also the many study group members who have contributed to the success of recent events. Most importantly, this book would not have been possible without the many young people who have participated in the various projects which make up this collection of papers.

Chapter 1

Introduction: Studying Young People in Late Modernity

MARK CIESLIK and GARY POLLOCK

Introduction

The last decades of the twentieth century has witnessed considerable change. We have seen the restructuring of the key institutions of welfare, employment, family and community as well as developments in information and communication technologies. The reshaping of cultural and economic processes have meant that we all now live in an increasingly globalized culture and society. For some these changes suggest the emergence of a post-modern era (Jameson, 1984), others talk of Post-Fordism (Brown and Lauder, 1997) and recently many have discussed the notion of late modernity and with it the concept of a risk society (Beck, 1992; Giddens, 1990, 1991). With such changes youth researchers have suggested that new patterns of identities and transitions have emerged bringing with it the creation of new opportunities as well as divisions and inequalities amongst contemporary youth. The election of new governments in Europe as we saw with the election of the British Labour Party in 1997 and 2001 also promised the beginning of a new social policy agenda for young people. In Britain, as in other countries with social democratic traditions of government there has been the emergence of the so-called Third Way philosophy which would marry the older socialist concerns for social justice with the Neo-Liberal or New Right concerns for economic efficiency and market policies. In the light of these changes many youth researchers agree on the need for new ways of exploring the impact of these developments on the lives of young people – new research agendas with an innovative approach to research problems, theories and methods (MacDonald et al., 1993; Cohen and Ainley, 2000). One of the key aims of this book therefore is to illustrate some of the most recent research with young people in the context of late modernity and risk societies. It also sets out to explore the impact on young people of some of the new social policies emerging from the Labour government of Tony

Blair. In so doing it seeks in a modest way to contribute to a new youth research agenda for the new millennium.

Risk and Risk Society

The concepts of risk and risk society are interesting as they have implications for how we understand social identities, the wider structure and organization of societies and also the key concepts which underpin the social sciences (Luhmann, 1990, 1995). One of the first writers to popularize the concept of risk was Mary Douglas (1966, 1983, 1992). Douglas illustrates how the category of risk operates as a key part of the classification system in contemporary cultures and that this has emerged because of the recent transformation of western societies. An important point made by Douglas is concerned with the process of social construction which underpins the use of risk categories in modern societies. The ways in which some practices or groups or places are constructed as 'risky' or 'at risk' inevitably involve political, ethical and moral judgements by some in relation to others. Some members of society then, have the resources and the power to define others and make such definitions stick, despite the efforts of those labelled to resist such categorization. The concept of risk and its operation is so effective and has become so pervasive Douglas suggests, as it draws on older categories such as sin, danger, cleanliness, purity and pollution. As sin and danger did in the past the concept of risk works today as a way of categorising social membership and in the process helps to maintain social order in modern societies. Significantly, such a system of categorization and the role of risk have become necessary because of the dynamism of contemporary societies. As Beck (1992) and Giddens (1991) were to later argue the reshaping of families, employment and communities in part through the pressures of globalisation creates uncertainties over identities and social membership. Such processes continually (re)create new marginal groups and thus contribute to the recasting of boundaries between those who belong and those who do not- the established and the outsiders. For Douglas, risk has become embedded in contemporary culture as it serves as a key 'forensic resource' (Lupton, 1999) for managing the disputes, uncertainties and anxieties over social membership in modern societies.

In contrast to Douglas who understood risk as a social category and an element of social classification, Beck and Giddens have developed the wider argument about the emergence of risk societies as a stage in the development of societies in late modernity. As such they make claims about the distinctiveness of risk societies in relation to earlier forms of industrial societies. For Beck (1992) a distinctive feature of risk society is the growth in manufactured hazards because of the pursuit of wealth through industrial production. These take a bewildering form – such as environmental pollution, food poisoning, anxieties over medical procedures and drug treatments as well as concerns over dangerous transport systems. These hazards create great uncertainty as their pervasiveness and global origins mean that they are often difficult to escape from. Moreover, the very fact that expert knowledges such as science and technology are used in the industrial processes which have created these risks have contributed to a growing scepticism in the power of expert discourses to offer solutions to these hazards.

Risk society is also characterized by other features which create a sense of uncertainty. Long term processes of cultural change – detraditionalization – means that those norms and values which act as collective cultural guides in our lives are waning in influence and this is reflected in a much more fluid understanding of families, employment and community life. In the place of these collective guides and traditional institutions are much more individualized identities and biographies where individuals have a greater scope beyond traditional markers of class, race and gender to create complex subjectivities and lifestyles.

The growth of new global hazards and the uncertainties of detraditionalization have created a world in which individuals increasingly have to become much more reflexive about their daily practices. This reflexiveness for Beck is the key way in which people manage their lives in risk society. When confronted by new global hazards, the restructuring of civil society and a growing critique of expert knowledges, individuals are compelled to become more involved in processes of 'self-confrontation' (Gudmundsson, 2000) or much more 'self-conscious' about their daily lives and practices if they are to successfully manage their biographies in contemporary societies.

A further development of the risk society concept by Giddens emphasizes the transformation of time and space and the impact this has on the lives of every citizen. Global capitalism has helped create a mediazed world where interaction is increasingly mediated by information and communication technologies (ICTs) and less and less through face-to-face interaction. This process of disembedding of social relationships creates a variety of problems (and indeed opportunities) for individuals – in particular around the issue of the trust that can or cannot be placed in the absent individuals which make up the lifeworld of citizens. The insecurity that people feel in a mediazed society, Giddens suggests, is compounded by wider processes of detraditionalization as outlined by Beck above. Those once predictable institutions which made up the fabric of modernity – the family, employment, welfare and community become increasingly fluid and unpredictable. The processes of detraditionalization and disembedding combine to produce an environment characterized by ontological insecurity – doubts about one identity, careers and biography. In such a world Giddens suggests, following Beck, that people have no alternative but to develop individualized and reflexive approaches to the management of their life projects – in their search for trust and ontological security.

The Third Way and Social Policy

In the twenty-first century governments have the difficult task of helping their citizens to meet the challenges presented by risk societies. One way of doing this is by developing innovative social policy which is suited to the dynamic, globalized societies in which we live. For some years now there has been an ambitious socio-political project in many European countries which has been exploring the possibility of moving beyond the old political and ideological divisions of Left and Right that have characterized politics for much of the twentieth century. These calls have been made as most western societies are struggling to find new ways of dealing with deeply ingrained problems of growing social exclusion and material inequalities as well as a crisis in the fabric of civil society. Many modern societies are experiencing the profound reshaping of institutions such as the family but also a growing cynicism about, and disengagement from, local and national political processes.[1] There is a need then to redemocratize contemporary societies. However, in their respective ways, we are told, the older social democratic and neo-liberal projects are both unsuited to risk society (Giddens, 1998). In Britain, Thatcherism's championing of the market and minimal state may have helped the economy adjust to global markets but has been unsuccessful in coping with the attendant social dislocation, particularly the growth in inequality and deterioration of many local communities. By promoting economic individualism Neo-Liberal policies have helped undermine the social solidarity that is essential to any society. In contrast social democratic governments have traditionally used state intervention to resist the effects of the global economy using welfare expansion and economic management to pursue egalitarian policies, usually via the goal of full-employment. Under this approach, the reliance on the state to furnish solutions to social problems has led to the growth of welfare dependency and the erosion of individual liberties through burgeoning state bureaucracies.

As developed by Giddens (1998, 2000) and championed by Tony Blair and others (for example the Democratic Party in the USA and the SPD in

Germany), the Third Way is an effort to reshape the social democratic political project in the context of risk society. At its heart is the aim of promoting social solidarity and social justice which were a feature of old Labour socialist policies whilst also maintaining the individual's freedoms and liberties which the New Right championed through the market based policies of Thatcherism. The Third Way aims to do this via several concepts which in turn have subsequently influenced current policy-making. A key concept is that of 'active citizenship' where there is the understanding that individuals can exercise their rights to welfare support only if they recognize their responsibilities to the wider community- 'the hand up not hand out' approach. Individuals then should look for work if unemployed, parents must take some responsibility for their child's welfare and all of us must make more of an effort to participate in our local communities. The Third Way also argues for a mixed economy where the state, private business and voluntary organisations can bring their respective expertises and work together to manage the economy and provide welfare services. The partnership approach is a way of involving a wider group of people in democratic processes of policy-making and implementation so as to check the current apathy which is felt by many about such issues. A partnership approach is also a way of empowering a wider range of people to become involved in the governance and policy process avoiding the problems associated with top-down initiatives which many feel ignore the views and interest of those it is supposed to represent.

There have been a range of social policies aimed at young people which reflect this current Third Way approach to government in risk societies. For example the British Labour government has revamped the careers advisory system creating in its place the new 'connexions' service which aims to provide support for young people managing what are now much more fragmented and extended transitions through education, training and work. In mainstream education the British government hopes to distance itself from the previous Conservative governments by using its policies to tackle social exclusion and promote social justice. Policies such as Education Action Zones, Excellence in Cities and Surestart are explicitly focused on delivering a range of flexible learning opportunities to those children, young people and their families who are living in areas of multiple disadvantage (see Simpson and Cieslik, 2000). Yet at the same time these policies are different to earlier Old Labour initiatives as they incorporate many of the market based initiatives of previous Conservative administrations. The Labour government, for example has done little to change the competitive ethos of the secondary school system, based as it is on student testing, open enrolment and league tables of examination results. Moreover in such a system, parents and young people have to exercise a key responsibility in making an informed choice about the sort of education they wish to receive. The introduction of student loans and tuition fees in higher education implies that parents and students now have financial as well as moral responsibilities when it comes to their participation in state education. At all levels of the education system the government promises to provide a quality system of education which is integral in the fight for social justice only if at the same time parents and young people play their part in this quest. Government will provide the key services which underpin citizenship only if citizens play an active part in such provision – the concept then of 'active citizenship' which is central to the philosophy of the Third Way.

The principles underlying this Third Way approach and in particular the concept of active citizenship can be seen in the New Deal initiative as Percy-Smith illustrates in his chapter in this volume. This particular initiative is based on the government, in partnership with a variety of local stakeholders, offering young people a choice of quality training and employment placements- a key departure from previous conservative schemes, yet at the same time insisting that young people take greater responsibility for making these choices and securing their long term employment. Yet as Percy-Smith's empirical data suggests, the aim of empowering young people to improve their own credentials and employability may in fact be undermined by the political imperatives and bureaucratic logic which underpins the delivery of New Deal programmes. As has happened with earlier training schemes the New Deal initiative may be compromized by the desire of politicians and officials to meet unrealistic performance targets set within a hopelessly ambitious timeframe.

The Crime and Disorder Act (1998) is also illustrative of Third Way policy making, in that for the first time it enshrines the prevention of youth offending in statute and with it a much wider focus on the social context and causes of youth crime. Consequently, the act, which has been the catalyst for a welter of new initiatives promotes the use of community based multi-agency intervention in the fight against the incidence of youth offending. New initiatives then, as with those in education and welfare, include provision for the establishment of local partnerships between the voluntary sector, local authorities and community groups. In aiming to tackle the long term cause of offending, new policies are intended to be much more holistic than in the past and so issues such as the role of social exclusion and the place of social justice have been incorporated into policies on youth justice for the first time. The characteristic Third Way principle of providing quality services, yet requiring individual responsibility, features strongly as the Act specifies the importance of young offenders' responsibilities to their victims as well as the parents role in the regulation of their children's conduct.

The Changing Face of Youth Research, Policy and Practice

The changes to society in late modernity and the emergence of debates around risk society and Third Way have provoked a variety of responses from those involved in youth research, policy and practice. Some youth researchers have actively engaged with political and social policy debates- notably those exploring youth transitions- whilst others have been more circumspect about debating the place of social policy in the lives of contemporary youth (Cohen, 2000; Bennett, 2000). Some have been enthusiastic about the notion of post-modernity (Redhead et al., 1993; Polhemus, 1999; Muggleton, 2000) suggesting that such societal change has encouraged the growth of much more diverse consumer orientated youth cultures and lifestyles which defy the once traditional (class-based) forms of analysis. Others have been much more sceptical about arguments for a post-modern society suggesting instead that contemporary societies are more likely to be a later stage of modernity rather than one which represents a clear break with earlier industrial and modern society (Miles, 2000). Many of this latter group of youth researchers, in Europe (Ziehe, 1989; Fornas, 1995; Wallace and Kovatcheva, 1998; Gudmundsson, 2000) and in Britain (Cohen and Ainley, 2000; France, 2000) have also more recently come to explore the notion of risk, risk society (and its related concepts) and the implications these have for young people. Concepts such as individualization, reflexivity and detraditionalization have in recent years increasingly began to feature in youth research projects (Helve and Bynner, 1996; Evans et al., 2000; Green et al., 2000). Although, as might be expected in the social sciences, there are still many undertaking youth research who have neglected or criticized the use of such concepts (Wyn and White, 1997; McDonald, 1998; McDonald et al., 2001).

The chapter by Nichols in this volume is just one example of how the concepts of risk and trust can be applied to the study of young people. In his research with young offenders Nichols shows how young people can explore and begin to reshape their identities and with it challenge their offending behaviour by working through the difficulties they face on outdoor adventure courses. By having to establish a level of trust with other participants so as to overcome the risks associated with activities such as rock climbing, and orienteering these young people are able to build self-esteem and explore other ways of being a young person. The chapter illustrates how these adventure programmes together with other forms of support can over time help prevent these young people from re-offending.

Youth Transitions

Many youth researchers in recent years have been keen to rethink the key concepts which underpin their work as well as contribute to new research and policy agendas not least because the changes associated with late modernity presents many new challenges to, as well as opportunities for, young people. Both British and overseas researchers (Roberts and Jung, 1995; Helve and Bynner, 1996; Heinz, 1999; Wyn and Dwyer, 1999; Bynner, 2001) point to the restructuring of youth labour markets (Ashton et al., 1990), the insecurity of employment (MacDonald, 1988), the expansion of post-compulsory education and training (Mizen, 1995) and changing patterns of family formation (Jones and Wallace, 1992; Coles, 1995) which have led to the wider reshaping of young people's lives and their transitions to adulthood. Accordingly, there has been a shift in how transition has been understood, from the use of crude typologies of youth careers in the 1970s (Ashton and Field, 1976) through to trajectories in the 1980s (Banks et al., 1992) to more recent concepts such as niches and navigations (Evans and Furlong, 1997), cyclical transitions (Craine, 1997), de-standardized transitions (EGRIS, 2001) and reversible transitions (Du Bois Reymond, 1998). Though for some writers, as we see with the work of Jeffs and Smith (1998) and Skelton in this volume, such reworking of the transition concept has not gone far enough. Indeed, Skelton suggests the concept inevitably has connotations of a crude and linear progress from one state to another and is thus unsuited to studying the lives of young people in late modernity. Moreover, it is often used in a normative and zero-sum way where there are only successful and failed transitions which fails to do justice to the complexity of young peoples identities and experiences today.

It is commonly accepted by researchers today that young people make a variety of different transitions to adulthood (such as education and employment, housing and relationships) which are now greatly extended when compared to earlier generations (Bynner et al., 1997b). Moreover, the increasing length and diversity of transitions has increased their complexity and the scope for young people themselves to make more decisions about their lives. For example, young people construct their biographies in a way which reflects a blending of various experiences – full-time students are often in waged employment, those in full-time employment undertake training, those receiving welfare participate in the informal economy (Allat and Dixon, 2001; Du Bois-Reymond, 1998). In this volume Sue Heath's chapter classically illustrates such transitions showing the impact of changing patterns of family formation and organization of relationships on the lives of young people. More and more young people are eschewing the conventional couple-based living arrangements opting instead to share various forms of accommodation and to experience different forms of residence with friends and lovers over longer periods of time. These trends have been the result partly of changing attitudes towards marriage but also as a result of the process of individualisation where young people increasingly organize their relationships and residence to meet their own rather narrow personal desires and needs.

The individualization of transitions presents young people with new opportunities as well as new dilemmas about how they should monitor and manage their biographies. Some researchers see such developments in a positive light suggesting the reshaping of attitudes towards employment, education and relationships means that many young people may have more freedom than in the past to experiment with their social identities and lifestyles (Polhemus, 1999; Muggleton, 2000). Other commentators are perhaps not as optimistic (Roberts, 1996, 2000), elaborating the notion of structured individualisation and the continuing significance of structuring processes (such as material resources and discourses around ethnicity and gender) to the lives of young people. Yet others (Furlong and Cartmel, 1997), have discussed how young people may now experience the impression of greater personal autonomy because of processes of individualization but that these impressions mask the underlying structuring of young people's lives - the so-called epistemological fallacy thesis.

Many transitions researchers therefore document how young people are often unable to make the most of the new opportunities for self-actualisation that individualized transitions now offer instead focusing on how new divisions and inequalities are created amongst young people in western societies. Through the 1990s researchers from many countries (Wallace and Kovatcheva, 1998; CYRE, 1998) have documented the difficulties facing young people as they experience poverty and disadvantage leading to marginalized lifestyles and the wider polarisation between the affluent and the poor. Bynner et al. (1997b) for example document how amongst their sample of twenty somethings in the UK in the mid-1990s, just 30 per cent were 'getting on' whilst the rest were 'getting by' (30 per cent) or 'getting nowhere' (40 per cent). Numerous other surveys both in the UK (YCS, 1999; Pilling, 1990; Hagell and Shaw, 1996; Pollock, 1996) and further afield (Evans and Heinz, 1994; Chisholm et al., 1995; Roberts, 1998) have illustrated similar findings in recent years and which have led to a renewed interest in the ways in which young people adapt culturally to processes of marginalization and experiences of social exclusion. Such an interest has given rise to research in the UK into status zero youth (Williamson, 1997), a youth underclass (Murray, 1994), alternative careers (Craine, 1997) and fiddly jobs (McDonald, 1994) as well as other ways in which young people try and cope with the experience of multiple disadvantage (Cieslik, 1997, 1998).

Youth Cultures and Identity

It has been an exciting time for those researchers studying youth cultures and identities as many suggest that such concerns have taken on a greater significance in recent years. The changes associated with late modernity such as increasing reflexivity, globalization and individualization all point to a greater scope for young people to carve out much more complex forms of identity and patterns of cultural association than seen in earlier times. The critique of foundational and structural approaches in the social sciences as well as the influence of postmodernist thinkers such as Baudrillard (1983, 1988), Jameson (1984) and Derrida (1978, 1981) has also given researchers a new vocabulary with which to examine youth cultures and identities. These developments in turn have led to a great expansion in the numbers of projects exploring the cultural lives of young people (see for example Rowe, 1995; Blackman, 1995; Malbon, 1999; Muggleton, 2000).

The individualization of transitions for many of these researchers suggest that young people now have a more active role to play in the shaping of their identities than in the past. Commentators have noted the efforts young people go to in order to create distinctive styles and looks from a bewildering array of sources (McRobbie, 1994; Wulff, 1995). Changing cultural traditions over roles and identities (by gender, race, ethnicity, place, sexuality and class) have also helped this process so that young people can exercise more freedom and creativity over the ways in which they map out a sense of self offering the possibility of creating hybridized and transgressive identities (Rattansi and Phoenix, 1997; Polhemus, 1999). Research has also documented the ways in which young people draw on local and global influences when creating particular styles of dress, music and forms of association (Bennett, 1997, 1999b). This meeting of the local and global has for many raised important questions about the emergence of new diasporic cultures and youth ethnicities (Mirza, 1992; Brah, 1996) as well as the growing significance of the temporal and spatial in the creation of youth cultures and identities (Skelton and Valentine, 1998; Hall et al., 1999).

Carrington and Wilson in this volume concern themselves with some of the problems of exploring the impact of globalization on youth cultures and on dance music in particular. Using the empirical example of rave music in the 1980s and 1990s they argue for the need to go beyond crude notions of the local and the global if we are to understand how young people are influenced by wider cultural flows and in turn then use such resources for their own purposes. The concept of 'scapes' (mediascape, ethnoscape, etc.) as developed by Appadurai (1990) is used to show how the dissemination of music products, the growth of tourism and media coverage of dance are all significant in the emergence of particular youth cultural formations such as dance and rave. In the slightly different context of illicit drug use, Shildrick's chapter however reasserts the importance of local knowledges and traditions to youth cultural identities. Although writers such as Carrington and Wilson argue for the increasing significance of global influences on the lives of young people, Shildrick suggests as Hirst and Thompson do (1999) that patterns of association and cultural life are still very much shaped by local class cultural experiences.

The changes associated with late modernity and the theoretical influences of post-structuralism have led youth researchers to seek new ways of conceptualizing youth identity and youth cultures. As Rattansi and Phoenix (1997) suggest, there has been a shift in recent years away from the more structural, reified and unitary notion of identity as exemplified by the use of typologies (see Brown [1987] for an example of this) to one where identity is understood as much more unstable and hybridized. Indeed, identity can only be understood relationally, in the context of more complex notions of 'difference' and 'the other'– in other words, identity has become de-centred. Furthermore, the authors suggest, drawing on Foucault (1977) that youth identities are constituted by an array of discourses (power-knowledge relationships) so that it is no longer tenable, as was the case in the past, to view youth identities simply in relation to economic processes or class cultures. Youth research therefore has seen a shift away from the earlier preoccupation with how work, employment and collective class cultural experiences ultimately shape youth cultures and identities to focus more on the increasingly autonomous and individualized patterns of experience rooted in consumption and leisure (Furlong and Cartmel, 1997; Bynner et al., 1997a; Roberts, 1996). This culturalization of young people's lives and with it youth research has resulted in young people being seen today much more as, 'consumer citizens rather than worker citizens' (Bynner, 1998, p.437).

The recasting of research into youth cultures and identities has rekindled theoretical debate about how these phenomena should be studied which has also led to a renewed interest in subcultural theory and particularly that employed by the Centre for Contemporary Cultural Studies (see Bennett, 2002). In recent years there has been the emergence of a number of different approaches to the study of youth cultures and identity. There are many who still employ the concept of subculture (though usually with some modification) in their research (White, 1999; Locher, 1998; Sardiello, 1998). Others have offered a more radical reworking of the subculture concept as we see in Muggleton's use of post-subcultures (Muggleton, 2000), Thornton's use of the concept of subcultural capital (Thornton, 1997), and Redhead's use of the concept of clubcultures (Redhead, 1997). Several others have studied youth cultures and developed very different alternatives to the subcultures concept as we see in Skeggs (1997b) and Fornas and Bolin (1995) who draw on Bourdieu's work on cultural capital. In a similar vein Miles' (2000) and Bennett's (2000) work on consumption and dance music uses concepts such as lifestyles and neo-tribes to explore youth cultures and identities. One reason for this retheorization has been the argument that in late modernity youth identities and patterns of association have become decoupled from wider class cultures. Those who have tried to retain elements of subcultural theory therefore are those who still believe that youth cultures have some form of structural relationship with wider class cultures. Whereas, the more radical rethinking of youth cultures as we see in concepts such as lifestyles and as discussed by Miles in his chapter tend to view this structured relationship between class culture and youth cultures as far too mechanical and deterministic for the realities of life in late modernity.

The current debates over the use of subcultural theory illustrate the continuing significance of issues such as the structure-agency problematic for youth researchers today. On the one hand there are those who suggest the individualization of transitions offers new positive opportunities for young people to generate a sense of self-efficacy and agency. These writers tend to downplay the problems of disadvantage young people can experience in risk societies. For example, Miles sees consumption as a key part of young people's lifestyles projects which allow them to survive the ontological insecurity endemic in risk society (Miles, 2000). But, as his chapter in this volume shows, the participation in education and training can also be understood as an important part of a young person's lifestyle project. Lifestyles allow young people to create fluid identities and also create and maintain the all-important relationships with their peers. In a similar way Holland's suggests the reshaping of transitions in recent years has meant that increasingly young people are socialized into ways of life and forms of identity through their leisure activities (such as 'going out' to pubs and clubs) rather than the older traditional forms of association through waged employment. Others such as Smith and Maughan (1998) and Bennett (2000) have documented the role that musical forms (often drawn and fused from disparate contexts) can play in offering resources for young people to use, as a way of making a living as well as offering new and positive vocabularies for representation.

On the other hand and in contrast to these more positive interpretations of youth in risk society there are those who tend to emphasize the more problematic nature of young people's lives today. Shildrick's chapter for example suggests how the experience of social exclusion can inform the transition from recreational drug use to more problematic patterns of drug taking. Willis (1990) and Furlong and Cartmel (1997) both suggest that new media technologies and processes of globalization of production can offer as many new possibilities for large corporations to increase their profits as they offer new identity possibilities for young people. Recent demonstrations against global capitalism perhaps points to the growing realisation of this fact by many young people today.[2]

Criticisms of the Risk Society and Third Way

Theories around risk and risk society are not without their criticisms. Perhaps the most common is the argument that risk theorists are wrong to suggest that risk society represents a distinctive stage in the development of western societies. Most of these critics raise doubts about whether contemporary societies are any more risky than earlier times or that a risk culture is more prevalent than in earlier industrial societies (Turner, 1994, 1997; Culpitt, 1999). Although there is the acceptance that key institutions have been reshaped as part of wider globalizing processes these commentators call for much more empirical work to be undertaken by risk theorists before they are able to claim the emergence of risk society. As a result many critics suggest the risk society thesis is as much futurology as it is discourse on the present state of late modern societies. Accordingly, there are those who suggest that writers such as Beck and Giddens neglect the continuing importance of face-to-face relationships and patterns of association, which have resisted the disembedding processes of modern societies (Savage, 2000). For many, the risk society discourse neglects the continuing role of economic and class based divisions in contemporary societies (Ray and Sayer, 1999). A variety of research projects have illustrated the significance of these traditional patterns of association for people in general and for young people in particular (Sennett and Cobb, 1997; Skeggs, 1997a).

A further criticism of the risk society thesis is that it has led some social scientists to become preoccupied with research projects which focus on the lives of individual young people abstracted from the wider social context in which they live. Although commentators such as Adam and Van

Loon (2000) suggest that sociology in risk societies has to become much more holistic than in the past other researchers have ignored such arguments to focus instead on young people's agency and reflexivity almost wholly unconstrained by wider social structures. Critics suggest that some recent research into youth lifestyles and youth cultures explores in minute detail the elaborate forms of identity formation amongst young people whilst ignoring the more traditional yet mundane matters of how access to opportunities and resources can structure their long term life chances. Recent youth cultural research therefore, may have become preoccupied with issues of ontological security at the expense of issues around economic security and insecurity (Cieslik, 2001).

There are as many criticisms of the Third Way thesis as there are of risk society. A major area of disagreement focuses on the ability to combine two differing political and social policy traditions without one of them taking the ascendancy. In its latest incarnation with Giddens and New Labour some commentators suggest that it is the Neo-Liberal strand which has come to be dominant (Hall, 1998). Though to be fair such comments depend greatly on the position of the writer – right wingers pointing to the socialistic tendencies in New Labours current philosophy and Old Labour activists arguing that behind the rhetoric of social justice lies the reality of Neo-Liberalism. Such views are also shaped by time. On coming to power in 1997 many writers pointed to New Labour's focus on social justice as a key way of differentiating them from previous Conservative governments. Since then however, the very same writers have increasingly rounded on the similarities between New Labour and earlier Thatcher and Major administrations (Hall, 1998; Ryan, 1999). Irrespective of such considerations some writers suggest there are very real problems in combining the old socialist values for social justice with the market based economic philosophy which seems to have become an orthodoxy amongst many western governments (Hall, 1998). At its most simple it is difficult to ensure the wellbeing of all citizens whilst at the same time restricting welfare expenditure and arguing that it is impossible for national governments to intervene in globalized labour markets. The values of social justice will always be hard to maintain when combined with an economic theory which promotes economic individualism.

Risk Society and the Crisis in Youth Research?

Whilst for some, the emergence of debates around risk society and the Third Way have been a catalyst for developing new approaches to youth work, policy and research, for others in Europe (Gudmundsson, 2000), and

Britain, it has led to a greater scepticism about the future of youth studies. This latter viewpoint is illustrated by Jeffs and Smith (1998) who argue that as the concept of 'youth' and its associated professional discourses emerged as an historically specific concept with industrial society then in the very different society of late modernity they are increasingly becoming an anachronism. The authors suggest that with such phenomena as 'tweenies' and the emergence of extended and cyclical transitions then those who were once defined as youth now have as much in common with children and those in their 20s and 30s as their peers of their own age.[3] This blurring of the concept of youth is accompanied by deficiencies in the theories which underpin the study of young people, and in particular around transitions and youth cultures. The notion of transition suggests a linear progression from one status to another but such straightforward transitions are seldom made in contemporary societies. Such a concept then has little empirical purchase on the lives of the majority of young people today. Similarly, subcultural theory says more about visible and spectacular forms of youth culture than it does about the majority of young people's rather ordinary and mundane forms of association. For these authors, youth research is in terminal decline and they go onto suggest that the ways in which youth professionals have responded to this decline simply adds to their problems. By concentrating on young people as 'problem youth' or 'at risk' in order to secure funding for research and initiatives youth professionals end up embroiled in a cycle of short-term and ineffective social policy interventions. Moreover, the focus on 'problem youth' misrepresents the majority of young people's lives, fuelling the mediazed moral panics we often see about young people today. This in turn contributes to the development of often authoritarian and punitive social policy initiatives such as curfews, school exclusion and workfare type welfare programmes.

There have been several other commentators who have echoed Jeffs and Smiths views on the state of contemporary youth research. Cohen and Ainley (2000) have spoken about the marginal position of youth studies and its declining influence on social policy debates, in part because of the inability to develop new theoretical approaches and research agendas. Others have suggested (Griffin, 1993; Piper and Piper, 1998; Kelly, 2000) that the weaknesses of current youth research, policy and practice are almost inevitable as youth professionals are part of a wider system of discourses which, usually in unintended ways, come to define and regulate the lives of young people. Hence, it is very difficult to develop truly emancipatory youth research, practice and policy as professional discourses reflect the interests of professionals (such as winning funding for initiatives and research) as much as the interests of young people. As a result such professional discourses are implicated in the surveillance of young people and the social construction (of rather narrow archetypes) of what it is to be a young person in contemporary societies.

Outline of the Book

The remainder of the book is loosely divided into two sections, the first (chapters two to five) includes chapters which explore young people's identities and youth cultures in relation to issues such as drug use, education and training and dance music. In various ways the authors examine whether there is a need to rethink some of the existing theories and concepts which have informed the study of youth cultures and identities. The sorts of questions the authors pose are: do subcultural theories still offer an adequate way of examining young people's involvement in substance (ab)use and participation in dance music? Alternatively, can concepts such as lifestyles or risk, provide a greater empirical purchase on the lives of young people in late modernity than these older approaches?

The second section of the volume (chapters six to nine) is concerned with how young people experience 'transitions', in relation to such topics as employment, sexuality and household formation. The chapters also raise important theoretical questions about the usefulness of the transition concept in late modernity. These papers illustrate how the reshaping of key institutions in late modernity has had a profound effect on the sorts of transitions young people make today. For example there are discussions of the growth in shared housing amongst young people in Britain and the role of New Deal programmes in shaping career trajectories of British youth. In addressing such issues and experiences the authors examine the potential contribution that concepts around risk and risk society and new Third Way social policy initiatives can have to contemporary youth studies.

Notes

1. See for example the low turnout by voters in parliamentary and local government elections. In the UK the average turnout for the 2001 parliament election was just 60 percent. For local government elections the figures are even lower.
2. The recent 'anti-capitalism' demonstrations in Seattle, Gothenburg and Genoa against the World Trade Organisation (WTO), General Agreement on Tariffs and Trade (GATT) and the G8 group of industrial nations are illustrative of this trend.
3. The term 'tweenies' has been coined by various commentators in the mass media to represent those children (aged 12 and under) whose lifestyles appear very much like the teenagers of previous generations, particular in relation to their forms of dress and patterns of consumption.

References

Adam, B. and Van Loon, J. (2000), 'Introduction: repositioning risk; the challenge for social theory', in Adam, B., Beck, U. and Van Loom, J. (eds), *Risk Society and Beyond: Critical Issues for Social Theory*, London, Sage.

Allat, P. and Dixon, C. (2001), 'Mundane matters: The shaping of a local political economy of post-16 education' paper presented at *The BSA Annual Conference, '2001 A Sociological Odyssey'*, April 9-12th.

Appadurai, A. (1990), 'Disjuncture and difference in the global cultural economy', in *Theory, Culture and Society*, vol.7, pp.295-310.

Ashton, D. and Field, D. (1976), *Young Workers*, London, Hutchinson.

Ashton, D et al. (1990), *Restructuring the Labour Market: The Implications for Youth*, London, Macmillan.

Banks, M. et al. (1992), *Careers and Identities*, Milton Keynes, Open University Press.

Baudrillard, J. (1983), *Simulations*, New York, Semiotext.

Baudrillard, J. (1988), *The Ecstasy of Communication*, New York, Semiotext.

Beck, U. (1992), *Risk Society: Towards a New Modernity*, London, Sage.

Bennett, A. (1997), 'Bhangra in Newcastle: Music, ethnic identity and the role of local knowledge', in *Innovation*, vol.10, no.1, pp.107-111.

Bennett, A. (1999a), 'Subcultures or neo-tribes? Rethinking the relationship between youth style and musical taste', in *Sociology*, vol.33, no.3, pp.599-617.

Bennett, A. (1999b), 'Hip, hop am Maim: The localisation of rap music and hip-hop culture', in *Media, Culture and Society*, vol.21, pp.77-91.

Bennett, A. (2000), *Popular Music and Youth Culture*, London, Macmillan.

Bennett, A. (ed.) (2002), *After Subculture*, London, Palgrave, forthcoming.

Blackman, S. (1995), *Youth Positions and Oppositions: Style, Sexuality and Schooling*, Aldershot, Avebury.

Brah, A. (1996), *Cartographies of Diaspora: Contesting Identities*, London, Routledge.

Brown, P. (1987), *Schooling Ordinary Kids: Inequality, Unemployment and the New Vocationalism*, Tavistock, London.

Brown, P. and Lauder, H. (1997), Education, globalisation and economic development', in Halsey, A.H. et al. (eds), *Education, Culture, Economy, Society*, Oxford, Oxford University Press.

Bynner, J. (1998), 'Youth in the information society: problems, prospects and research directions', review article in *Journal of Education Policy*, vol.13, no.3, pp.433-442.

Bynner, J. (2001), 'British youth transitions in comparative perspective', in *Journal of Youth Studies*, vol 4, no.1, pp.5-24.

Bynner, J. et al. (eds) (1997a), 'A new agenda for youth research', in Bynner, J. et al. (eds), *Youth, Citizenship and Social Change in a European Context*, Aldershot, Ashgate.

Bynner, J. et al. (eds) (1997b), *Twenty Something in the 1990s*, Aldershot, Ashgate.

Cartmel, F. and Furlong, A. (2000), *Youth Unemployment in Rural Areas*, York, Rowntree Foundation.

Chisholm, L. et al. (1995), *Growing up in Europe: Contemporary Horizons in Childhood and Youth Studies*, Berlin, De Gruyter.

Cieslik, M (1997), *Youth, Disadvantage and the Underclass in South Wales*, Unpublished PhD Thesis, University of Kent at Canterbury.

Cieslik, M. (1998), 'Lifelong learning and multiple disadvantage in South Wales', in Walther, A. and Stauber, B. (eds), *Lifelong Learning in Europe: Options for the Integration of Living, Learning and Working*, vol.1., Neuling Verlag, Tubingen, Germany.

Cieslik, M. (2001), 'Researching youth cultures: some problems with the cultural turn in British youth studies', in *Scottish Youth Issues Journal*, vol.1, no.2. pp.27-48.
Cohen, P. (2000), '"There must be some way out of here": Some reflections on method', paper presented at the *BSA Youth Study Group Conference, 'Researching Youth: Issues, Controversies and Dilemmas'*, University of Surrey, England, July.
Cohen, P. and Ainley, P. (2000), 'In the country of the blind? Youth studies and cultural studies in Britain', *Journal of Youth Studies*, vol.3, no.1, pp.79-96.
Coles, B. (1995), *Youth and Social Policy*, London, UCL Press.
Craine, S. (1997), 'The "Black Magic Roundabout": cyclical transitions, social exclusion and alternative careers', in McDonald, R. (ed.), *Youth, the Underclass and Social Exclusion*, London, Routledge.
Crime and Disorder Act (1998), *Youth Framework Document*, London, Home Office/HMSO.
Culpitt, I. (1999), *Social Policy and Risk*, London, Sage.
CYRE (1998), *European Yearbook of Youth Policy and Youth Research*, vol.2, Berlin, De Gruyter.
Derrida, J. (1978), *Writing and Difference*, London, Routledge.
Derrida, J. (1981), *Positions*, London, Athlone Press.
Du Bois-Reymond, M. (1998), '"I don't want to commit myself yet": young people's life concepts', in *Journal of Youth Studies*, vol.1, no.1, pp.63-80.
Douglas, M. (1966), *Purity and Danger: An Analysis of Pollution and Taboo*, London, Routledge.
Douglas, M. (1983), *Risk and Culture*, Berkeley, University of California Press.
Douglas, M. (1992), *Risk and Blame: Essays in Cultural Theory*, London, Routledge.
EGRIS (2001), 'Misleading trajectories: transition dilemmas of young adults in Europe', in *Journal of Youth Studies*, vol.4, no.1, pp.101-118.
Epstein, J. (ed.) (1998), *Youth Culture: Identity in a Postmodern World*, Oxford, Blackwell.
Evans, K. and Heinz, W. (eds) (1994), *Becoming Adults in England and Germany*, London, Anglo-German Foundation.
Evans, K. and Furlong, A. (1997), 'Metaphors of youth transitions: niches, pathways, trajectories or navigations', in Bynner, J. et al. (eds), *Youth, Citizenship and Social Change in a European Context*, Aldershot, Ashgate.
Evans, K. et al. (2000), *Learning and Work in the Risk Society*, London, Macmillan.
Fornas, J. (1995), *Cultural Theory and Late Modernity*, London, Sage.
Fornas, J. and Bolin, G. (eds) (1995), *Youth Culture in Late Modernity*, London, Sage.
Foucault, M. (1977), *Discipline and Punish*, Harmondsworth, Penguin.
France, A. (1998), 'Why should we care: young people, citizenship and questions of social responsibility', in *Journal of Youth Studies*, vol.1, no.1, pp.112.
France, A. (2000), 'Towards a sociological understanding of youth and their risk-taking', in *Journal of Youth Studies*, vol.3. no.3. pp.317-332.
Furlong, A. (1998), 'Youth and Social Class: Change and Continuity', review article in *British Journal of Sociology of Education*, vol.19, no.4, pp.591-597.
Furlong, A. and Cartmel, F. (1997), *Youth and Social Change: Individualisation and Risk in Late Modernity*, Milton Keynes, Open University.
Giddens, A. (1990), *The Consequences of Modernity*, Cambridge, Polity Press.
Giddens, A. (1991), *Modernity and Self-Identity*, Cambridge, Policy Press.
Giddens, A. (1998), *The Third Way: The Social Renewal of Democracy*, Cambridge, Polity Press.
Giddens, A. (2000), *The Third Way and Its Critics*, Cambridge, Polity Press.
Green, E. et al. (2000), 'Conceptualising risk and danger: an analysis of young people's perceptions of risk', in *Journal of Youth Studies*, vol.3, no.2, pp.109-126.
Griffin, C (1993), *Representations of Youth*, Oxford, Polity.

Griffin, C. (1997), 'Youth research and identities: same as it ever was?', in Bynner, J. et al. (eds), *Youth Citizenship and Social Change in a European Context*, Aldershot, Ashgate.

Gudmundsson, G. (2000), 'Youth research at the crossroads: sociological and interdisciplinary youth research in the Nordic countries', in *Journal of Youth Studies*, vol.3, no.2, pp. 127-166.

Hagell, A. and Shaw, C. (1996), *Opportunity and Disadvantage at Age 16*, London, PSI.

Hall, S. (1998), 'The great moving nowhere show', *Marxism Today*, Nov/Dec. pp.9-14.

Hall, S. and Jefferson, T. (eds) (1978), *Resistance Through Rituals: Youth Subcultures in Postwar Britain*, London, Hutchinson.

Hall, T. et al. (1999), 'Self, space and place: youth identities and citizenship', in *British Journal of Sociology of Education*, vol.20, no.4, pp.501-513.

Heinz, W. (1999), *From Education to Work: Cross-National Perspectives*, Cambridge, Cambridge University Press.

Helve, H and Bynner, J. (1996), *Youth and Life Management: Research Perspectives*, Helsinki, Helsinki University Press.

Hirst, P. and Thompson, G. (1999), *Globalisation in Question*, 2nd edition, Cambridge, Polity Press.

Hollands, R. (1995), *Friday Night, Saturday Night: Youth Cultural Identification in a Post-Industrial City*, Newcastle, Newcastle University Press.

Jameson, F. (1984), 'Postmodernism or the cultural logic of late capitalism', in *New Left Review*, no.146.

Jeffs, T. and Smith, M. (1998) 'The problem of youth for youth work', in *Journal of Youth and Policy*, Autumn/Winter, no.62, pp.45-66.

Jones, G. and Wallace, C. (1992), *Youth, Family and Citizenship*, Milton Keynes, Open University.

Kelly, P. (2000), 'Youth as an artefact of expertise: problematising the practice of youth studies in an age of uncertainty', in *Journal of Youth Studies*, vol.3, no.3, pp.301-316.

Locher, D. (1998), 'The industrial identity crisis: the failure of a newly forming subculture to identify itself', in Epstein, J. (ed.), *Youth Culture: Identity in a Postmodern World*, Oxford, Blackwell.

Luhmann, N. (1990), *Essays of Self-Reference*, New York, Columbia University Press.

Luhmann, N. (1995), *The Sociology of Risk*, Berlin, De Gruyter.

Lupton, D. (1999), *Risk*, London, Routlege.

MacDonald, R. (1988), 'Out of town, out of work: research on post-16 experiences in two rural areas', in Coles, B. (ed.), *Young Careers: The Search for Jobs and the New Vocationalism*, Milton Keynes, Open University Press.

MacDonald, R. (1994), 'Fiddly jobs, undeclared working and the "something for nothing" society', in *Work, Employment and Society*, vol.8. no.4. pp.507-530.

MacDonald, R. (ed.) (1997), *Youth, Social Exclusion and the Underclass*, London, Routledge.

MacDonald, R. (1998), 'Youth transitions and social exclusion: some issues for youth research in the UK', in *Journal of Youth Studies*, vol.1, no.2, pp.163-176.

MacDonald, R. et al. (1993), 'Youth and Policy in the 1990s', in *Youth and Policy*, Spring, no.40, pp.1-9.

MacDonald, R. et al. (2001), 'Snakes and ladders: in defence of studies of youth transition', in *Sociological Research Online*, February.

Malbon, B. (1999), *Clubbing: Dancing, Ectasy and Vitality*, London, Routledge.

McRobbie, A. (1994), *Postmodernism and Popular Culture*, London, Routledge.

Miles, S. (1995), 'Towards an understanding of the relationship between youth identities and consumer culture', in *Youth and Policy*, pp.35-45.

Miles, S. (2000), *Youth Lifestyles in a Changing World*, Milton Keynes, Open University.

Miles, S. et al. (1998), 'Fitting in and sticking out: consumption, consumer meanings and the construction of young people's identities', in *Journal of Youth Studies*, vol.1, no.1, pp.81-96.
Mirza, H. (1992), *Young Female and Black*, London, Routledge.
Mizen, P. (1995), *The State, Young People and Youth Training*, London, Mansell.
Muggleton, D. (1997), 'The Post-Subculturalist', in Redhead, S. et al. (eds), *The Clubcultures Reader*, Cambridge, Blackwell Press.
Muggleton, D. (2000), *Inside Subculture*, London, Berg Press.
Murray, C. (1994), *Underclass: The Crisis Deepens*, London, Institute of Economic Affairs.
Pilling, D. (1990), *Escape from Disadvantage*, London, Falmer Press.
Piper, H. and Piper, J. (1998), '"Disaffected youth": a wicked issue: a worse label', in *Youth and Policy*, winter, no.62, pp.32-44.
Polhemus, T. (1999), 'In the supermarket of style', in Redhead, S. et al. (eds), *The Club Cultures Reader*, Cambridge, Blackwell.
Pollock, G. (1996), 'Unemployed and under 18: struggling between subsistence and destitution', in *Youth and Policy*, Autumn.
Rattansi, A. and Phoenix, A. (1997), 'Rethinking youth identities: modernist and postmodernist frameworks', in Bynner, J. et al. (eds) (1997a) op. cit.
Ray, L. and Sayer, A. (1999), 'Introduction', in Ray, L. and Sayer, A. (eds), *Culture and Economy After the Cultural Turn*, London, Sage.
Redhead, S. (1997), *Subcultures to Clubcultures: An Introduction to Popular Cultural Studies*, Cambridge, Blackwell.
Redhead, S. et al., (ed.) (1993), *Rave Off: Politics and Deviance in Contemporary Youth Culture*, Aldershot, Ashgate.
Roberts, K. (1995), *Youth and Employment in Modern Britain*, Oxford, Oxford University Press.
Roberts, K. (1996), 'Individualization and risk in East and West Europe', in Helve, H. and Bynner, J. (eds), *Youth and Life Management: Research Perspectives*, Helsinki, Helsinki University Press.
Roberts, K. (1998), 'School-to-work transitions in former Communist countries', in *British Journal of Education and Work*, vol.11, pp.221-238.
Roberts, K. (2000), 'The sociology of youth: problems, priorities and methods', paper presented at the *BSA Youth Study Group Conference, 'Researching Youth: Issues, Controversies and Dilemmas'*, University of Surrey, England, July.
Roberts, K. and Jung, B. (1995), *Poland's First Post-Communist Generation*, Aldershot, Avebury.
Roker, D. (1998), *Worth More Than This: Young People Growing Up in Family Poverty*, London, Children's Society and Trust for the Study of Adolescence.
Rowe, D. (1995), *Popular Cultures: Rock, Music, Sport and the Politics of Pleasure*, London, Sage.
Ryan, A. (1999), 'Britain: recycling the Third Way', in *Dissent*, 46/2, Spring, pp.77-80.
Sardiello, R. (1998), 'Identity and status stratification in deadhead subculture', in Epstein, J. (ed.), *Youth Culture: Identity in a Postmodern World*, Oxford, Blackwell.
Savage, M. (2000), *Class Analysis and Social Transformation*, Milton Keynes, Open University Press.
Sennett, R. and Cobb, J. (1997), *The Hidden Injuries of Class*, 2nd Edition, London, Fontana.
Simpson, D. and Cieslik, M. (2000), 'Expanding study support nationally: implications from an evaluation of the East Middlesbrough Education Action Zone's programme', in *Educational Studies*, Sept. vol.26, no.4.
Skeggs, B. (1997a), *Formations of Class and Gender*, London, Sage.

Skeggs, B. (1997b), 'Classifying practices: representations, capitals and recognitions', in Mahony, P. and Zmroczek, C. (eds), *Class Matters: Working Class Women's Perspectives on Social Class*, London, Taylor and Francis.

Skelton, T. and Valentine, G. (eds) (1998), *Cool Places: Geographies of Youth Cultures*, London, Routledge.

Smith, R. and Maughan, T. (1998), 'Youth cultures and the making of the Post-Fordist economy; dance music in contemporary Britain', in *Journal of Youth Studies*, vol.1, no.2, pp.211-228.

Thornton, S. (1997), 'The social logic of subcultural capital', in Gelder, K. and Thornton, S. (eds), *The Subcultures Reader*, London, Routledge.

Turner, B.S. (1994), *Orientalism, Postmodernism and Globalism*, London, Routledge.

Turner, B.S. (1997), 'From governmentality to risk: some reflections on Foucault's contribution to medical sociology', forward to Peterson, A.R. and Bunton, R. (eds), *Foucault, Health and Medicine*, London, Routledge.

Wallace, C. and Kovatcheva, S. (1998), *Youth in Society: The Construction and Deconstruction of Youth in Eastern and Western Europe*, London, Macmillan.

White, R. (1999), *Australian Youth Subcultures: On the Margins and in the Mainstream*, Hobart, Australian Clearinghouse for Youth Studies.

Williamson, H. (1997), 'Status Zero Youth', in MacDonald, R. (ed.), *Youth, Social Exclusion and the Underclass*, op. cit.

Willis, P. (1990), *Common Culture*, San Franciso, Westview.

Wulff, H. (1995), 'Inter-racial friendship: consuming youth styles, ethnicity and teenage feminity in South London', in Amitai, V. and Wulff, H. (eds), *Youth Cultures: Cross-Cultural Perspectives*, London, Routledge.

Wyn, J. and Dwyer, P. (1999), 'New directions in research on youth in transition', in *Journal of Youth Studies*, vol.2, no.1, pp.5-22.

Wyn, J. and White, R. (1997), *Rethinking Youth*, London, Sage.

YCS (1999), *Youth Cohort Study: The Activities and Experiences of 16 Year Olds: England and Wales*, March, London, DfEE.

Ziehe, T. (1989), *Ambivalences and Diversities: Texts on Youth, Education Aesthetics and Culture*, Copenhagen, Politisk Revy.

Chapter 2

Young Offenders, Risk and Personal Development Programmes[*]

GEOFF NICHOLS

Introduction

Many adventure programmes place young people in challenging or 'risky' situations in order to promote personal growth. However, it has been argued that young people are already confronted by an increasing range of risks in their daily lives and, paradoxically, some adventure programmes are directed towards young offenders who already face a disproportionate amount of risk. This chapter examines the use of risk in outdoor adventure programmes with young offenders undergoing drug rehabilitation. The research included interviews with programme participants, programme managers and probation staff and the findings illustrate the difficulties of risk management in programmes that require particular sensitivity to the disadvantages faced by clients. The major risks faced by clients were sustaining a new self-concept and lifestyle which excluded drug use. Experiences of outdoor adventure were not a direct substitute for drugs but they could act as a metaphor for overcoming the challenges of rehabilitation, provide a catalyst for changes in self-concept and the development of new trust relations, and the activities themselves could provide a new life interest. Thus, risk sensitively managed, could have positive outcomes for these young people.

Risk and Personal Development Programmes

There has been little published analysis of the process by which outdoor adventure programmes, in which participants experience perceived risk, leads to personal growth. A recent review concluded that, 'virtually none of the evaluations...attempted to define how the actual program components work to attain their intended results' (Reddrop, 1997, p.61). However, it is likely that practitioners will have developed their own practical understanding of what works and why. The most well developed published account of the process of adventure education, in which risk has a central role, (Hopkins and Putnam, 1993, ch.4) draws on a model of the 'adventure experience paradigm' devised by Priest and Martin (1991). This incorporates Mortlock's (1984) categorization of stages of adventure.

Figure 2.1 Priest's 'adventure experience paradigm'

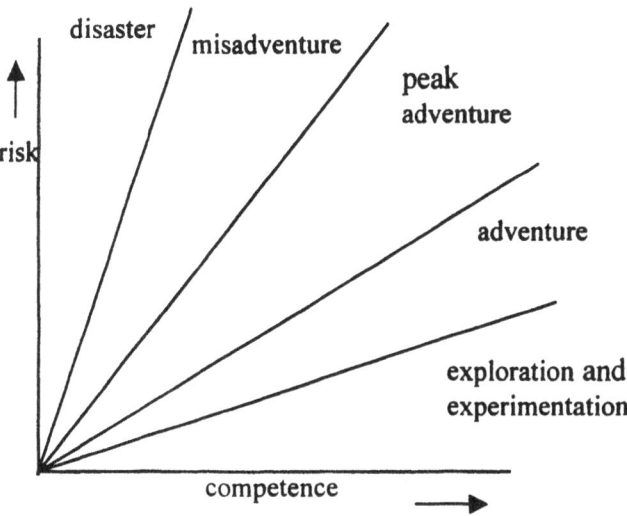

(Adapted from Hopkins and Putnam, 1993, p.70)

An individual's position on Figure 2.1 will depend on their perception of their competence in relationship to risk in any given situation. Where competence and perceived risk are balanced there is a state of 'peak adventure'. Misadventure occurs where risk exceeds competence and adventure can occur where competence exceeds risk. Priest gives examples of how the educator can use perceived risk (1991). If the participant lacks confidence the educator can set them up with an experience that is in the participant's perceived misadventure zone but which the educator judges they can cope with. When they manage to overcome the challenge their perceptions change such that through their achievement they realize that their capabilities are greater than they thought they were. Similarly, an overconfident participant could be set up with an activity that is actually beyond their competence. By failing at it they gain a more realistic perception of their own capabilities. The educator has to manage this process by matching the participant to the appropriate level of challenge. Participants' successes and failures need to be constructively reviewed to achieve a positive outcome.

Hopkins and Putnam (1993) argue that in a programme of personal development for young people, growth is facilitated through a succession of adventurous activities. During these the individual is encouraged to take personal risks as an adventure into the unknown of their own capabilities and those of other group members. Risk may be physical, social or emotional. A long-term result of the process would be that the individual would be willing to take charge of their own development by instigating their own risk-taking activities. Thus while Priest's model explains an educational process involving a realignment of perceived and real balances between risk and capability, Hopkins and Putnam take this further and claim that by pushing an individual into their perceived misadventure zone their competencies will be stretched. Personal growth through these situations is either achieved by the development of skills to cope with the higher level of challenge or by the realisation that one had previously underestimated ones own potential. The individual is then able to take on the higher level of risk, but now it is perceived as being within their peak adventure zone.

Personal growth is not just an incremental movement up the levels of peak adventure. Entering the area of perceived risk may produce dissonance in self-concept such that new patterns of behaviour and value systems are adopted (Putnam, 1985). Thus personal growth involves creativity in reconstructing self-perception (Baker-Graham, 1994) and Hopkins and Putnam (1993, pp.82-86) give examples of this change in self-concept. In this model it is important that activities on the programme can be used by the participant as a metaphor (Bacon, 1983) for others in their daily life. For example, the approach to overcoming a physical challenge could be a metaphor for other challenges, such as getting a job or staying off drugs.

A legacy of the historical development of programmes using adventure has been an emphasis on physical risk. Hopkins and Putnam (1993) have extended the range of risks to the social and emotional. This raises the question of whether the programme staff have comparable skills in managing these other dimensions of risk. Only very recently have articles considering the psychological risk felt by participants been published (Ringer, 1995 and 1997) and it is likely that educator's skills in managing these will be far less well developed, unless the literature lags considerably behind the practice.

Important points to note arising from the historical development of the use of risk in adventure education are; the traditional emphasis on physical risk and the use of particular activities; the relatively recent development of a model of the process in which perceived risk is used in adventure to lead to personal growth which may not necessarily be used by practitioners; and the extension in this model of the range of risk from the physical to the emotional and social, with the consequent demands on practitioners' skills to manage these other dimensions of risk. An important legacy is that of the value judgements of Kurt Hahn, the influential founder of the Outward Bound movement, who believed that it was educationally justifiable to impel young people to confront challenges they would not otherwise tackle and that (over 50 years ago) humanity was facing physical degeneration (Richards, 1991). This has influenced the justification of physical risk and the general perception that the major challenges of adventure programmes are physical.

Theorizing the Role of Risk in Personal Development Programmes

It has been argued, especially in relation to programmes designed to reduce offending behaviour, that risk in legitimate activities could be an effective substitute for risk in illegal ones. This understanding of the motivations for crime was implied by Lyng's (1993) concept of 'edgework'. Drawing on Katz's (1988) interviews with criminals Lyng concluded that they seek situations where the outcome is unpredictable but they will have to draw on all their resources of will power and determination to achieve a successful outcome. 'The goal is to transport yourself and your victim to the limits of an ordered reality and then use your transcendent power as a 'hardman' to control the ensuing chaos'. This could be seen as the criminal seeking risk induced excitement, corresponding to an intrinsically rewarding flow experience in the sense described by Csikszentmihalyi (1992). Katz's sample appears to have been taken from criminals with a well-established criminal career. Rosental (1982) used this explanation of criminal behaviour to understand the results of a study of juvenile offenders on an Outward Bound course who subsequently reduced offending; suggesting that adventurous activities could provide a legitimate substitute for criminal ones. But, as Putnam and Hopkins's model (1993) explains, and has been argued elsewhere (Nichols, forthcoming), the process of a physically demanding personal development course is much more complex. Roberts (1992) has suggested that merely providing legitimate risk will probably be insufficient to divert young people from offending behaviour. His explanation is that:

> Much delinquency and all other riotous incidents...can be exceptionally good fun for the perpetrators. Driving a stolen car is exhilarating...Pitched battles with the police can be particularly rousing...There really are no socially acceptable alternatives that deliver the same kicks. The same applies to heroin. (Roberts, 1992, p.11).

Roberts further asserts that such offences are committed because offenders are alienated from society and have no stake in it to lose.

So what does work in reducing offending behaviour and what sort of risks might be involved for programme participants? The success of a sports counselling programme for young probationers has been understood in terms of a redefinition of their self-identity (Nichols, forthcoming; Nichols and Taylor, 1996). Dissonance in self-concept occurred as a result of changes in self-esteem, new role models provided by the sports leaders on the programme and new peer groups. Changed self-concept has also been identified as important in research into those that desist from offending (Graham and Bowling 1995). Graham and Bowling's research found that desistance from crime involved a reappraisal of personal value systems. These studies indicate the importance of helping young people to take risks in self-concept and that this could lead to a reduction in offending. They also indicate the importance of taking a risk in a new relationship of trust with someone who becomes a significant role model; as was the case in the relationship between sports leaders and participants on the sports counselling programme.

The Nature of Risk Faced by Young People

Both Giddens (1991) and Beck (1992) argue that in a state of late modernity decisions are less rational and more risky because of the lack of knowledge about outcomes. It is not that there are necessarily more risks in modern society but for Giddens, the risks taken are of a different type. They involve having to cope with a general sense of anxiety because they are difficult to calculate. Giddens's (1991) major concern is the risk we must all take of continual self-definition. He does not make specific mention of adolescence but the establishment of self-identity has been seen by Hendry (1993, ch.1) as the major task faced at this age. The need to make choices and take risks has been accentuated by the individualization of society. Although divisions of class, gender and ethnicity may still have a determining effect on a young person's career path that effect is less certain (Furlong and Cartmel, 1997). Consequently, individuals have a sense of choice, and are forced to make choices, giving an impression of control, but those that start life with a disadvantage are likely to end with one. Thus we have a paradox where society appears more individualistic to actors but where traditional divisions still affect the life course.

Class position also influences the distribution of risk. The economically and socially disadvantaged are forced to take greater risks. They may have to live in a neighbourhood of high crime and may be forced to take risks which may lead to criminal behaviour. For example, a large proportion of young people carry a weapon for self-defence (Carvel, 1996), but victims of crime come disproportionately from the disadvantaged (Commission on Social Justice, 1994, p.50; Audit Commission, 1996, p.10). Young people involved in crime are likely to have experienced a combination of disadvantages (Stewart et. al., 1994) and disadvantaged young people are more likely to be forced into situations where they have to take risks, some of which will involve illegal activities. For example, Davies's (1997) account of young adolescent prostitution, drug taking and life in poverty shows how through a multitude of disadvantages young people may be put into situations where the only perceived options involve risk-taking. Through taking such risks they may become more skilled at judging them and avoiding them, although their position of disadvantage still leads to more inadvertent risk taking. The uneven distribution of risk leads to a questioning of the relevance of exposing young offenders to further perceived risk in adventure programmes. Adventure programmes may seek to inculcate a risk-taking attitude as part of taking responsibility for ones own further personal growth through learning from new challenges one has decided to tackle. However, young offenders may be more concerned to learn strategies for coping with or avoiding risks they have no option but to confront.

How Appropriate are the Risks Offered by Adventure Education Programmes for Young People at Risk?

Priest's model of adventure education, adapted by Hopkins and Putnam, was primarily concerned with physical risk. Even if it can be applied to personal growth involving a redefinition of self, as in the cases of young offenders rejecting offending behaviour, have those running the programmes the skills to manage this process and the risks involved? Do the activities on a programme provide a direct substitute for the excitement of crime or drug taking, or is their potential to do this limited? To what extent do the risk activities on a programme act as an effective metaphor for risks that offender's face in the rest of their lives? While the impact of adventure programmes may be more dramatic because of their novelty a significant change in self-concept, especially one that contrasts with that of former peers, may require considerable support after the programme. Does such a change in self-concept occur and is the support required available?

The following discussion draws on a case study of a residential outdoor centre in Wales, Hafotty Wen, run by Merseyside Probation service. The centre runs a wide range of programmes from one day visits to a series of training events that lead up to an attempt on all the 3000 ft. mountains in Wales over 24 hours, a considerable physical challenge. Clients may come from residential settings, such as bail hostels or drugs rehabilitation units, as well as other areas of probation service work. Interviews were conducted with four probation officers (two female and two male) who had extensive experience of sending a variety of clients on programmes at the centre. Interviews were also conducted with; five ex-clients (all male) who had used the centre over the last 14 years; three recent clients (all male) who had taken part in programmes at the centre in recent months; and the centre manager. Four of the ex-clients had successfully completed long-term drug rehabilitation programmes and are now involved in work with current drug users. The fifth had also been involved in drug related crime and now manages an organisation which also works with young offenders. Thus the ex-clients could comment on the role the outdoor programme took in their own rehabilitation and how they used it with others.

Managing Risk to Achieve Positive Outcomes

The skilful management of risk is important if the processes described by Priest (1991)˙and Hopkins and Putnam (1993) are to result in personal growth. Generally such programmes are associated with physical risk, especially by those that are unfamiliar with them. However, the centre manager thought that the physical challenge of the activities was not a very important component of the programmes, seeing it as valuable in initially bringing groups together. For some prospective participants the physical challenge was also not a concern but this was usually because they did not realize it's extent before they were involved in the activities; it was hard to imagine climbing a 3000 ft high mountain until one had tried it. For those in residential drug rehabilitation units a visit to the centre was seen primarily as a welcome change from a very structured routine so they might not consider the physical challenge until they were confronted by it.

For other prospective participants the physical element of the courses could be a source of apprehension. Young males whose physical condition had been affected by drug use might feel that their self-esteem would be challenged by being unable to live upto male stereotypes. A bail hostel warden explained how this was one of the apprehensions she had to reassure participants about before they attended a programme. An insensitive activity leader could set unrealistic physical expectations, and one example was given of where this had happened in the past. However, experienced probation staff were now able to liaise closely with the centre before visits which ensured the appropriate level of challenge was presented to all participants. For example, a drug rehabilitation officer described how:

> The mountains are a long day, some people may not be able to achieve that and we are not wanting to set people up to fail, so we will phone Hafotty and say, one or two are not going on this particular walk, one of our staff will stay behind, but rather than saying, 'maybe I should have gone', they will cook the tea, so when the group come back and they are tired they're all part of it.

The perception of the courses offered by the centre as mainly physical was a reason why some probation officers did not recommend them to their clients. This had resulted in a split within the probation service between officers who supported and did not support the centre. Those that used the centre regularly showed how the physical challenges, and other risks, could be made appropriate for the participants.

The most physically challenging programme offered by the centre was the 14 Peaks expedition, which several of the interviewees had undertaken. Although it involved two or three training events, participants still felt unprepared for the degree of challenge:

> Now, I look back now and look at my certificate and I can remember every single step of that 14 Peaks. I felt every step. I can remember getting out of the van as clear as I'm looking at you now...and it was absolutely teeming with rain. Going up Snowdon, I'd only taken about 20 steps and I was thinking, how have I got here, what am I doing? I really found it hard to motivate myself at that point because I just felt like turning back.

However, experienced probation staff showed an appreciation that there were many other aspects of risk than the physical. These needed to be carefully considered in designing the programme and preparing the participants for it. A bail hostel warden gave an example of how perceived risk could be managed and used constructively in the case of young men experiencing horse riding on a course:

> Now that in itself was another huge experience for residents because most of them had never seen a horse close up. But then they had to trust themselves on the back of this huge animal, and it was a very frightening experience. As I say you are talking about people who think nothing about bottling you in the face, but really, really having quite a hard time sat on the back of a horse. Actually it's about keeping your nerve, trusting the animal, trusting yourself, not doing

anything rash. In a very real way getting a grip of yourself and learning to control.

In this case the bail hostel warden purposely did not discuss the activity beforehand because:

Otherwise then the exercise becomes meaningless, you are just sat on a horse aren't you. But for them afterwards to talk about how they felt. They would say to you 'I was really scared, I really bottled it on that horse you know'. That is interesting because it is not a macho thing to bottle it on anything,...This is now quite a big step here for these guys because they are actually admitting to fear, it means that they can actually take a different way out of a situation other than going back...It's no good challenging the horse to go outside and have a fight is it?

In this example the hostel warden skillfully managed the participants' apprehensions to achieve an experience which would allow them to express their emotions and seek constructive ways out of difficulties rather than resorting to violence. The same warden spoke of many other fears of programme participants. These included being made to appear inadequate if they had to complete a written exercise due to low levels of literacy, fears of bed wetting due to physical conditions, fears of how they would cope without access to drugs and concerns about their arrangements for social security payments. This illustrates the great sensitivity that is required in managing risk for clients with a range of needs and conditions and who may well be lacking in self-esteem. It shows the importance of a worker who has detailed knowledge of the clients being able to liaise with the centre staff to ensure that the level and type of challenge is appropriate and managed. This bail hostel warden had learned the importance of this through having to deal with situations where a large number of residents had expressed an interest in attending courses but few had turned up on the day. This large drop-out rate had been remedied by sensitive preparation, but this did not happen in all bail hostels. It depended on the experience and commitment of the hostel staff, especially the warden. Thus the quality of risk management by probation staff was variable.

Even the experienced bail hostel warden quoted above was still surprised by some course outcomes. She gave an example of how the shared experience of a course by staff and a client had led to unpredicted emotional risk-taking by the client. A young female member of staff had been employed at the hostel [which was for males only] to try and help male residents experience and develop the capacity to have normal day-to-day relationships with people of the opposite sex. She was supported in this challenging role but one client had not managed to come to terms with this and continually verbally abused her. The hostel warden explained how this relationship changed on a course:

> Well she [the female member of staff] said it happened in the middle of a river and she was stuck, they were doing a river crossing. He turned back and helped her, she was not in physical danger, she was stuck...He was in front of her and he turned round and he saw her and she said 'can you give me a hand' and he went back for her, it was like that. You could not have set it up. Something happened in that moment...she had a very fruitful and productive relationship with him thereafter.

This illustrates how the experience on the course acted as a catalyst for this client to take the emotional risk of offering support to the female member of staff. A change in relationship had been achieved that had not been possible through other activities. The activities had been a catalyst for risk-taking and change, but in an unpredictable way. Similarly, another experienced probation officer reported that:

> I expect the Home Office would want to see a set of objectives, and we certainly need to justify what we are doing there, but I am one of the most experienced probation officers that have used Hafotty Wen. I have been going for 15 years, it is certainly the best facility the probation service has got, and that's from experience, but if I was taking somebody out there the real answer is I don't know what they are going to get out of it, I know they will get something, but depending on the individual, 'cos. you sit there, and say 'so and so is going to do this', and when you get there you find he does not do that, you find he is an entirely different person, with skills or a different attitude, or someone who will talk to you in the office in a monosyllabic conversation will sit down and tell you their whole life history. I have been amazed at some of the changes I have not foreseen.

Overall the analysis above shows the different perceptions of the centre manager and different probation staff of the risks taken by participants. These perceptions have consequences for the management of risk on the programmes. Where the perceptions are inadequate they may result in negative outcomes; an example being poor preparation of participants resulting in them not attending at all. The combination of disadvantages faced by participants required a particularly perceptive and sensitive appreciation of their apprehensions and management of the programmes, although even then, some positive outcomes were unpredictable.

Perceptions of Risk and the Benefits of Participation

While participants might have been apprehensive about the physical challenge, overcoming it was a source of satisfaction. In particular, the achievement of completing the arduous 14 Peaks expedition, recognized by a certificate, was of major significance to all participants:

> I was elated after we'd done. Once we'd got back to the centre it was just wanting to get into bed, obviously. The next day at the presentation it was, to be honest with you, it was like the biggest achievement of my life.

A client on one of the standard courses reported:

> You go up Snowdon. I'd never really done mountain walks before. I'd done hill walks but not mountain walks and I thought I'd never get to the top. At the beginning I really dreaded it, I really wasn't looking forward to it. Just going there in the van I thought , 'Oh, this is going to be testing'. I used to look how far ahead you've got to go and it used to kill me. The top was there in the distance many millions and millions of miles away from me. It did seem like quite a hurdle at that time, to get up a mountain. You come to realise that it's not so bad, it's quite good really. The feeling gets better as you get closer to the top, I've got to admit.

As noted above, there has been debate over the extent to which exciting physical activity can be a substitute for crime and drug use (Roberts, 1992; Lyng, 1993). For some participants mountaineering had become a major life interest and, in this sense, had replaced drug use, and for some an interest in outdoor pursuits had led to employment opportunities:

> It's given me an alternative to drugs but it's something that I enjoy more than taking drugs. You can say that it's a replacement but it's not a negative replacement, it's a positive thing because I've actually found something that I like doing that isn't having a detrimental effect on my health.

This participant 'enjoyed the adrenaline' of rock climbing, but for another participant, who also experienced satisfaction and excitement on the programme, this was not a crucial part of a substitute activity for drugs:

> Everybody's different and different things appeal to different people. The hard thing sometimes is finding what's on offer that will fill the void, if not to

the point that drugs did, quite close to it, that does give you a good feeling, does give you a purpose in life.

This was reflected in a quote from a participant who put the satisfactions of outdoor pursuits in perspective when related to taking heroin:

> ...actually taking drugs, you do get something out of it. It is a good feeling, the actual drug itself. I think if you asked people and say if heroin grew on trees, and in anyway didn't affect your lives or relationships with your mother or your family or your girlfriend or your wife or whoever, and give you this good feeling, I think there would be a large part of the population on it. At the end of the day it doesn't give you all that and it causes a lot of grief in your life. Therefore, sometimes it's hard to grasp what could give you an adequate feeling after drugs because you do tend to relate everything to the good feeling. Actually achieving something, actually just sharing, just being with people and doing outdoor pursuits, feeling good about yourself, that's a natural good feeling.
> When you get off drugs there's a big void there, for me there's a big void. I've lost the drugs to fill this empty space inside me that used to give me a good feeling and now the drugs have gone I haven't got that good feeling. I know it really does fill a gap inside me. In a way it is addictive but it is a positive one.

Having a new interest, and one possibly leading to employment opportunities, appeared to be more important than excitement and risk associated with drugs. These were similar characteristics to those experienced by successful participants in the sports counselling scheme evaluated by Nichols and Taylor (1996). Increased self-confidence, and support from probation staff, was required to help clients establish a new self-identity that might be in sharp contrast to that of their former associates. One participant, a former drug dealer, developed an interest in conservation work, which led to voluntary work and later full-time employment:

> I could not tell my friends and associates, 'that is a robin red breast there, and that does stay here in the winter, and that is a blackbird and that is a song thrush', that just would not have happened, it would not have gone down well, me street cred would have gone, so it was all suppressed, so coming here, people asking me, and what would I like to do personally, and it was like conservation, and it was great, there was no one judging me and saying, I don't like that.

This redefinition of self-concept is the main risk that Giddens (1991) thinks characterizes late modernity but in this case it is all the more challenging because it is in such a contrast to the participant's previous self-identity and that of his former peers. Hence it needed greater support to sustain. Similarly, those leaving the rehabilitation hostel to live independently needed support to redefine their lives.

Physical achievements especially the 14 Peaks expedition did act as a metaphor for participants who were undergoing drug rehabilitation or trying to start a new life:

> ...the first mountain I walked up, I kept tripping because I was looking at the peak and I was looking at the scenery and Simon said to me, look at your feet and every now and again you stop and check...and have a look back at the scenery. I thought that would be like coming off drugs that, if I look at where I'm going, I'll fall over and if I look at where I've been to I'll fall over so I need to look at my feet, you know, every day...So I translated that one thing he said, that on the surface was about mountain climbing, into the bigger thing.
>
> At one time I thought I'd never be able to get off drugs, I'll never be able to sort this one out. I often compare it with the 14 Peaks. I said that when I was just first walking up them first few steps, which really stopped me from going any further especially with drugs, it really stopped me from getting over that threshold. I honestly believe in my heart now that it can be done:

Experiences could also act as a metaphor to help clients put their relationship to nature and others in perspective.

> I found it quite humbling, a humbling experience, I realised in a positive way for the first time in my life, that I was actually deeply insignificant when put next to all this stuff. How that helped me was because for years I had a typical junky attitude and that the universe revolves round me and I am the most important thing in it which a lot of people need to drop before they become drug free. I have known quite a few other people have that experience at Hafotty.

The achievements on the courses, especially the physically demanding ones, could act as a metaphor for other challenges, such as coming off drugs. But this needed long term support because of the risk of relapse, which was not uncommon. A client who had relapsed reported:

> I had to go back into the same situation that I came out of, sort of old haunts really. It was eighteen months where I didn't actually use drugs but being offered it constantly. We get tested enough, ex drug addicts, on a day to day basis just walking along the road. You're always being tested in one way or

another. You try and minimise it as much as you can. I wouldn't go to a friend's house where I know he has his mates round all using heroin because I know that's just not a good idea, it's a simple as that. You try and minimise those times and keep it as rare as possible. If you can foresee a time where you can put yourself in a vulnerable situation you will try, or I will now, try and avoid them.

As illustrated above, the major risk facing those on drug rehabilitation is relapse. Ex-addicts were aware of the dangers of going back to live in the same place, but living somewhere else offered other challenges:

The problem is, most people, in rehabilitation you're wrapped in cotton wool, if you like. You're in an enclosed community, you're not dealing with the outside world. They do learn you skills to cope with everyday normality, whatever normal is. When you get outside, you get a flat and then you go pay your bills and stuff like that, you're unemployed, you haven't got a job because you've been out of work for years because you took drugs and it's like starting your life over, it's like leaving home all over again. You know how difficult is to get a job and most people look at it and think, I can't cope with this, I might as well go back to taking drugs. You've got no support, a lot of people feel isolated again because they took drugs for years, all they've ever known is other drug users and to suddenly come out of that subculture and come back into society, you tend to be isolated because society doesn't really want to know them because they're a drug user or former drug user, and you don't fit into the drug culture any more because you no longer want to use drugs. You're sort of caught in the middle and either go one way or the other, most of them tend to go back to what they know, which is drug use, what they're comfortable with.

The courses provided the catalyst for relationships of trust to develop between probation officer and client which could provide the long-term support required for drug rehabilitation. These moved towards 'pure relationships' in the sense used by Giddens (1991, p.89) which became independent from the social structure of the probation supervision context. Unprompted, all participants commented on the good relationship they had developed with the centre manager which for many had become a long term significant relationship as they visited the centre on repeated occasions:

...meeting Stan, he was from where I live, he's from Liverpool. He was born on...Road in Liverpool and I'm only five minutes away. Just being from the same place I felt I could relate to Stan a bit. I seem to have hit it off with Stan ever since. Every time we've had a good chin wag about when he used to live in Liverpool.

Both the centre manager and probation staff might become long term 'significant others'. A former client explained how his probation officer, who he had shared the 14 Peaks expedition with 14 years ago, had remained a close friend since then. This development of a trust relationship with an authority figure who acts as a role model is similar to the relationship between sports leaders and participants on the sports counselling programme (Nichols and Taylor, 1996) reported earlier. It may be of more importance to participants who have few other relations of trust.

Risk is Relative to Perception

The analysis above has contrasted probation service staffs' perception of risk on the outdoor programme and that of drug rehabilitation clients'. The risks on the programme have been placed in the context of the major risk faced by those on drug rehabilitation, that of relapse and the difficulties of establishing a new life and sustaining a new self-identity. Not only do probation staff have to be extremely sensitive to the risks as perceived by their clients but also how their perception of risk changes over time.

One participant who had taken up rock climbing as a result of being introduced to outdoor activities later gave it up when he realized how dangerous it could be. In contrast, while on drugs he,

> ...used to inject half grams of heroin which is a bigger gamble than the lottery. Basically what that type of behaviour says about somebody is that they don't care whether they live or die. I didn't at the time but I do now.

This illustrates that perceived risk is relevant to ones knowledge. In the same way that Beck's (1992) concern with risks of environmental disaster is a function of his awareness of the problem, this participants concern with the risks of rock climbing is a function of his awareness of the consequences of making a mistake. For some people this awareness of risk in rock climbing could enhance the experience, as in the rock climbers studied by Csikszentmihalyi (1992) in his understanding of the intrinsically satisfying state of 'flow'. Others may not choose to take these risks. A second point is that risk is relative to the value of potential loss and gain. The participant above took high risks with drugs when he did not value his life, but low risks with rock climbing when he did. Another ex-addict described the risks he took to get crack:

> Desperate for more crack I began stealing from the dealers. Letting myself in at three one morning I was pounced on by a dealer I owed £500 for a few grams of cocaine. He stripped me naked, trussed me like a pig and beat me with a claw-hammer for nearly two hours.

The risks were balanced against the benefits of getting the crack, as perceived at the time. An appreciation of this changing perspective on risk is useful in considering the validity of Roberts' (1992) argument that offenders would be less likely to commit crime if they had a stake in society to lose. The two examples above of drug addicts taking risks were people who felt they had nothing to lose, except their next fix. Drug addicts on rehabilitation realized the risks they faced through association with former peers and easy access to drugs when they felt insecure. Gaining employment, if they could, helped alleviate these, but they needed more than this stake in society. They needed help to 'start your life over', to become established as a new person.

Conclusion

Risk can be used constructively in outdoor adventure programmes for offenders but this requires particular care and skill to take account of the circumstances of the clients. The analysis above shows that the clients have very diverse needs that can only be appreciated by someone in long-term contact with them. Sensitive and skilled centre staff need to liaise closely with probation officers who know the clients to ensure that risk is used constructively. Probation staff need to prepare clients carefully for the risks they will take on the programme, but this needs to be part of a long term process of supervision. If this is done, physical, emotional and social risks can be managed to achieve positive outcomes such as improved self-esteem, improved relations of trust with probation staff, and possibly a new interest that could lead to employment opportunities. The model of personal growth through adventure (Hopkins and Putnam, 1993) is useful, but the skills of programme staff need to be particularly high to take account of the nature of risks faced by clients and the considerable need for support.

Because the clients are disadvantaged they will face greater risks and therefore need greater support for a longer time; for example, those leaving drug rehabilitation for independent living. While for advantaged young people it may be reasonable for outdoor adventure courses to use risk-taking to promote personal growth, for disadvantaged participants it maybe more valuable to minimize or avoid risk; for example, avoiding former associates involved in drug use.

There is little support for the idea that risk activities can offer intrinsic satisfactions that substitute for drug use. The role of the activities as a medium for development is more important, but they can also offer a constructive, legal, leisure interest; and for some, this may lead to employment opportunities. However, it is still possible that for criminals with different motives not related to drug use, for example, those studied by Katz (1988), risk activities could provide a closer substitute for offending behaviour. This illustrates the difficulty of generalizing between effective programmes for different offenders. A limitation of this study is its concentration on those involved in drug related crime and its all male sample of clients. This sample's perceptions of risk therefore may be very different from other groups of young people. However, the probation officers interviewed had experience of working with male and female clients.

It is necessary to understand not only what the client perceives as a risk but also the perceived balance between benefits and rewards, which is specific to situation and level of knowledge. A drug addict may take considerable risks to obtain drugs or when taking them even when they know what those risks are. On the other hand, prospective programme participants may volunteer to climb a mountain but will not realize the scale of this challenge before they undertake it.

Overall the study indicates the difficulty of generalizing about perceived risk in the way that Giddens (1991) and Beck (1992) have. If risk is a function of awareness then one can only generalize about the perception of environmental disaster, as Beck does, to the extent that everybody shares the awareness of the factors that will lead to that. Giddens is more justified in generalizing about the risks of having to continually redefine self-identity because of the common experience of social change. However, Giddens, unlike Beck, puts little emphasis on the unequal distribution of risk and does not note the particular needs of adolescents to establish an independent self-identity. Thus, as discussed above, an ex-drug dealer redefining himself as a conservationist will face a disproportionate challenge if he tries to establish himself in his old community.

Giddens's concern with self-definition can be incorporated into Hopkins and Putnam's (1993) model of personal growth through adventure. A particular strength of outdoor adventure experiences can be its catalytic power in transforming self-concepts. This change can be guided through relations of trust – Giddens's 'pure relationships'. Sharing outdoor adventure provided a catalyst for these trust relationships developing between clients, centre staff and probation officers. Outdoor activities were not a direct substitute for drugs in terms of the satisfactions they gave. Climbing a mountain did not give a comparable experience to taking heroin. But outdoor pursuits could become a central life interest in a new life style. Where drug rehabilitation had been successful changed lifestyle, self-concept and peers had led to changed behaviour; reduced drug use and reduced offending. The sensitive use of risk in outdoor adventure programmes with young offenders can be justified by these positive outcomes.

Note

* This chapter was originally published in, *Journal of Youth Studies* as, 'Is risk a valuable component of outdoor adventure programmes for young offenders undergoing drug rehabilitation?' (1999), vol.2, no.1, pp.101-117. Reproduced with the permission of Carfax Publishing, Taylor and Francis Ltd, Rankine Road, Basingstoke, Hants, http://www.tandf.co.uk.

Acknowledgements

I would like to acknowledge the value of discussions with Paul Wiles in the research leading to this paper and the time and assistance given by interviewees.

References

Audit Commission (1996), *Misspent Youth: Young People and Crime*, Abingdon, Bookpoint.
Bacon, S. (1983), *The Conscious Use of Metaphor in Outward Bound*, Denver, Colorado Outward Bound School.
Baker-Graham, A. (1994), 'Can outdoor education encourage creative learning opportunities?', in *Journal of Adventure Education and Outdoor Leadership*, vol.11, no.4, pp.23-25.
Beck, U. (1992), *Risk Society: Towards a New Modernity*, London, Sage.
Carvel, J. (1996), 'Third of boys aged 15 carry arms', *The Guardian*, 15 May.
Csikszentmihalyi, M. and Csikszentmihalyi, I. (1992), *Optimal Experience: Psychological Studies of Flow in Consciousness*, Cambridge, Cambridge University Press.
Commission on Social Justice (1994), *Social Justice, Strategies for National Renewal*, London, Vintage.
Davies, N. (1997), *Dark Heart. The Shocking Truth About Hidden Britain*, London, Chatto and Windrus.
Furlong, A. and Cartmel, F. (1997), *Young People and Social Change*, Buckingham, Open University Press.
Giddens, A. (1991), *Modernity and Self-Identity*, Cambridge, Polity.
Graham, J. and Bowling, B. (1995), '*Young people and crime*', Home Office research study *145*, London, Home Office.
Hendry, L. et al. (1993), *Young People's Leisure and Lifestyles*, London and New York, Routledge.
Hopkins, D. and Putnam, R. (1993), *Personal Growth Through Adventure*, London, David Fulton.

Katz, J. (1988), *Seductions of Crime: Moral and Sensual Attractions in Doing Evil*, Basic Books, New York, in Lyng, S. (1993), 'Dysfunctional risk taking: criminal behaviour as edgework', in Bell, B. and Bell, W. (eds), op cit.

Lyng, S. (1993), 'Dysfunctional risk taking: criminal behaviour as edgework', in Bell, B. and Bell, W. (eds) (1993), *Adolescent Risk Taking*, London, Sage.

Mortlock, C. (1984), *The Adventure Alternative*, Cicerone Press.

Nichols, G. (forthcoming), 'Developing a rationale for sports counselling projects', in *Howard Journal*.

Nichols, G. and Taylor, P. (1996), *West Yorkshire Sports Counselling, Final Evaluation Report*, Halifax, West Yorkshire Sports Counselling Association.

Priest, S. and Martin, A. (1991), 'The adventure experience paradigm', in Miles, J. and Priest, S. (eds), *Adventure Education*, State College, PA, Venture Publishing.

Putnam, R. (1985), *A Rationale for Outward Bound*, Rugby, Outward Bound Trust.

Reddrop, S. (1997), *'Outdoor programs for young offenders in detention – an overview'*, Hobart, Tasmania, National Clearinghouse for Youth Studies.

Richards, A. (1991), 'Kurt Hahn', in Miles, J. and Priest, S. (eds), *Adventure Education*, State College, PA, Venture Publishing.

Ringer, M. and Gillis, H.L. (1995), 'Managing psychological depth in adventure programming', in *Journal of Experiential Education*, vol.18, no.1, pp.41-51.

Ringer, M. and Spanoghe, F. (1997), 'Can't he see me crying inside? Managing psychological risk in adventure programs', in *Zip Lines*, Summer 1997, pp.41-45.

Roberts, K. (1992), 'Leisure responses to Urban Ills in Great Britain and Northern Ireland', in Sugden, J. and Knox, C. (eds), *Leisure in the 1990s: Rolling Back the Welfare State*, Eastbourne, Leisure Studies Association.

Rosental, S.R. (1982), 'The fear factor', in *Sport and Leisure*, No.23, p.61.

Stewart, J. et al. (1994), *Understanding Offending Behaviour*, Harlow, Longman.

Chapter 3

Young People and Illicit Drug Use in Postmodern Times?[1]

TRACY SHILDRICK

Introduction

This chapter looks at the issues of youth culture and illicit drug use. Young people's relationship with illicit drugs goes back a long way, although the advent and popularity of the dance club cultures which emerged in the later 1980s were to cement this relationship once and for all. Historically youth cultures have often been understood as a class-based phenomenon, and notably through the concept of subculture (Hall and Jefferson, 1976). A sophisticated and influential theoretical approach for understanding these youth subcultures was produced by the Centre for Contemporary Cultural Studies (CCCS) in the late 1970s and early 1980s. The approach was extensively criticized at the time and more recently by youth cultural researchers (see Miles, 2000; Bennett, 2000).

As a consequence of criticisms of the CCCS and together with the increasing popularity of postmodern social theory youth cultural researchers have moved away from class-based analysis, and tried instead to draw upon notions of tribes and lifestyles as meaningful ways to understand young people's experiences. This chapter starts with a brief review of the literature on youth culture. It then moves on to explore the issue of youthful drug use as an example of the ways in which aspects of postmodern social theory have been used to try to understand young people's lives. It has been suggested that young people's use of illicit drugs may be indicative of processes associated with postmodernity, as fragmented and pick 'n' mix lifestyles become embedded in the ways in which young people use illicit drugs (Parker et al., 1998).

This chapter draws upon qualitative research material collected for a doctoral study. The study had two main aims: to explore the nature of youth cultural identification and experience; and to examine the potential relationship between such experiences and the use of illicit drugs. The next part of this chapter presents findings from this project in relation to illicit drug use. Most of young people who took part in this project were aware of the availability of illicit drugs and many had been in situations where they had been offered drugs, supporting the notion that today many young people are drug wise (Parker et al., 1998). When it comes to drug consumption, however, the picture is less straightforward. Almost half of the 76 young people in this project had never tried any illicit drugs. Of the small majority who had used illicit drugs, experiences varied significantly from those young people who had tired cannabis just once to those who had used a much wider range of illicit drugs, which for a small number included heroin.

Three broad stylistic groupings of young people were apparent in this research,[2] with one group, the 'trackers', being widely known to the other young people who took part in the project. Significantly, it was within the 'tracker' group that the use of solvents, prescription tablets and heroin was observed. There are two important points to note here: firstly there is perhaps too rigid a distinction between recreational drug use and more chaotic, dependent, daily use which underpins contemporary explanations of young people's drug use as we see in Parker's (1998) notion of normalization. Certainly for the 'trackers' this division was less clear and evidence from the these young people suggests that such monolithic distinctions may be weakening, with some groups of young people, especially those like the 'trackers' crossing over from earlier recreational use (of solvents, cannabis, amphetamines etc.) to later dependent use (of heroin) in the course of their individual drug using careers (Johnston et al., 2000); and secondly that for some groups of young people, in this project the 'trackers', there appears to be a link between socio-economic background and patterns of illicit drug use; 'trackers' socio-economic location corresponds most closely to that which has been described elsewhere as a youth 'underclass' (see MacDonald, 1997, for a review of these debates).

This chapter suggests that attempts to link contemporary patterns of drug use to the concept of postmodernity are not especially helpful in trying to fully understand youthful drug use. By merging a significant proportion of young people's drug use under the concept of recreational use, nuances and detail of attitudes and experiences will never be revealed. Furthermore, by presenting drug use as a phenomena which is largely untouched by traditional inequalities such as social class, it is difficult to explore the ways in which structural disadvantages, or indeed other dimensions of inequality, may correspond to particular patterns, or experiences of drug consumption.

Postmodernism, Youth Culture and Illicit Drug Use

Over the last twenty years wide ranging social and economic changes have led to the suggestion that we now live variously in high modern (Giddens, 1996), late modern (Furlong and Cartmel, 1997) or post-modern (Baudrillard, 1993) society. All too often though, such changes tend to be subsumed under the catch all phrase postmodernity, a term which is, as a consequence, frustratingly elusive to define (Featherstone, 1992). Contemporary youth researchers, particularly those interested in the more cultural aspects of the youth experience, have tended to draw, to varying extents, upon what might broadly be described as 'postmodern' theoretical approaches as a way of understanding young people's lives. As noted elsewhere in this volume youth research is generally thought to fall into two broadly differing camps. Whilst one might argue over the extent to which the apparent rift between the two is more imagined than real (see MacDonald et al., 2001 for a fuller discussion) most youth researchers accept that some differences exist between those approaches which explore youth transitions and those which examine the more cultural and lifestyle aspects of young people's lives. Structural explanations of young people's experiences tend to be central to transitions research and in the past have also been important for youth cultural research. In the late 1970s and early 1980s the CCCS produced a sophisticated theoretical approach for understanding youth subcultures which had social structures and more specifically social class at its very core (see Hall and Jefferson, 1976). Subsequent criticism however, have led contemporary youth cultural researchers to draw upon newer theoretical ideas to try and understand young people's lives.

Postmodern theory tends to discard or downplay previously accepted indicators of social experience and stress the more fragmented, reflexive and individualized nature of contemporary social life. People's lives seemingly become more fraught with risks (Beck, 1992) and structural factors became less obvious or important. For example, social class, which was once the most widely used concept in British sociology (Edgell, 1993) has moved to a position where its usefulness and explanatory value is increasingly challenged (Pakulski and Waters, 1996; Pahl, 1989). Youth cultural researchers have been keen to move beyond the older class-based theoretical approach of the CCCS and generally agree that their approach is empirically unworkable (Thornton, 1994) or simply unsuitable in attempting to understand the 'postmodern consumers, who wish to construct their own identities through the wearing of 'stylistic masks' (Muggleton, 2000, p.39). Moreover, the apparently fragmented and individualized nature of young people's experiences may lend itself more easily to newer theoretical persuasions. The fragmentation of identity is key here as it raises questions about traditional class-based notions of collectivity and suggests instead the use of concepts such as 'tribes' (Maffessoli, 1996) or neo-tribalism (Bennett, 1999) which are argued to be more relevant to contemporary youth experience. The concept of neo-tribalism has proved useful to some contemporary youth researchers who have argued that in direct contrast to the class-based youth subcultures of the past the contemporary cultures of youth are more fleeting and transitional and organized around individualized lifestyle and consumption choices. Here it is the fragmented and individualized ways in which young people are alleged to construct their identities, which is of significance. As Bennett suggests:

> I put forward a new theoretical framework for the study of the cultural relationship between youth, music and style using the Maffessolian concept of neo-tribalism...Neo-tribalism provides a much more adequate framework as it allows for the shifting nature of youth's musical and stylistic preferences and the essential fluidly of youth cultural groups. Such characteristics have been a centrally defining, if developing, aspect of consumer based youth cultures since the establishment of the post-war youth market...I have endeavored to illustrate how urban dance music and its attendant sensibilities of consumption, although appearing to have inspired a new chapter in the history of post-war youth culture, is actually the product of neo-tribal sensibilities which have characterized young people's appropriation of popular music and style since the immediate post-war period, such sensibilities being an inevitable aspect of later modern consumer society (Bennett, 1999, p.614).

For some, postmodern youth move swiftly through a succession of styles like tins of soup on a supermarket shelf (Polhemus, 1994), exhibiting a 'stylistic promiscuity which is breathtaking in its casualness' (Polhemus, 1994, p.131). Developing these themes it has been suggested that 'lifestyles' (Bennett, 1999; Miles, 2000) may be a more appropriate tool to help understand the complexity of contemporary youth identities. In this vein Miles has suggested that:

> Young people are having to deal with the dilemmas of rapid social and cultural changes as a routine part of their everyday lives and a primary means by which they deal with this situation is through the maintenance of consumer lifestyles. Consumer lifestyles effectively provide a vehicle or a currency through which fluid identities are constructed. A consumer imperative has therefore emerged as a fundamental means of stabilizing young lives at the turn of the century. Such stability is not manifested in the form of a deep-rooted sense of sameness, but in a flexible, mutable and diverse sense of

identity which consumerism appears to present the only viable resource (Miles, 2000, p.158).

The concept of lifestyle has importance for understanding youthful drug use, as drugs become simply another commodity for consumption in similar ways to fashion, music and other leisure pursuits. Youth cultures have long been associated with drug use (see Muncie, 1999 for a review) and recent trends in theorizing young people's use of drugs provide a good empirical example of how developments in postmodern theory are alleged to aid understanding of the reality of young people's lives. The increasing importance of consumption, accompanied by an apparent loosening up of traditional social structures is argued to produce fragmented and individualized lifestyles and this has led to new ways of understanding young people's relationship with illicit drugs:

> Throughout the 1960s the connection between drugs and youth culture became more closely interwoven with top pop groups such as the Rolling Stones, Small Faces, Jimi Hendrix and The Who openly stating that they used drugs and making drug references (Blackman, 1996, p.183).

The advent of the dance club scene in the mid 1980s was to cement this relationship once and for all with the close association between participation in this culture and the use of ecstasy, amphetamines and cannabis (Release, 1997). The rave scene emerged in the UK in the mid-to-late 1980s and was succeeded by a diverse club dance scene. Whilst changes in patterns of drug usage have long been associated with ebbing and flowing of changes in youth culture, the advent of the rave scene was different in a number of ways to the subcultures which had preceded it. For the first time it seemed that subculture had moved from the marginal to the mainstream with a larger number of young people being involved in this culture then ever before (Merchant and MacDonald, 1997). It was argued that this particular culture included diverse groups of young people and unlike the subcultures of the past, where participants were argued to come from similar backgrounds participants in this culture emanated from a diversity of backgrounds and cultures (Redhead et al., 1997).

An attendant consequence of the widespread popularity of dance club cultures is that drugs and drug use have moved from 'marginal subcultures to the situation where they are widely sampled and used in late modern consumer culture' (South, 1999, p.3), developments which, in part, underpin the sustained interest in the concept of normalization. Indeed it has been suggested that processes of normalization are underpinned by wide ranging 'social transformation' (Parker et al., 1998, p.2) where the contemporary drug using experiences of young people provide further evidence of postmodernizing trends. It is argued that postmodern theory, with its emphasis upon fragmentation and choice, is best placed to help us to understand a situation where young people from 'all social and educational backgrounds' (Parker et al., 1982, p.1) become drug users. Moreover it is suggested that social changes, such as those associated with post-modernity, have resulted in a situation where young people embrace drug use as an integral aspect of their leisure and cultural landscape. In essence, Parker and colleagues suggest that the 1990s were remarkable because:

> Most adolescents and young adult users merely fit their leisure into busy lives and then in turn fit their drug use into their leisure and 'time out' to compete alongside of sport, holidays, romance, shopping, nights out, drinking and most importantly of all having a laugh with friends (Parker et al., 1998, p.157).

As such, drugs are no longer deemed to part of an unknown, deviant and unorthodox world which is alien to the majority of 'ordinary' young people but shift into a position where they are an accepted and integral aspect of the cultures and contexts which most young people inhabit. Taylor argues that 'young people increasingly see the use of illegal drugs as a lifestyle choice' leading to a situation where 'the use of drugs in a recreational context, is regarded by young people as normal feature of everyday life, regardless of whether they approve of it or not' (Taylor, 2000, p.333).

It is suggested that 'social changes represented within some elements of contemporary social theory *(postmodernity)*, are crucial to understanding how the nature of being an adolescent in Western Europe is changing and why drug use is becoming a feature of modern leisure and consumption' (Parker et al., 1998, p.22) and furthermore it widely accepted that:

> Any explanation of changes in young people's attitudes and behaviour are more likely to evolve from aspects of social theory found in the post-modernity debate and less likely to be found in older social class or unmodified subcultural explanations (Parker et al., 1998, p.27).

In summary current trends in the use of illicit drugs mirror and perhaps reflect many of the trends which are associated with the dawn of postmodernity:

> The new widespread availability of a whole range of drugs packaged and marketed for the 1990s mimics the processes of commodification and global trading and consumption patterns identified in contemporary social theory. The way in which drug use has interwoven itself into fashion, music, dancing,

partying and indeed drinking, right across Europe, corresponds with theoretical ideas about global markets, the ascendancy of consumption and the transportability and transnationalization of youth culture (Parker et al., 1998, p.31).

Central to these ideas is the proposition that young people take more individualized and reflexive approach to their drug taking, being more aware of the risks, and the importance of successfully negotiating such risks (alongside of others) on a daily basis. Increasingly young people take a pick 'n' mix approach to their drug use much as they might with other aspects of their lives such as alcohol use (Parker et al., 1998). Theses changes in patterns of drug use as reflective of the broader social changes which have rendered the youth or transitional phase as more risky and uncertain.

The Research

The fieldwork for the research reported here was conducted in the period May 1996 to January 1998. The research was conducted in a town located on the coast of the North East of England. Forty-nine in-depth, semi-structured interviews with seventy-six young people, along with a number of episodes of participant observation were carried out. The participants in the project were aged between 16 and 26, and 45 were male and 31 were females. The young people were variously, in further and higher education (full and part-time), engaged in various forms of youth training, in employment (full or part-time), unemployed and a small number were engaged in voluntary work. One young man was self-employed. One participant was of Asian origin and all other participants were white. The young people came from a range of social, economic and social class backgrounds. There was no explicit attempt to involve only young drug users in the project, but rather to try to explore a range of experiences and attitudes of an 'ordinary' group of young people. A key aim of the project was to explore how young people's youth cultural experiences were related to illicit drugs and he utility of using postmodern theoretical approaches as a means of understanding these experiences.

From the Critical to the Tolerant: Young People's Accounts of Illicit Drug Use

One aim of the project was to explore young people's youth cultural identification alongside their attitudes towards, and experiences of, illicit drugs, whilst at the same time taking account of the broader context of young people's lives in terms of family background, housing careers, education, work careers and social class. The intention was to try to provide a more holistic and integrated understanding of young people's experiences rather than to follow in the path trodden by so many others and dissociate young people's cultural and leisure lives from their broader, more structural life (style) experiences (Muggleton, 2000; Bennett, 1999, 2000; Miles, 2000). By exploring youth cultures alongside drug using careers and also the wider socio-economic context it was possible to make comparisons across leisure, youth cultural style, drug use and socio-economic backgrounds. The attitudes and experiences of the young people who participated in this study were diverse in nature and defy any one overarching explanation. Their attitudes ranged from being cautious or critical about drug use, to being tolerant and accepting and likewise their drug using experiences extended from regular and indulgent users, to desisters, occasional and non-users. In broad terms, however their accounts could be mapped onto their wider experiences of youth cultural identification. There were three stylistic groupings apparent in the research. These were 'Spectacular youth', such as those who adopted a widely recognized youth cultural style such as Goths. Then there were the 'Trackers' who were well known locally, in part through their style of dress – the wearing of tracksuits. Finally, the 'Ordinary youth' who described themselves as 'just normal' or 'just ordinary'.

'Ordinary' Young People

The drug using experiences of the 'ordinary' young people were the most limited across the sample and the majority had not tried any illicit drugs. Although, in the main they were drug wise (Parker et al., 1998) in so far as they were aware of drugs in the environments which they inhabited and many had been in situations where they had been offered drugs. Interview data provided many descriptions of these sorts of experiences:

> I have been offered them plenty of times in nightclubs. Someone will be smoking it [cannabis] and saying 'do you want half of this' or someone

coming up to you and saying 'do you want to buy some?' or whatever. It's common you just get used to it (Tim, 'ordinary' youth).

Only a minority of these 'ordinary' young people had any direct experience of drug use and as such most drew upon a range of sources of knowledge to inform their views and opinions. These included the media, stories and rumours which circulated in the local area and drugs education at schools (although most had little recollection of this). A smaller number of the ordinary young people had tried a drug at least once, and here experiences ranged from those who had tried cannabis occasionally or once to those who had infrequently used a wider range of illicit drugs including ecstasy, LSD and/or amphetamines. Claire was one of the very few 'ordinary' young people who had tried a wider range of illicit drugs:

> I've tried acid, cannabis, ecstasy and speed. It's not like a regular thing. I wouldn't take them very often but it is alright to try as I am a curious person. If you don't try you wouldn't know...you take a quarter as an experiment. Me and me boyfriend we got one [ecstasy tablet]. We knew we wanted to try it...it was purely out of curiosity that we took a quarter (Claire, 'ordinary' youth).

Curiosity is the key factor which the majority of 'ordinary' young people cited as their motivation for using drugs. Most typically in this group, drug users describe their consumption as occasional and in no cases was drug consumption described by these participants as regular. This was borne out by the fact that none of the ordinary young people were using drugs at the time of the research (in so far as they had not used a drug in the previous week). The boundaries between acceptable and unacceptable drug use were clear and relatively rigid within this 'ordinary' group of young people who for the most part only accepted the use of cannabis. Cannabis use was deemed to be relatively harmless (by both users and non-users) although the acceptance of the use of other drugs such as amphetamines was apparent in the accounts of a much smaller number of 'ordinary' youth. Many of the 'ordinary' young people were critical of the use of ecstasy and perceived it to be 'very dangerous'. Such views were clearly informed by the media campaign which took place after the death of Lea Betts and is indicative of the ways in which 'ordinary' young people had relatively little direct experience of illicit drugs and their opinions were often clearly (mis)informed by popular national and local discourses. Heroin was, perhaps predictably perceived as a drug to be avoided at all costs. Overall the use of drugs by ordinary young people was limited and they overwhelmingly possessed either a cautious or a critical approach to the use of illicit drugs.

'Spectacular' Youth

'Spectacular' youth were different to the ordinary young people in a number of respects: they were more explicitly aware of drugs and the use of drugs by young people around them, and as such their attitudes were more often informed by direct knowledge and experience; and secondly they were more likely to have used illicit drugs themselves. Whilst a small number of the 'spectacular' youth had never used any drugs the majority did have some experience of drug consumption. For many of the spectacular youth their experiences extended beyond the use of cannabis to the use of amphetamines, LSD and/or ecstasy. Typically they had used drugs on a number of occasions, although the majority were not regular drug users, for example Nicola who was part of a Goth youth cultural grouping:

> I have used cannabis a few times...well perhaps a dozen or so. I mean it's not really classed as a drug. But then the others...well I tried LSD at a friends and I have taken amphetamines a few times. It's not like a regular thing, you know, but well it does go on...it's not really any big deal.

The boundaries which were rigid and clear within the ordinary group were more blurred with spectacular youth who were on the whole relatively tolerant of what they perceived as recreational drug use. The 'spectacular' youth who participated in this project were, however, very clear about the acceptability of certain types of drug and levels of consumption. Occasional or irregular consumption of recreational drugs such as cannabis, ecstasy and amphetamines was generally described as being largely unremarkable. Regular or poly-drug use was deemed to be much less acceptable within this group, as was the use of heroin, which was perceived as a particularly bad drug.

Overall the 'spectacular' youth who took part in this project were more likely to have used a range of illicit drugs, including cannabis, ecstasy, LSD and amphetamines. In general, both drug users and non-drug users in this group processed attitudes which were tolerant of the use of certain illicit drugs, such as cannabis and ecstasy and amphetamines.

'Trackers'

The drug using experiences of the 'trackers' was distinctive in a number of respects: they tended to describe drug consumption as a much more accepted, regular and common place part of their cultural lives. For many of the trackers drug use was a relatively 'normal' aspect of their cultural lives and this was evident in the ways in which many of them described their 'time-out' and leisure experiences. Unusually and in contrast to the other participants in the project, a significant number of them referred to the use of drugs unprompted, for example when asked about what sorts of things he did in his spare time Darren ('Tracker') told me:

> Well, like I said we just hang around. There will be some alcohol, maybe some blow. I don't know...if we're lucky someone will get hold of some jellies [temazepam]...it's just what you do.

For many of the 'trackers' their accounts suggest that they did 'fit' drugs into their leisure experiences in much the same way as Parker suggests. However, they did not accommodate drugs use alongside holidays, sport and nights out, but rather alongside of alcohol and simply 'hanging around' the streets and generally 'doing nothing' (Corrigan, 1976).

The range of drugs which are used by the 'trackers' is more complex than that which was described by any of the other young people who took part in this project. Solvents are well known for their association with lower-working class males (Tyler, 1986) and for many of the male 'trackers' in this study solvents provided an early initiation into the use of illicit drugs. Michael ('tracker') explained how he started using solvents at around 12 years of age:

> When you're fucking bored yeah nought to do on the streets, It's when you can't find your mates and you have no money, no nought and you see a tin of Linx [deodorant] up on the top [bathroom shelf] and you just do it...you just take the top off and wrap a t-towel up and sniff it and all the butane it comes up – it's a right one.

'Trackers' were unusual in so far as prescription tablets (for example temazepam) appear in their accounts as a relatively unremarkable and accepted part of their drugs repertoire. Jane ('Tracker') recounted:

> One night I took a pill...well it just looked the same, but I was dead bad. Me sister was going to take us up the hospital but I got all right in the end...I found out after it was a tablet for epilepsy (Jane aged 17, tracker).

The 'problematic' experience which Jane described was not especially uncommon in the 'trackers' accounts and many of them described incidents where they personally, or someone they knew had experienced 'problems' after taking drugs. Such 'problems' ranged from suffering a 'whitey' (feeling sick and faint) to falling down and knocking oneself unconscious.

For a smaller number of the 'trackers' their drug use had become especially problematic resulting in addiction to heroin. As with previous research in this area, findings from this project suggest that heroin abuse was confined to those, 'young people who are socially excluded or who live in disadvantaged neighbourhoods' (Parker, Bury and Eddington, 1998, p.30).

To summarize, at the outset of this project there was no intention to include young people who were known for their drug use. Instead the aim was to explore how illicit drugs may (or may not) be linked to youth cultural identification and experiences. The young people in this project exhibited a broad and wide range of attitudes and experiences of illicit drugs although in many respects these could be mapped onto their wider youth cultural identifications and experiences. At the simplest level the 'ordinary' young people are the least likely to exhibit attitudes and experiences which were in any way indicative of a process of normalization, (except in relation to cannabis). The accounts of the 'spectacular' young people were more likely to be aware of, and tolerant of, 'recreational' drug use by either themselves or those around them. 'Trackers' accounts indicate that they tend to use a wider range of drugs on a more regular basis than the other young people who took part in the project.

Discussion

This chapter has used the example of youthful drug use to try and shed some light on the analytical value of attempting to use post-modern theory to try and understand contemporary youth cultural experiences. Whilst not wishing to wholly discount the value of contemporary theoretical approaches described above, I want to suggest that one should also be mindful of how older, perhaps more structurally informed analysis, may also still be of use. Contemporary accounts of youth cultural identity and illicit drug use tend to under-state the structurally differentiated nature of the contemporary youth experience whilst at the same time broadly over-stating the eclectic and individualized nature of young people's experiences. Similarly, attempts to link postmodernizing trends to patterns of drug use tends to obscure the ways in which traditional patterns of inequality may impact upon some young people's experiences and patterns of illicit drug use.

The vast majority of young people (in this study) who had used illicit drugs were 'ordinary' in so far as they were not targeted for their known use of illicit drugs and the vast majority of drug users were not 'problematic' (in the sense of being known to professionals/agencies as drug users, or being officially addicted to drugs) but rather they were 'recreational' drug users. Patterns of 'recreational' drug use are not necessarily obvious and what constitutes recreational use for one young person may represent 'problematic' use to another. The experiences of the young people here, especially the 'trackers' suggests that 'recreational' drug use may be more complex than has previously been imagined. It follows that the distinction between 'recreational' and 'problematic' use may also be less exact than previous accounts might suggest. For many of the 'trackers' their use of drugs had been problematic for them in one way or another and it was not difficult to imagine that more of them could in the future progress from the use of recreational drugs to the use of other more addictive drugs such as heroin. Whilst not wishing to deny that postmodern theory may be helpful in explaining some young people's relationships with some illicit drugs it was suggested that such approaches do not help us to understand *all* recreational drug use. In particular most of the trackers could be defined as recreational users. They are, however, not recreational users of the nature which Parker et al. and others have described them. In particular their use of tranquilizers and solvents set them apart from other recreational drug users. Most interestingly the trackers are different to the other young people in the research in terms of their socio-economic backgrounds. They are living in areas of the town, which are known to be deprived and disadvantaged. The parent(s) of the Trackers were either unemployed or engaged in unskilled or low-skilled part-time, temporary or unofficial work. Trackers themselves were either unemployed or on youth training schemes. Few had any school qualifications.

This raises questions about attempts to link contemporary drug use to wider notions of postmodernity (Parker et al., 1998; South, 1999). Whilst normalization purports to move beyond one-dimensional meta-narratives which can explain youthful dug use, by its very nature the concept of normalization imposes its own meta-narrative upon young people's experiences negating the opportunity for multiple understandings or explanations. Although traditional dimensions of inequality, such as social class and gender, which were once prime indicators of drug usage, may no longer be useful when looking broadly at the use of drugs. For example it is clear that being middle class no longer prevents young people from taking illicit drugs, indeed the latest research suggests that living in more affluent areas may infact increase the likelihood of using illicit drugs (Ramsay and Partridge, 1999). Once we move beyond this rather primitive concern with prevalence, however, a more complex picture emerges. For some groups of young people, in this study the trackers, there was a very clear relationship between socio-economic factors, and patterns of drug consumption. The most disadvantaged young people, in this study 'trackers' were most likely to use a wider range of drugs on a more regular basis and to experience more 'problematic' incidents than other young people were. For these young people living in a disadvantaged area and spending time on the streets also meant that they were more likely to come into contact with drug users at an earlier age.

Significantly the 'trackers' 'choice' of drugs illustrates the problems with existing theories of youthful drug – taking. Recreational drug use does not take place in a vacuum, where all young people make 'informed choices' about whether or not to consume drugs and which drugs to consume. The availability of drugs remains a key influence upon the types of drugs which are consumed. As Measham, et al. (1998) argue where young people are involved in street centred networks they are more likely to gain knowledge about and access to illicit drugs. At an even simpler level there is also the issue of cost and for the 'trackers' the use of prescription tablets was clearly influenced by the ready availability and the cheapness of these drugs.

Conclusions

This chapter has explored illicit drug use and its relationship to youth cultures and in particular how postmodern theory has been used to try to shed some light on the empirical reality of young people's lives. The young people in this research project fell broadly into three different groups: 'ordinary' youth, 'spectacular' youth and 'trackers' and their drug using experiences could be mapped onto their wider youth cultural identities. In the case of the trackers they were also connected by their disadvantaged socio-economic position. It is argued that the use of post-modern theory limits the ways in which we can understand how various forms of inequality impact upon young people's lives and in particular their drug use.

Exploring the ways in which structural factors affect young people has in some areas become unfashionable. Very few studies of young people's youth cultural lives pay more than fleeting attention to how wider social and economic factors may impact upon young people's experiences (see Hollands, 1995 for an exception). This trend is not altogether unsurprising. Historically studies of youth culture have been criticized for being overly structurally determined and the perceived lack of connection between the empirical reality of young people's lives and the theories which purport to describe them have all, perhaps rightly, served to open the way for newer theoretical approaches. Indeed, some aspects of some young people's lives may well best be understood by using postmodern theoretical approaches.

To date, however, we lack the empirical evidence to either wholly support of completely refute this. Many studies are lacking in empirical evidence (Redhead, 1993) whilst others which are more empirically grounded tend to neglect the wider socio-economic contexts of young people's lives (for example Bennett, 1999; Miles, 2000). It is my view that for some groups of young people, in this research the 'trackers', socio-economic factors may have a significant impact on their broader youth cultural and drug using experiences. We must be sceptical of studies which neglect the wider socio-economic contexts of young people's lives when undertaking research. Any assumption that such factors are less important than in the past should be supported by empirical data. Roberts makes the point very well:

> It is in the course of making school-to-work and family transitions that social class, gender and ethnic divisions amongst young people widen, deepen and are re-consolidated. These divisions are then reproduced in other areas of young people's lives. This is just one respect in which it is impossible to explain what is occurring elsewhere until the sub-structure of young people's lives (their school to work and family/housing transitions) have been analyzed properly (2000, p.6).

The gap between the rich and the poor continues to widen and many young people bear the brunt of rapidly changing social and economic environments. If we are serious about the need to understand the reality of young people's lives we would be unwise to neglect the wider socio-economic contexts in which young people find themselves today.

Acknowledgements

I am grateful to the University of Teesside and Deighton NHS Trust for funding this research. I would also like to thank the editors, Mark Cieslik and Gary Pollock for their useful comments on an earlier draft of this chapter.

Notes

1. An earlier version of this chapter appeared in the Journal of Youth Studies, vol.5, no.1, March 2002.
2. Three broadly differing youth cultural groups were identified in this research project. These were 'ordinary' youth, 'spectacular' youth and 'trackers'. It is not suggested that these groups are subcultural in the sense in which subcultures have been described in the past (Hall and Jefferson, 1976) or that they are coherent groupings with fixed boundaries. Rather these groupings emerged from young people's *own* accounts of their youth cultural identifications and stylistic preferences. Whilst stylistic differences were key to many young people's accounts, similarities of leisure experiences and

attitudes and experiences of drugs were also noted. In the case of the 'trackers' social class background was also noted to be a significant factor (See Shildrick, 2000 for a fuller discussion).

References

Baudrillard, J. (1992), *Simulations*, New York, Semiotext.
Beck, U. (1992) *Risk Society: Towards a New Modernity*, London, Sage.
Beck, U. (2000), 'Living your own life in a runaway world: Individualization, globalization and politics', in Hutton, W. and Giddens, A. (eds), *On the Edge. Living with Global Capitalism*, London, Jonathan Cape.
Bennett, A. (1999), 'Subcultures or neo-tribes? Rethinking the relationship between youth style and musical taste', in *Sociology*, vol.33, no.3, pp.599-617.
Bennett, A. (2000), *Music and Popular Identity*, Basingstoke, Macmillan.
Blackman, S. (1996), 'Has drug culture become an inevitable part of youth culture? A critical assessment of drug education', in *Educational Review*, vol.48, no.2 pp.131-142.
Coffield, F. and Gofton, L. (1994), *Drugs and Young People*, London, Institute for Public Policy Research.
Corrigan, P. (1976), 'Doing nothing', in Hall, S. and Jefferson, T. (eds), *Resistance Through Rituals*, London, Althone.
Edgell, S. (1993), *Class*, London, Routledge.
Featherstone, M. (1992), *Consumer Culture and Postmodernism*, London, Sage.
Furlong, A. and Cartmel, F. (1997), *Young People and Social Change*, Buckingham, Open University Press.
Giddens, A. (1996), *Social Theory and Modern Sociology*, Cambridge, Polity Press.
Hall, S. and Jefferson, T. (1976), *Resistance Through Rituals*, London, Althone.
Holland, R. (1995), *Friday Night, Saturday Night: Youth Cultural Identification in the Post-Industrial City*, Newcastle, University of Newcastle-upon-Tyne.
Hutton, W. and Giddens, A. (eds) (2000), *On the Edge. Living with Global Capitalism* London, Jonathan Cape.
Johnston, L., MacDonald, R., Mason, P., Ridley, L. and Webster, C. (2000), *Snakes and Ladders: Young People, Transitions and Social Exclusion*, Bristol, Policy Press.
MacDonald, R., Mason, P., Shildrick, T., Webster, C., Johnston, L., and Ridley, L. (2001), 'Snakes and Ladders: in Defense of Studies of Youth Transition', in *Sociological Research On-Line*, vol.5, no.4.
MacDonald, R. (ed.) (1997), *Youth, the 'Underclass' and Social Exclusion*, London, Routledge.
Maffesoli, M. (1996), *The Time of the Tribes*, London, Sage.
Measham, F., Parker, H. and Aldridge, J. (1998), *Starting, Switching, Slowing and Stopping*, London, Home Office.
Merchant, J. and MacDonald, R. (1992), 'Youth and the rave culture, ecstasy and health', in *Youth and Policy*, no.45, pp.16-38.
Miles, S. (2000), *Youth Lifestyles in a Changing World*, Buckinghamshire, Open University Press.
Muggleton, D. (2000), *Inside Subculture*, Oxford, Berg.
Muncie, J. (1999), *Youth and Crime*, London, Sage.
Pahl, R. (1989), 'Is the Emperor Naked? Some questions on the adequacy of sociological theory in urban and regional research, in *International Journal of Urban and Regional Research*, vol.13, no.4, pp.709-720.
Pakulski, J. and Waters, M. (1996), *The Death of Class*, London, Sage.

Parker, H., Aldridge, J. and Measham, F. (1988), *Illegal Leisure*, London, Routledge.
Parker, H., Measham, F. and Aldridge, J. (1995), *Drug Futures: Changing Patterns of Drug Use amongst English Youth*, London, Institute for the Study of Drug Dependence.
Parker, H., Bury, C. and Eddington, R. (1998), *New Heroin Outbreaks Amongst Young People in England and Wales*, London, Home Office.
Polhemus, T. (1994), *Street Style*, London, Thames and Hudson.
Ramsay, M. and Partridge, S. (1999), *Drug Misuse Declared in 1998: Results of the British Crime Survey*, London, Home Office.
Redhead, S. (1993), *Rave Off*, Aldershot, Avebury.
Redhead, S., Wynne, D. and O'Connor, J. (eds) (1997), *The Clubcultures Reader*, Oxford, Blackwell.
Release (1997), *Drugs and Dance Survey: An Insight Into the Culture*, London, Release.
Roberts, K. (2000), 'The sociology of youth: problems, priorities and methods', presented at *British Sociological Association Youth Study Group Conference*, University of Surrey, July 2000.
Shildrick, T. (2000), 'Youth Culture, the "Underclass" and Social Exclusion' *in Scottish Youth Issues Journal*, Issue 1, Autumn 2000, pp.9-30.
South, N. (ed.) (1999), *Drugs, Controls and Everyday Life*, London, Sage.
Taylor, D. (2000), 'The word on the street: advertising, youth culture and legitimate speech in drug education', in *Journal of Youth Studies*, vol.3, no.3, pp.333-352.
Thornton, S. (1995), *ClubCultures*, Cambridge, Polity.
Tyler, A. (1986), *Street Drugs*, London, New English Library.

Chapter 4

Victims of Risk? Young People and the Construction of Lifestyles

STEVEN MILES

Introduction

Young people's experience of life in a risk society is all too often portrayed as entirely negative in nature. There is an alarming tendency to imply that young people do not actively engage with the risk society, but that they are powerless victims of that society. The argument I want to present in this paper is that in some respects at least, young people actively engage with the power structures that surround them, and that, moreover, they often use such structures as a positive force for change in their lives. Authors elsewhere in this volume have indicated that the experience of 'youth', if we can still usefully deploy that term, is increasingly risky in the sense that pressures that would previously have been dissipated by social support mechanisms such as the family, community and religion, are falling squarely on young people's shoulders (see also Furlong and Cartmel, 1997). This may well be the case, but it should not be assumed that young people's lives will be made radically more difficult as a result. The intention of this chapter is therefore to consider the suggestion that young people are not victims of their own transitions, but that in a sense they actively collude with elements of the risk society in order to construct a coherent sense of identity in what is an ever-changing world (see Miles, 2000).

The sociology of youth is haunted by a discourse that valorizes the notion of the transition. It is indeed, important to note that the transition is not tangible in any real sense. It is only actually of any use as a means of conceptualizing the 'big picture' (Wyn and Whyte, 1997). It is patronizing to suggest that young people do go through a 'transition' because the word transition implies a unitary and channelled experience, a process in which young people have no creative input. This is a discourse that implies that young people aspire to travel from point A to B and that the only satisfactory conclusion is to reach some sublime state of adulthood. This is a simplification and reflects a world in which young people, and what it actually means to be a young person, is changing more rapidly than those people who are entrusted with the task of researching these changes. My suggestion is that the dependence on notions of the 'transition' has created a set of circumstances in which young people's experiences are portrayed, inaccurately, as fixed and immutable. Many of such approaches go to great pains to deny such criticism (e.g. MacDonald et al., 2001), but the underlying problem here is that the 'transition' is almost inevitably presented as problematic. There is an underlying assumption that the transition is inevitably difficult, that it is never straightforward and that young people will inevitably struggle as a result. This vision of a problematic transition creates its very own process of transference to the extent that young people themselves are portrayed as victims of processes that are well and truly beyond their personal control. But just because aspects of the so-called transition have a strong hold over young people's lives, does not mean that they cannot develop their own strategies to deal with such problems. In the remainder of this chapter I want to develop this particular argument, notably in light of the concomitant divide that exists between structural and cultural approaches to young studies. I will then propose a discussion of lifestyle as a means of coming to terms with what it means to be a young person in a risk society. I will illustrate this point through a brief discussion of some of my own research which looks at young people's experience of youth training.

The Structural Versus the Cultural

More than anything else the sociology of youth and indeed, youth research, is the product of a fissure that has served to mould the character of, if we can call it such, the 'sub-discipline' of 'youth studies'. Though not necessarily terminal in nature this fissure is fundamentally damaging and is characterized by the enormous gulf that divides structural and cultural analyses of young people's lives. This gulf helps to perpetuate a particular image of young people. As I pointed out above, there is a tendency to portray young people as victims. While it is true to say that many young people are in some sense disenfranchized from society in some shape or form, this vision of victimhood is reinforced by the fact that sociologists of the transition are, on the whole, not particularly interested in the arenas in which young people react or negotiate with structural change. As a result sociologists of youth perpetuate an image of young people as powerless victims whose youth cultural experience is nothing more than an apparently straightforward escape from structural woes. Sociologists of the transition are interested in the impact of structure upon young people's lives. They are not generally interested in aspects of youth culture, when ironically youth culture represents the very arena in which young people negotiate structures. Meanwhile, at the other end of the spectrum, sociologists of youth culture have limited input to debates about the structural conditions in which young people live. What I want to suggest is that one of the major obstacles to an adequate understanding of young people's relationship to the risk society, is the fact that at a conceptual level the sociology of youth is predisposed to see young people's experience of social change as necessarily risky or problematic. Before I consider this proposition in more detail I want to outline further the nature of the fissure I have identified.

Structural approaches to young people tend to focus on one of three areas: employment, training and education, with some corollary concern for young people's changing experience of family relationships (see Miles, 2000). All these issues are clearly of central concern not only to sociologists of youth, but to sociologists in general. The significance of these issues is manifest. What is a matter of concern, however, is the precise way in which the sociology of youth addresses such matters. Our understanding of the actual impact of these particular contexts through which young people relate to social change is undermined by the fact that broad patterns of employment and education are, all too often, prioritized at the expense of potentially more informative discussions about how young people experience and invest meaning in these aspects of their lives. While commentators on youth continue to refer to the fluid and predictable nature of young people's experience, the data they use is actually bound up with a very static, categorical definition of youth. In short, there is a very limited understanding of the fluid ways in which young people interact with static aspects of employment, training and education. The end result of this process is that an orthodoxy has emerged in which the nature of youth experiences are grossly over-generalized. Let us consider one such example.

The question of unemployment is perhaps the key concern of contemporary sociological approaches to youth. This is reflected by a whole raft of statistics which illustrate that young people constitute the most vulnerable sector of the labour market. In his influential work on employment and unemployment in Britain, for instance, Ken Roberts (1995) identifies a decline in youth employment in the 1980s and early 1990s at a much faster rate than the rise of general unemployment between those dates. According to Roberts then, young people are exceptionally vulnerable to the ups and downs of economic restructuring, most notably in the aftermath of the recession in the early 1980s which itself reflected global changes in the demand for labour. In this context, Brinkley (1997) describes young people as 'under-worked and under-paid', the problem being that deregulation and the freedom of the marketplace have not necessarily benefited young people as much as might have been hoped. Indeed, Brinkley points out that the relative position of the under 25s in Britain has worsened during the 1990s. In particular, the gap between the unemployment rate for all ages and that of the under 25s seems to be greater in the 1990s than it was in the 1980s. Young people are relatively worse off employment wise than the workforce as whole. In fact, young people make up 35 per cent of the long-term unemployed. Meanwhile, young people appear to be especially susceptible to a mismatch that exists between the sorts of jobs on offer and the sorts of jobs they are actually seeking. The move towards part-time and temporary employment has hit young people particularly badly as they are arguably the most vulnerable sector of the labour force and as such are increasingly having to take-up jobs or 'McJobs' which require less qualifications than they have actually attained. The problem then, seems to be that youth unemployment is highly sensitive to overall economic conditions.

Not only can young people be described as an index of social ills and a barometer of social change, but also as beacons of economic stresses and strains. In this context, Brinkley argues that deregulation simply does not work and that the main source of hope for the future of youth employment depends on the long-term impact of the minimum wage which was first introduced in 1999. But regardless of what might be said in the future, the very least that can be said is that in recent years the youth labour market has been radically transformed, to the extent that some commentators go as far as to argue there is no longer any such thing as a 'youth' labour market (Maguire and Maguire, 1997; Skilbeck et al., 1994). The personal implications of youth unemployment are enormous and create a situation in which,

> The effect is to drive thousands of young people off benefit and out of the mainstream economy altogether, either into an indefinite dependency on their families or into illicit forms of money making. Enforced economic dependency takes away young people's cultural, social and personal autonomy and denies them any semblance of citizenship (Rutherford, 1997, p.120).

Young people, from this point of view are increasingly dependent as they struggle to gain a foothold in a society in which they apparently do not belong. This period of dependency in youth is prolonged by an extension of training and education, the shrinkage of the youth labour market and a reduction in state support (Jones, 1995, p.30). Young people are therefore victims of economic change. This is all well and good, but an approach to young people's relationship to the job market which prioritizes the accumulation of statistics on unemployment will inevitably construct a vision of young people as powerless. It is predisposed to do so because an emphasis on unemployment figures is bound to bring bad news. Moreover such an approach gives no indication of how young people negotiate a route through the ups and downs of the transition. In short, while there are examples of research that address young people's actual experiences of the 'transition' (e.g. Griffin, 1993), there is a limited understanding of how young people normalize what on the surface may appear to be negative experiences on an everyday basis. The experience of aspects of social division and inequality are highly personal, but the sociology of youth has, up to now, presented a highly impersonal view of young people as victims of social change. I want to make it clear that I am not suggesting here that traditional notions of the transition are redundant, but rather that the transition needs to be conceived in a far more imaginative and reflective fashion than is currently the case. The tendency at present is to perceive the transition as a process external to young people. Young people are apparently forced to live by the rules which the transition sets. But what is potentially far more interesting are the strategies young people adopt to cope with aspects of structural change. The transition is not forced upon young people, however much this may appear to be the case on the surface. Young people actively engage with the transition, some aspects of which they have more control over than others. The challenge for the sociology of youth is for it to come to terms with this level of creative complexity.

The first point to make about cultural approaches to youth is that these too, have tended to be predisposed towards an analysis of the subordinacy of youth. There is, or at least has been an overwhelming tendency to see youth sub-cultures as deviant or debased. Although researchers have, in effect, used youth as a vehicle for the systematic study of the cultural (which in itself is a more than worthwhile exercise), by doing so they have labelled and therefore framed, social formations to the extent that the relationship between the sub-ordinate and the dominant culture (and those that might actively abide by that culture) have become increasingly blurred. In this context, authors such as Wyn and White (1997) have noted how the tendency to categorize young people, as if age represents the central feature characterizing young people's lives has tended to portray masculine, white, (and rebellious) middle class experience as the norm. Often, when we think about cultural approaches to youth, the work of the Centre for Contemporary Cultural Studies in Birmingham comes to mind (see Epstein, 1998 for a detailed discussion). Basing their conception of young people very much upon what it is to be deviant, the Birmingham School argue that young people establish who they are through a process of labelling. By combining the insights of symbolic interactionism, structural functionalism and semiology the Birmingham School tried to move away from mass media portrayals of spectacular youth cultures in order to establish a more grounded, realistic and objective portrayal of young people's lives which were seen to be resistant to hegemonic cultural forms. In other words, the Birmingham School were concerned with the ways in which the young expressed themselves in opposition to a culture in which their voice was rarely heard. Could it not, however, equally be the case that the world in which young people live has changed so much that young people currently actively use aspects of youth culture to legitimize dominant power structures. Young people, at least on the surface, are actively immersing themselves in hegemonic visions of the world, because those visions serve the very purpose of allowing them to survive in a so-called risk society. Before taking this argument further I want to consider criticisms of the CCCS in more depth. Perhaps the most relevant and important criticism, as Muggleton (2000) notes, is that what he calls 'the CCCS approach' (with the possible exception of Paul Willis's [1978] work 'Profane Culture') neglects the subjective viewpoints of those young people who partake in particular youth sub-cultures. Muggleton (2000) goes on to quote Caroline Evans (1997) who suggests in turn, that:

> Subcultures, in all their complexity, are generally not studied in any serious, empirical way within cultural studies because of the state of British academic life. It is cheaper to do theory than ethnography, at least in the field of popular culture (p.185).

The implication of this process has been that young people have been portrayed as mere pawns of economic history. The problem as Muggleton (2000) points out is that the CCCS has attained the status of an orthodoxy. The innovative nature of recent ethnographic analyses of youth subcultures by authors such as Widdicombe and Wooffitt (1995), Thornton (1995), Blackman (1995) and Malbon (1999) have at least to an extent challenged this orthodoxy. But nonetheless, "the CCCS approach continues to provide the benchmark against which contemporary developments are measured" (Muggleton, 2000, p.4). But there is a problem with Muggleton's approach, as much as there is a problem with that which he critiques. Muggleton is arguing that in the context of analyses of youth culture, theory maintains a privileged position over ethnography to the extent that:

> Ethnographic evidence on the lives of young people is treated less as a representation of their subjective experiences than as an expression of their 'subjectivities' – the texts, discourse, frameworks and social positions through which their lived reality is 'spoken' (Muggleton, 2000, pp.3-4).

Two wrongs do not, however, make a right. Yes, theory has in a sense been lionized in this context, but ethnography is nothing if it does not reflect the social structures with which young people interact. Subcultural aspects of youth are of interest in their own right, but they are of more interest as part of symbiotic relationship with broader aspects of social change.

Sociologists of youth need to go about ensuring a balance in which ethnographic approaches to youth culture speak for themselves *and* in doing so speak for broader aspects of young people's lives. A study of youth culture should therefore enliven a study of youth transitions and vice versa. In this context, youth subcultures are more than simply 'a symbolic violation of the social order' (Hebdige, 1979, p.19). They are a vivid expression of young people's attempts to negotiate the ups and downs of social change. This negotiation takes many forms, and as such, the tendency to assume that youth cultures are necessarily rebellious is a damaging one. The implication that young people who do not rebel are somehow not 'doing their job' is a ridiculous one. Youth cultures do not reflect the relative rebelliousness of young people, but rather the often creative ways in which young people interpret the structural and cultural changes that surround them. They should not, therefore, be subjected to value judgements. It is in this sense that ethnographies of youth cultures should speak for themselves.

In constructing this argument I do not want to make the misleading suggestion that the sociology of youth culture is still dependent upon Birmingham-style subcultural analyses, but its influence is clearly still evident. It is also fair to say that disaffection with the term 'subculture' has become increasingly prevalent in Britain. Sadly, however, this is as a reflection of what Redhead (1997) describes as "the virtual disappearance of a 'field' of 'appreciative' contemporary sociological and cultural studies of youth culture" (p.3). In effect, the sociology of cultural aspects of young people's lives has appeared in the past fifteen years or so to have lost its impetus, arguably because there are simply less 'committed' youth upon which sociologists can focus their subcultural attention in a world where 'ordinary' youths are the norm. My point is that as authors such as Brown (1987) have illustrated this 'ordinariness' is in itself fascinating. And yet there is a strong tendency for sociologists of youth culture to focus their attention on the more melodramatic of youth cultural forms. Hence, the disproportionate attention given to young people and dance. What may actually be of more interest is the fact that the majority of young people do not partake in subcultural modes of behaviour. The fact that they do not may be a telling indication of how young people relate to the nature of social change.

In considering the above, there is clear evidence that the gulf between structural and cultural approaches to young people's lives is a damaging one. However, there is evidence that at least some commentators are beginning to address the problem. Indeed, as I noted above and as MacDonald et al. (2001) point out, there are examples of research that has sought to inform an understanding of structural change through young people's lived cultural experience (e.g. Bates and Riseborough, 1993; Hollands, 1990; Blackman, 1995) In this context, MacDonald et al. (2001) argue that the notion of the 'transition' should continue to play a key role in the sociology of youth. Using a qualitative study of young people growing up in Teesside, in Northeast England to back up this position, MacDonald et al. argue that a focus on transition does not, in fact, necessitate the use of overly deterministic models of young people and, indeed, actively includes young people's cultural experiences and identities, notably through an analysis of young people's leisure and social network 'careers' (MacDonald and Marsh, 2000; Shildrick, 2000). To an extent, this may be so, but there remains a long way to go before the structural and the cultural are equal partners in this equation. The transitions orthodoxy is so well ingrained that even in these examples the often unspoken implication is that young people's cultural identities are simply a *reflection* of more fundamental structural aspects of young people's 'transitions'. I would argue, in contrast, that young people's cultural experiences represent the actual area within which they seek to cope with and at times *defy* the ups and downs of structural change.

'Youth' Lifestyles

Having identified what I feel is the most pressing concern for the sociology of youth, I want to consider in more detail, one means of addressing this problem. I want to argue that the problem is essentially a conceptual one and that in turn, this problem lies not so much in the subject of study, but in who it is that is undertaking this study. That is, youth researchers are generally content to pursue the same methodological and conceptual avenues that they have always pursued. They do not feel the need to address structural and cultural simultaneously, because the longer they continue to follow their route, the more they seem to be able to establish its orthodoxy. This is not necessarily a criticism, but it does represent an obstacle to a well-rounded conceptualization of the 'state' of youth in a risk society. The experience of that society is played out through the cultural arena. For that reason the notion of lifestyles may prove especially enlightening.

If we accept, as several authors in this volume appear to have done, that the process of individualization represents a key aspect of young people's experience of social change, then it would make sense to suggest that this process is most readily expressed in the context of market dependency. This argument is developed most effectively by Ulrich Beck (1992) who identifies a new mode of socialization, a 'metamorphosis' or 'categorical shift' in the make-up of the relationship between the individual and society. In particular, there is apparently an increasing focus on the individual as a reproduction unit for the social in his or her life-world. In other words, the traditional forms of social support upon which young people used to be able to depend are no longer available. But this process is accompanied by a dual process in which the market is extended into every aspect of social life which serves to further undermine traditional sources of social support to the extent that the individual becomes as standardized as he or she is individualized. The key arena within which young people's experience of the cultural and the structural are transposed therefore appears to be that of consumer culture. Indeed, any sociological assessment of the notion of lifestyle has tended to concentrate on a broad amorphous notion of lifestyle as a 'way of life' which is somehow associated with individualized aspects of consumer culture.

Lifestyles are not simply about our relationship with consumer culture. Nor are they simply the outward expression of consumerist principles. The danger with an analysis of lifestyles is that they are indeed perceived as trivial and uncritical. There is a danger that they are portrayed as nothing more than consumerism in action. I mentioned above the possibility that the apparent lack of a rebellious streak to young people today could be read off as a kind of political impotence. Rather I would prefer to suggest that young people are rebelling from within. In an individualized society the opportunities to 'rebel' are less obvious than they were in the past. Rather, young people call upon aspects of consumer culture which they can use to construct their identities, whilst rejecting those aspects which they do not relate. Young people are not passive. Their 'opposition' to the status quo has, at one level at least, just been individualized. Young people may not be politically vocal, but they can use the resources provided for them by consumer culture to cope with the rapidity of social and structural change. I therefore prefer to define lifestyles as the cultural arena in which young people navigate through aspects of personal, structural and social change. Lifestyles are, in effect, lived cultures in which individuals actively express their identities, but in direct relation to their position as regards the dominant culture. If it is to have any sort of sociological value the notion of lifestyle needs to be addressed in specific contexts through the analysis of the specific meanings constructed by agents of social life and how they relate to the dominant culture.

This emphasis on the ways in which young people actively engage with structural and cultural contexts is essential if the sociology of youth is to be effective, precisely because more traditional ways of looking at young people implicitly assume that those young people are 'disadvantaged', 'dominated' or 'powerless'. Of course, in many respects this much may be true, but what is important here are not necessarily the power relationships young people find themselves entwined in, but how they actively deal with those relationships as individuals. A sociology of lifestyles is promising, insofar as it can potentially enlighten an understanding of the inter-play between structure and agency which operates in the context of young people's everyday lives. This paradoxical situation is manifested most readily through young people's lifestyles which are an active expression of their relationship with the risk society. In short, young people's lifestyles reflect that while on the one hand the opportunities open to young people in a global society appear to be immense, on the other there are structural constraints that inevitably constrain their ability to be 'free'.

But the key question remains: how do we actually go about studying young people's lifestyles? Do we actually know what lifestyles are to begin with? The problem with the whole debate about 'lifestyles' is that up to now it has been used in a far too lackadaisical fashion. The term lifestyle does not on its own mean anything – it has firstly to be given meaning by actors. Perhaps the key point, as Johansson and Miegel (1992) note is that in contemporary society the individual has gained greater freedom to choose and create his or her own specific lifestyle:

> This is not to say, however, that structure and position no longer play a significant role in the making of lifestyle...in modern society neither structure, position, nor the individual, is the sole determinant of lifestyles. Modern lifestyles are the result of a complex interplay between phenomena at all three of these levels (Johansson and Miegel, 1992, pp.37-38).

Lifestyles in Action

In order to illustrate the above point I want to briefly discuss an example of youth lifestyles as expressed through a recent piece of comparative research funded by the European Union. This project was concerned with the nature of youth training in Great Britain, Germany and Portugal. The intention was to evaluate three particular projects each of which took an apparently unconventional approach to youth training. Two of these projects were based in theatre schools and the third in a Portuguese Circus School. It may seem odd to look at a training programme as a means of addressing youth lifestyles, but I do so precisely because lifestyles are not purely cultural, neither as I pointed out above are they simply an outlet for consumer culture. They are the direct cultural expression of the negotiation of social change. The qualitative research which I conducted with my colleagues Rui Manuel Bargiela Banha, Maria do Carmo Gomes, Axel Pohl, Barbara Stauber and Andreas Walther constituted an effort to look at how young people actively engage with their transitions through the conduct of their lifestyles.

The UK portion of the research was concerned with appraising an organization called 'Hope Street' which is located in Liverpool and which provides disadvantaged young people with what on the surface at least, appears to be training in the performing arts. However, having interviewed many of the young people concerned and one of the leaders of the project over a period of two years, it became clear that this was not a training programme in performing arts at all. It was far more than that in as much as it sought to provide an arena in which young people could 'find' themselves. Many conventional forms of youth training could be criticized on the grounds that they prioritize economic imperatives. In other words, they could be said to be concerned with the needs of the economy first and those of young people second. Hope Street is an example of an organization that provides training which actively offers young people at least the possibility of a future and a career. In effect, it engages with young people's lifestyles. The technical skills young people learn at Hope Street are undoubtedly useful, but the less explicit skills were more important in the long term. These included: how to work in a group; meeting deadlines; how to conduct research; working independently; making decisions; admitting your mistakes; discipline and time-keeping; the ability to listen; basic report-writing skills; communication skills and above all, confidence. In short, Hope Street provides an environment in which young people are encouraged do develop the generic skills associated with life in a so-called 'risk' society.

But a more important issue here is the fact that the young people I interviewed did not simply accept the structural conditions in which they found themselves. Yes, the problems associated with individualization and risk were important to them, but their relationship with such processes was reflective in nature. They actively constructed a lifestyle and a way of looking at the world around the opportunities that there experience of this particular training centre, Hope Street, provided them. They did so by taking ownership of their own training and by making it the centre of their lives. Hope Street provided young people with the opportunity to 'find themselves'. Prior to Hope Street these young people were largely resigned to the fact that they would be lucky to get any job at all, let alone a career. Hope Street provided the conditions in which these young people were able to realize themselves and they did so through the construction of lifestyles, the particular way in which they came to approach their lives. The training became the focus of many of these young people's lives and they appeared to actively define themselves by fitting into the mono-culture that Hope Street invited them to join. The important point to remember here is that young people did not have to take advantage of the opportunities provided for them by Hope Street. They could easily have gone through the motions of completing the course, but they did more than that. They incorporated the course into their lifestyles. There is an inherent danger that young people perceive youth training as a necessary (or unnecessary evil) and in some cases they undoubtedly do. But if youth training conceives young people as active authors of their own training biographies and provides the conditions for young people to negotiate their transitions, then it becomes clear that the whole process of the transition is not as top-down as it may seem on the surface. As one respondent commented:

> It gives you a go this course. We've all had a chance to have a go. Like when you go outside now to get a go, you will have a go. Before we might not of.

Drama provided a forum within which these young people were free to make the mistakes necessary to begin a very complex journey. Young people were impressed by the training they received because it was more than just a training course, it was a way of life. Hope Street provided a cultural context within which young people could play out their relationship with structural change. Take this example,

> See we had this lad on the first block of the course. He was really shy and never said anything to anybody. Very quiet. There was improvement in him: the rest of the group got behind him a lot. Help him with his voice. We dragged him along to the pub. He started to make excuses at first, but you could see he really wanted to go. He was a bit on his own. So eventually we insisted he came, almost carried him at one point to come out with us. Yeah, we brought him out of his shell eventually. That's another good thing about this place. Even if you don't want to be an actor maybe, if you're quiet and maybe you need more confidence this is somewhere to come. After that first block we couldn't shut this bloke up, he was really into it. 'Acting Up' was brilliant for him.

Hope Street appears to provide a context within which young people can 'find themselves'. These young people are not simply training units, but individuals whose fears about the future and feelings of helplessness can be dealt with in a positive and constructive fashion through the medium of drama. Young people took on the training provided by Hope Street by making it theirs and by claiming authorship of it. This lifestyle was communal in nature. It emerged out of a sense of mutual responsibility. But it amounted more than simply regular attendance to a training course. Rather, performance became a key focus for the construction of these young people's identities. The young people concerned felt that this training would only succeed if they invest their whole selves in it,

> That's what Hope Street does. It gives you the vehicle to travel to the place you want to be if you wanna be there. And if you don't really wanna go that vehicle will break down.

Another young person described the Hope Street experience as 'explosive' in both an emotional and a physical sense.

> The course itself could become overpowering because you become immersed in it. It just becomes everything to you. It just means everything. It's just your destiny in life to complete it.

In a way then lifestyles are a psycho-social construct. They provide a sense of belonging, meaning, and coherence, that is less about the expression of a consumer identity and more about an expression of personal and social identity which is often constructed in contrast to consumer culture. In a sense, the structural circumstances in which these young people found themselves, were transported into a cultural context within which they could take control. Hope Street, in particular, provides a means of creating what can be described as a 'sense of coherence' (Antonovsky, 1987). It provides a mode of belonging; a legitimate setting for the playing out of 'identity work' (Keupp, 1997). This was also reflected in the Portuguese segment of the research in which the young people concerned actively constructed their lifestyles around training in performance to the extent that by the end of the training they looked *physically* similar. They had adopted a particular subcultural style that was expressed through the way they dressed. But the way these young people looked only goes so far in explaining the ways in which they were negotiating their experience of the risk society. Young people's lifestyles were actually more overtly expressed through how they felt about their training. This training became the centre of their lives and altered their whole perspective on not only the present, but also the future. The way these young people related to each other, the whole focus of their everyday lives, the material expression of their identities in relation to the dominant culture became more than simply functional but rather an active cultural expression of their relationship with structural change.

Concluding Comments

Various authors such as Jeffs and Smith (1998) and Cohen and Ainley (2000) have pointed out the pitfalls of a static sociology of youth and the need for youth research that directly addresses the shared experiences manifested through young people's meanings. By presenting a flavour of some of the empirical material which I collected, my intention was not to convince the reader that a sociology of lifestyles should constitute the future of the sociology of youth, but rather to have illustrated the benefits of addressing the meanings which young people invest in their experience of the risk society. The Hope Street example is more than simply an evaluation of a training programme. For many of the young people concerned joining Hope Street was in itself a risk. It was a decision that many of them had to ponder because it was a decision they often had to make alone. They might succeed or they might fail during their time on the programme. They were fully aware that a commitment to performance and potentially a career in performance is a tenuous one. But the point is they were prepared to make a positive decision to put themselves in a situation in which they were vulnerable. They were making positive choices about how to cope with the risks associated with extended 'transitions'. They confronted that risk and the vast majority of them came out the other end. And they were able to do so, through constructing a supportive lifestyle which was reflected in not only the way they dressed, but also in their changing attitudes, their determination to succeed, their dedication to performance and their sense of group solidarity. These young people were in it together and regardless of the potential pitfalls and the lack of jobs available to them on completion of the course, they were determined to succeed. That determination was a direct consequence of the fact that Hope Street was not simply a training programme, but an absolutely core aspect of these young people's lifestyles. Hope Street and training programmes like it, can therefore be regarded as what Wenger (1998) would describe as 'communities of practice', social settings where meaning is produced by action and interaction: a space in which young people are able to take responsibility for their own choices. By participating in a drama group young people adopt roles that actively impact upon their lifestyles. Young people are therefore embedded in a setting of mutual responsibility and interdependence. The common enterprise provided by drama provides a source of meaning. The potential of training programmes which address young people's own needs, aspirations and sense of self are, in this context enormous. These young people were actively impinging their own lifestyles and their own personalities on their training programme and as such, far from being passive recipients of risk, they were actively confronting that risk.

There are considerable dangers inherent in adopting a mind-set which means one is predisposed to see young people as victims of social change. There is no doubt that in many respects young people are relatively powerless. But it does not follow that they are passive recipients of the structures that surround them. Whether or not the notion of lifestyles provides any solutions to the division between structural and cultural approaches is a matter for debate. But what is certain is that the meanings which young people invest in their everyday experience of social change remain under-researched. Young people's experience of the risk society is complex and sophisticated. The concepts and methods which sociologists use to address these issues should be equally so.

Acknowledgements

I would like to acknowledge the support of the European Union and that of my colleagues, Rui Manuel Bargiela Banha, Ana Micaela Gaspar, Maria do Carmo Gomes, Axel Pohl, Barbara Stauber and Andreas Walther.

References

Antonovsky, A. (1987), *Unravelling the Mystery of Health*, San Francisco, Jossey-Bass.
Bates, I. and Riseborough, G. (eds) (1993), *Youth and Inequality*, Buckingham, Open University Press.
Beck, U. (1992), *Risk Society: Towards a New Modernity*, London, Sage.
Blackman, S. (1995), *Youth: Positions and Oppositions: Style, Sexuality and Schooling*, Aldershot, Avebury.
Brinkley, I. (1997), 'Underworked and underpaid', in *Soundings*, vol.6, pp.161-171.
Brown, P. (1987), *Schooling Ordinary Kids*, London, Tavistock.
Cohen, P. and Ainley, P. (2000), 'In the country of the blind? Youth cultural studies in Britain', in *Journal of Youth Studies*, vol.3, no.1, pp.79-96.
Epstein, J.S. (ed.) (1998), *Youth Culture: Identity in a Postmodern World*, Oxford, Blackwell.
Evans, C. (1997), 'Dreams that only men can buy, or, the shy tribe in flight from discourse', in *Fashion Theory: The Journal of Dress, Body and Culture*, vol.1, no.2, pp.169-188.
Furlong, A. and Cartmel, F. (1997), *Young People and Social Change*, Buckingham, Open University Press.
Griffin, C. (1993), *Representations of Youth: The Study of Youth and Adolescence in Britain and America*, Cambridge, Polity.
Hebdige, D. (1979), *Subculture: The Meaning of Style*, New York, Methuen.

Hollands, R. (1990), *The Long Transition: Class, Culture and Youth Training*, Basingstoke, Macmillan.
Jeffs, T. and Smith, M.K. (1998), 'The problem of "youth" for youth work', in *Youth and Policy*, no.62, pp.45-66.
Johansson, T. and Miegel, F. (1992), *Do the Right Thing: Lifestyle and Identity in Contemporary Youth Culture*, Malmo, Graphic Systems.
Jones, G. (1995), *Leaving Home*, Buckingham, Open University Press.
Keupp, H. (1997), Diskursarena Identiät: Lernprozesse in der Identitätsforschung, in: Keupp, Heiner/Höfer, Renate (Hg.) Identitätsarbeit heute – Klassische und aktuelle Perspektiven der Identitätsforschung, Frankfurt a. M, Suhrkamp.
MacDonald, R. and Marsh, J. (2000), 'Employment, unemployment and social polarisation: young people and cyclical transitions', in Crompton, R., Devine, F., Savage, M. and Scott, J. (eds), *Renewing Class Analysis*, Oxford: Blackwell.
MacDonald, R., Mason, P., Shildrick, T., Webster, C., Johnston, L. and Ridley, L. (2001), 'Snakes and ladders: In defence of studies of youth transition', in *Sociological Research Online*, vol.5, no.4, http://www.scoresonline.org.uk/5/4/macdonald.html.
Maguire, M. and Maguire, S. (1997), 'Young people and the labour market', in MacDonald, R. (ed.) (1997), *Youth, the 'Underclass' and Social Exclusion*, London, Routledge.
Malbon, B. (1999), *Clubbing: Dancing, Ecstasy and Vitality*, London, Routledge.
Miles, S. (2000), *Youth Lifestyles in Changing World*, Buckingham, Open University Press.
Muggleton, D. (2000), *Inside Subculture: The Postmodern Meaning of Style*, Oxford, Berg.
Redhead, S. (1997) (ed.), *Post-Fandom and the Millenial Blues*, London, Routledge.
Roberts, K. (1995), *Youth Employment in Modern Britain*, Oxford, Oxford University Press.
Rutherford, J (1997), 'Introduction', in *Soundings*, vol.6, pp.112-126.
Shildrick, T. (2000), 'Youth culture, the 'underclass' and social exclusion', in *Scottish Youth Issues Journal*, vol.1, no.1.
Skilbeck, M., Connell, H., Lowe, N. and Tait, K. (1994), *The Vocational Quest: New Directions in Education and Training*, London, Routledge.
Thornton, S. (1997), *ClubCultures: Music, Media and Subcultural Capital*, Cambridge, Polity.
Wenger, E. (1998), *Communities of Practice: Learning, Meaning, and Identity*, Cambridge, Cambridge University Press.
Widdicombe, S. and Wooffitt, R. (1995), *The Language of Youth Subcultures*, London, Harvester Wheatsheaf.
Willis, P. (1978), *Profane Culture*, London, Routledge and Kegan Paul.
Wyn, J. and Whyte, R. (1997), *Rethinking Youth*, London, Sage.

Chapter 5

Global Clubcultures: Cultural Flows and Late Modern Dance Music Culture

BEN CARRINGTON AND BRIAN WILSON

Welcome to the global dance...Once only weird kids wanted to dress up and dance all night – now this kind of clubbing is a mainstream leisure activity everywhere: from Tokyo to Telford, Birmingham to Bali...In the past decade, major British clubs such as Ministry of Sound, Cream and Gatecrasher have become international youth culture brands, big business selling CDs, magazines and clothes and organizing parties all over the globe...[The scene] has also bred a new kind of tourism – clubbers who travel the world less to see the sights than to experience the nights (The Guardian, 2000, p.2).

Introduction

Like all youth cultures, and especially those formed through associations with music cultures, the evolution of 'club cultures'[1] around the world can be attributed, in part, to the ongoing global processes of cultural borrowing. Iain Chambers, speaking more generally about the dynamics of cultural hybridity, (inter)mixture and exchange, has argued that the 'international medium of musical reproduction underlines 'a new epoch of global culture contact'. Modern movement and mobility, whether through migration, the media or tourism, have dramatically transformed both musical production and publics and intensified cultural contact' (1994, p.80). DJs and promoters travel to foreign countries, are exposed to fresh varieties of music and nightclubs, and ultimately integrate ideas gleaned from these experiences into their domestic dance music cultures. Touring DJs and imported albums influence local music-makers who combine the new material with their current work, thus creating something 'new again'. Images and ideas extracted from mass and alternative media are incorporated into local music production, fashion styles and club venues. In retrospect, what has emanated from years of this cultural 'cutting and mixing' (Hebdige, 1987) is a fascinating but hazy relationship between a 'global' club culture and various 'local' club cultures.

While core members of the world's various dance music communities might have a shared understanding of the origins of their 'global scene' – about internationally renowned DJs and clubs, and about key club-related websites and magazines – the various national and regional club communities still maintain a 'local' knowledge/flavour, complete with a (somewhat) unique history and distinct dance music culture. Yet, at the same time, these 'local scenes' are becoming increasingly difficult to define, in part, because club culture has become fragmented as musical styles (and clubbers' tastes) have evolved and specialized. As the epigraph to this chapter suggests, the increasing tendency for youth to travel to foreign scenes as 'post-rave tourists' has meant that local cultures are becoming further defined by their diverse and transient membership. These mobile formations might well be described as *reflexive* communities (c.f. Lash, 1994) in the extent to which they dissolve the boundary between producers and consumers, are actively entered into by their members rather than being proscribed by social location, are not delimited by simple time-space boundaries, and are based on cultural and symbolic – rather than formally material – practices.

Emerging from this brief overview are key questions about the various ways that dance music flows into and through local clubcultures around the world, the trans-local forms of cultural resources this offers young people, and the ways these resources are adapted in the ongoing process of identity construction. This includes queries about the ways that certain styles of music, clothing, DJing, or club décor are 'distributed' worldwide, interpreted locally, and then redistributed by youth themselves. These new spaces of economic activity, opened up by the globalization of disorganized capitalism, mean that opportunities for cultural intermediaries and producers – DJs, promoters, event managers, club designers and so on – are being created by young people themselves, operating within and sometimes against the dictates and logic of the mainstream commercial music industries.

These general questions are especially pertinent considering that existing research has generally focused on the ways that local dance cultures interpret and use global influences as a way of creating a distinct local culture, but seldom examine the ways in which dance music culture enters, influences, and exits these local scenes. This is certainly not to say that the global flows of dance music culture have not been identified and acknowledged. Authors like Bennett (2000), Krus (1993) and Slobin (1993) have discussed, at least in a cursory way, how travel and mass media exposure have impacted local music scenes. Terms like 'trans-local subculture', 'trans-regionalism' and 'trans-locality' have emerged in this context.

This chapter is concerned with tracing the nature of these 'global flows' as a way of understanding the current state of late modern (globalized) youth subcultures. More specifically, the chapter seeks to position these issues within current debates about the relationship between local (youth) cultures and global processes, and to identify departure points for studying the global flows of dance music culture. The underlying argument presented here is that globalizing processes evident within contemporary late modern youth cultures are not adequately explained through conventional sociological approaches to the cross-cultural analysis of youth. Such approaches often take localized youth cultures as discrete cultural entities, have an essentialized understanding of 'place' and locality, and often fail to account for the cultural, political and economic complexities of 'global-local' interactions in *constituting* local cultures in the first place. Rather, it is precisely the constellation of wider social relations that give meaning to 'the local'. As Doreen Massey (1994, p.156) has argued the specificity of 'place' only emerges from the fact that 'each place is the focus of a distinct mixture of wider and more local social relations'. What is required, she continues, from those concerned to theorize the nature of spatialized identity in this context, is 'a global sense of the local, a global sense of place' (ibid.). To be clear, this is not an argument against localized studies but rather for more reflexive and nuanced accounts of the dialectic between the local/global and the wider context within which the local is made meaningful. As Caspar Melville notes, like all other cultural forms:

> Dance music is always related to a socio-political context. It may embody global aspirations but it always has a local manifestation: dancing takes place somewhere, with particular kinds of people present, in a particular socio-historical moment (2000, p.41).

Despite the encouraging contributions of an emerging tradition of ethnographically-informed analyses of youth cultures that are sensitive to the links between localized practices and broader social and cultural developments, tensions surrounding the notion of the 'the local' (particularly in relation to theories of political economy) remain unresolved and understudied. Whilst such new work has rightly displaced the (often narrow) preoccupation with the class location of the subjects studied found in earlier work on youth, they have themselves been tied to a notion of locality that is itself limited by its own fixity. That is, 'the local' remains a bounded and hermetically sealed entity, albeit one from which more diverse and fluid identities can be constructed. The notion of the local itself being a discursive construction which is produced and shaped by particular ideologies and flows – cultural, political and economic – is often seriously underplayed.

With these objectives in mind, we have organized this chapter into four sections. In the first, a brief overview of attempts to explain youth cultural activity is provided. Particular attention is paid to the ways that contemporary understandings of global processes and local cultures have been dealt with in this literature, including attempts to conduct cross-cultural research. In the second, we provide a more detailed overview of theories that describe the global flows of (youth) culture, concentrating on the ways that culture is transmitted to youth around the world, the ways it is interpreted and used by youth consumers/cultures, and the way it is (re)distributed by these same youth. In the third, we illustrate some of these global flows through an historical overview and discussion of the British and Canadian club scenes. Fourth and finally, we outline some theoretical, empirical, and substantive departure points for future work on global flows and the reflexive communities that have emerged in the context of global clubcultures.

Approaching Youth Culture in the Global and the Local

Early Work in the American Delinquency and British Subcultural Traditions

There have been various attempts to explain youth subcultural involvement. Researchers who worked out of the University of Chicago in the 1920s and 30s and subsequently those associated with the American 'delinquency' tradition focused on the ways that youth react to their sometimes marginalized social position (e.g., as working class youth in educational systems dominated by middle-class values). They showed how subcultural groups are formed by youth who share this social position, and how these groups construct alternative value systems that allow youth-members to 'measure themselves' against more accessible 'counter middle-class' standards (Cohen, 1955; Merton, 1938; Sutherland, 1947; Shaw and McKay, 1927). Those working out of the Centre for Contemporary Cultural Studies (CCCS) in Birmingham, England, extended these seminal formulations by describing how youth 'reactively and proactively' express their dissatisfaction with the status quo of post-war British society. By articulating themselves through spectacular forms of 'style' (e.g., the extreme fashions of punks and skinheads), youth were believed to be symbolically and creatively 'resisting', and in so doing, finding 'solutions' to their problems. CCCS theorists called these 'magical solutions' as a way of recognizing that subcultural involvement is only a temporary form of empowerment and escape that does not (necessarily) substantially challenge the dominance/hegemony of the ruling classes (P. Cohen, 1972; Hall and Jefferson, 1976; Hebdige, 1979; Willis, 1977).[2]

Although these works provided a crucial foundation for subsequent work on youth culture, they have been subject to systematic critique (see Bennett, 2000; Tanner, 1996). The shortcoming most pertinent to this chapter is that there was little attention to understanding the relationships *between* youth cultures in America, Britain, and other countries (i.e., cross-cultural research) and, as noted earlier, there was 'a failure to consider local variations in youths' responses to music and style' (Bennett, 2000, p.23). Moreover, and with the exception of Brake (1985) and Hebdige (1979), there was insufficient attention to the ways that youth cultures were influenced by subcultural traditions in other countries, and an extreme paucity of work that attempted cross-cultural comparisons that were informed by any rigorous empirical research. Even Brake's work was limited theoretically because, while it recognized that youth culture in countries like Canada is 'largely derivative' and reliant on 'elements of borrowed culture' (1985, p.145), as Young and Craig (1997, p.177) note, Brake 'apparently overlooks the fact that *all* subcultures, including early British articulations, tend in some way to borrow from the cultural expressions of other groups' (see also Osgerby, 1998).

Although there was a growing literature on the impacts of mass mediated messages on audiences at this time (e.g., Morley, 1980), such work was seldom integrated into youth cultural studies. This lack of rigorous attention to the ways that youth subcultures could be theorized as 'interpretive communities' (Fish, 1979; Radway, 1984) meant that the various impacts of global cultural forces *within* local youth cultures was left understudied. This crucial critique, along with Young and Craig's and Osgerby's, has been pursued by Bennett (2000) in his work on popular music and youth culture. Bennett takes theorists like Hebdige (1979) to task for their tendency to dismiss any culture that has been taken up by the market as 'inauthentic', arguing that Hebdige's inflexible view of authenticity 'automatically closes off any consideration of the regional variations and local levels of significance that such styles acquire once they become more widely available as commercial products' (Bennett, 2000, p.24).

Post-CCCS Developments

Several key approaches to understanding youth cultural activity arose following these seminal developments in the 1970s. The most notable trend was for theorists to emphasize the subtle 'everyday' strategies that youth adopt to either 'get back at' the establishment or to help them cope with the various difficulties faced by adolescents at the end of the century (e.g., McRobbie, 1993; Willis, 1990; see also de Certeau, 1984). Some key works in the symbolic interactionist tradition (c.f., Blumer, 1969) similarly point out that youth negotiate their identities in their 'social worlds' in generic ways, often tactically manipulating adult-created systems to their advantage, thus creating their own 'idioculture' (an interactionist version of subculture) within mainstream organizations like schools or sports leagues (Fine, 1987; Fine and Mechling, 1993; Prus, 1996). These interactionist approaches have sometimes been criticized, though, for not adequately accounting for the social and historical context that underscores all subcultural involvement.

For many contemporary theorists the *fin de siècle* socio-historical backdrop is key to any explanation of the emergence and development of rave culture (and its descendant clubculture). Steve Redhead (1990) for example has challenged conventional understandings that the mass media and commercial culture 'incorporated' and, in turn, 'robbed' rave culture or other subcultures of their authenticity. Instead, he suggests that after the 1970s, subcultural authenticity became 'impossible' because of contemporary culture's tendency to be self-referential, shallow, flat and hyppereal (i.e., a culture of effervescent, spectacular, fast moving, ever-present, 'better than real' images). Muggleton (1997, 2000) has extended this argument, suggesting that this era of 'postmodernity' is inhabited by 'postsubculturalists' whose identities are multiple and fluid, whose consumption is no longer 'articulated through the modernist structuring relations of class, gender or ethnicity' and who are defined by their fragmented/multiple stylistic identities (p.52). That is to say, they have a low degree of commitment to any subcultural group and high rates of subcultural mobility, a fascination with style and image, are generally apolitical, and have a 'positive attitude toward media and a celebration of the inauthentic' (2000, p.52). This view is akin in some respects to those espoused by other post-CCCS authors such as Bennett (1999, 2000) and Malbon (1998, 1999) who have adapted Maffesoli's concept *tribus* to illustrate how 'neo-tribal' identities in postmodern times are unstable, temporal, and driven by consumer culture. It is no coincidence that Bennett and Malbon were both studying urban dance (club/rave) music culture; which is prevalently considered to be the archetypal late century subculture.

As noted previously, underlying these updated understandings of youth activity is the assumption that contemporary society is somehow culturally distinct from 'earlier times'.[3] Those who support this view usually point to the acceleration of 'globalization' processes, focusing on the ways that national boundaries have become less meaningful as exclusive markers of cultural identities, as mass media and consumer culture have become increasingly pervasive (see Featherstone, 1995). Theorists have identified various potential impacts of these processes. The characteristics outlined by Muggleton and Redhead (described above) represent the strand of thought that emphasizes the impacts of increased exposure to market/media culture on consumers who tend to create 'identities' through their eclectic consumption of products and styles, instead of affiliating themselves with and committing to any particular social group.

Miles (2000) perceptively notes the tension between optimistic and pessimistic interpretations of these developments. On one hand, he describes how rapid advancements in technology and communication might be empowering for youth 'whose social lives are increasingly individualized' and who now have 'a semblance of control over their personal biographies' (p.53; drawing on the works of Tinning and Fitzclarence, 1992 and Cote and Allahar, 1994). On the other hand, he points out that authors like Best and Kellner (1997) express concern that the combination of mass media exposure/interaction with existing social plights only magnifies the rift between 'reality' and any movement toward improving social conditions.[4]

Departure Points for Comparative Work

This abbreviated overview of post-CCCS developments unveiled several encouraging trends. For example, many of the above noted works tend to account for the lived experiences of youth in an increasingly globalized culture and provide often compelling (ethnographically-informed) discussions of the ways that local identities are negotiated and forged. Further, some key works have offered insightful suggestions for updating and challenging orthodox views of subcultural 'resistance', while at the same time offering revised models for understanding the types of involvements that youth have in cultural life that avoids perceiving young people as cultural dupes.

Some of the more ambitious empirical projects such as Bennett's (2000) and Mitchell's (1996) work on popular music, and Skelton and Valentine's (1998) and Amit-Talai and Wulff's (1995) more general – youth-related edited collections – are cross-cultural examinations. Most often authors who adopt a cross-cultural view of youth cultures either provide a collection of studies conducted in various countries/regions and discuss the similarities and differences between these studies, or provide a general summary of 'international' research on youth. The seminal work of Brake (1985) is the usual departure point for talking about the ways that local conditions influence, and to a certain extent determine, how youth use cultural resources (or subcultures) as a way of defining their identities. These works are progressive endeavors with the admirable aim of attaining a more geographically/culturally sensitive and inclusive understanding of youth culture.

This body of 'cross-cultural' work has its shortcomings, however. Only some of this research engages with theoretical issues related to 'the global and the local'. Often 'the local' is left relatively undefined, with little regard for the fact that local identity is inherently a *relational* identity that can sometimes refer to regional and national identities. At the same time, cross-cultural work seldom develops micro-interactionist models that allow researchers to organize and more fully develop understandings of the generic social processes of youth group life. That is to say, the 'comparative' component of these studies remains theoretically underdeveloped.

In other cases, micro-analyses powerfully describe local experiences with 'global resources', yet provide little detail about the process through which these global resources enter youth scenes, or about how these 'interpreted resources' are rearticulated and redistributed to other cultures. So, while the notion of cultural borrowing is central to one level of analysis in much of this work, the overall lack of research on cultural *flows* or 'channels of influence' has meant that the concept has been left underdeveloped. Moreover, and underlying these concerns about the dearth of in-depth comparative work is a relative lack of attention to issues of political economy, social stratification and inequality in these cross-cultural studies. It is almost as if, in the desire to move on from the perceived and actual inadequacies of the CCCS work on youth culture, the broader attempt to map the diffusion of political and economic ideologies through the contested terrain of popular culture has been abandoned in the process. This tension, between locating the agency within the diffuse lifestyle choices of the young, against the (over)determining interpellation of individuals into particular subject positions set within the context of late capitalism's embrace of culture, is necessarily difficult both theoretically and empirically. However, and despite the challenges that inevitably emerge in any analysis of 'structure and agency' in youth cultural studies, we argue that glib dismissals of 'economic reductionism' are inadequate as methods of resolution. A further concern is that cross-cultural studies only sometimes consider the *same* cultural phenomenon in different contexts.

These studies also neglect the ways that subcultures that share similar 'roots' and cultural resources *interact with one another* while developing/maintaining their distinctly 'local' scenes.

Global Flows and Local Cultures

Theorizing the Transmission and Interpretation of (Popular/Youth/Music) Culture

As noted above, understanding globalization processes is crucial for understanding the clubculture phenomenon. Although debates are ongoing about whether globalization processes contribute to the accelerated 'homogenization' or 'heterogenization' of (popular) culture (see Carrington et al., 2001; Jackson and Andrews, 1999), Lull (2000) outlines a convincing case for mapping the complex and *interactive* relationship that local cultures have with pervasive and imposing cultural, economic and political (globalizing) forces. He argues:

> Globalization does not mean that some universal, technology-based super-society covers the globe and destroys local social systems and cultures. Despite technology's awesome reach, we have not, and will not, become one people. It is true that potent homogenizing forces such as English, Chinese, Arabic, and other dominant languages, military weaponry, advertising techniques, Internet protocol, media formats, international airports, and fashion trends undeniably affect consciousness and culture in every corner of the world...But these political-economic-cultural influences do not enter cultural contexts uniformly. They always interact with local conditions to produce diverse and dynamic consequences (Lull, 2000, p.233-234).

Underscoring Lull's argument, and a key postulation in this chapter, is that while global cultural forces impact local (youth) scenes and communities, these forces are interpreted and used in both intended and unintended ways by consumers/audiences (i.e., unintended by the media producers), though necessarily of course, under conditions rarely chosen by young people. With these basic assumptions, we attempt in the remainder of this section to identify and conceptualize the dynamics that underlie the development of clubcultures by turning to key works that have focused on the processes of cultural transmission and interpretation.

Transmission of Culture

Among the various attempts to describe the dynamics of global cultural transmission, Appadurai's (1990) 'five dimensions of cultural flow' remains one of the most comprehensive and useful guides for analysis. Underlying this model is the key assumption that the new global economy is a 'complex, overlapping, disjunctive order,' which is more aptly described as 'disorganized capitalism' (Lash and Urry, 1987). Appadurai suggests that these five dimensions, or what he calls 'scapes', work in ways that prevent the construction of a homogenous culture. These 'scapes' are: ethnoscapes, mediascapes, technoscapes, finanscapes, and ideoscapes. Ethnoscapes refers to the flow of people around the world (e.g., tourists, immigrants, refugees, exiles, guestworkers and other moving groups). Technoscapes refers to the flow of technology (e.g., the export of technology to countries as part of transnational business relocations). Finanscapes refers to the patterns of global capital transfer. Appadurai (1990) argues that the global relationship between these three scapes is:

> Deeply disjunctive and profoundly unpredictable, since each of these landscapes is subject to its own constraints and incentives...at the same time as each acts as a constraint and a parameter for the other (Appadurai, 1990, p.298).

Augmenting these first three scapes are mediascapes and ideoscapes. Mediascapes refers to mass media images, to the modes of image distribution (e.g., electronic or print media), and to the ways that these images allow viewers to gain access to other parts of the world – and thus become part of 'imagined communities'. Crucial to the current chapter is Appadurai's suggestion that these media narratives:

> Can and do get disaggregated into complex sets of metaphors by which people live as they help to constitute narratives of the 'other' and proto-narratives of possible lives, fantasies which could become prolegomena to the desire for acquisition and movement (Appadurai, 1990, p.299).

Ideoscapes refers to images that are invested with political-ideological meaning (e.g., the images presented by governmental groups justifying a military action, or images created by social movements attempting to overthrow power groups). The crux of Appadurai's framework is the assumption that the various 'disjunctures' or interactions that occur between global cultural flows (as they relate to the various scapes) provide the analyst with crucial information about the complex ways that local cultures relate to global forces.

The Interpretation/Reception of Culture

Although there has been a historical tendency within certain (elitist) traditions of critical social theory to view consumers as cultural dupes, recent work has been careful to acknowledge that audiences knowingly interact with media messages, and that audience members sometimes appropriate media-derived resources for their own purposes. The classic work on subcultures from the CCCS (Clarke, 1976; Hebdige, 1979) acknowledged this in their adoption of the concept 'bricolage', a term which was used to describe how youth often invest meanings in cultural objects that do not necessarily cohere with those intended by the object's producer, sometimes placing and using these objects in ways that are subversive and shocking (e.g., the punk's use of a tampon as a jacket ornament). The deconstructionist work conducted in the subculture literature that extends this premise tends to focus on the ways that subcultures and subcultural styles take on various and often diverse meanings for youth in different countries. Bennett (2000), for example, has described the various cross-cultural formations of punk, considering the varying levels of cultural significance that punk had for Hungarian youth (referring to work by Szemere, 1992) and German youth (from Hafeneger et al., 1993 and Muller-Wiegant, 1990) as well as British youth (from Laing, 1985).

Another relevant body of work generally known as 'reception studies' or 'media audience research' is more attentive to the complexities of interpretive difference. Although this research tradition has evolved through a series of debates since its emergence in the late 1970s (Alasuutari, 1999), a notable assumption underlying most key works is that one's tendency to interpret a media 'text' (e.g., television commercial, magazine article, song) in a certain way relates not only to one's social position in terms of class, 'race', and gender-related identities, but also to any variety of cultural experiences or social circumstances that frame an individual's life history. In the same way, the traditional types of 'background variables' that might previously have been used to 'predict' an individual's preference or taste for certain types of cultural resources, lifestyle choices or political affiliations are often seen to be of limited use in explaining the ways and extent that these resources are integrated into an individual's everyday life and world view (c.f., Buckingham 1993, 1997; Miles, 2000; and Wilson and Sparks, 1996).[5]

Returning to our discussion of dance music cultures, this more elaborate approach to theorizing 'the local' encourages researchers to consider the intricacies of youth tastes (e.g., preferences for various genres of dance music, such as house or jungle or trance), interpretations of this music (e.g., as an escape, as a form of resistance), and uses of it (e.g., making a living in a dance music-related occupation). This more flexible and integrated interpretive framework also allows the analyst to consider how youth might simultaneously be interpreters *and producers* of culture – creating 'alternative' media that both reflects youths' understandings of global culture, while contributing to this same culture (see Duncombe, 1997).

British and Canadian Club Cultures

Histories and Cultural Flows

The history of rave and club culture is a topic of interest for many popular music commentators. Authors like Collin (1998), Garratt (1998), Kempster (1996), Reynolds (1998) and Rietveld (1998) have provided detailed accounts of the various developments that led up to and followed the 'second summer of Love' in 1988 in Britain; which has been pinned as the 'official' beginning (and for many the end) of the 'rave' phenomenon. For the most part, these histories tend to trace the origins of the British rave scene to the 1970s and early 1980s in New York City, Chicago and Detroit. In New York and Chicago in particular, at gay and black all-night dance clubs, early forms of electronic dance music were being developed by 'mixing' different songs together and sometimes integrating synthesizer-generated sound effects, while at the same time amphetamines and Quaaludes ('uppers and downers') were being used by some club-goers to help enhance the atmosphere and the music (and to enable all-night dancing). Even in these early stages, variations of dance music were emerging, with some DJs playing more 'soulful' up-tempo forms of dance (e.g., the 'house' music that renowned DJ Frankie Knuckles was playing at his famous club 'the Warehouse') while others were playing more 'raw', 'speedy' forms (e.g., less polished forms of house music associated with Chicago's Powerplant club and DJ Ron Hardy). Some forms of this music were eventually integrated into mainstream formats and commercialized as Disco, although the underground/alternative styles and parties continued during and after the Disco era of the late 1970s.

While the evolution of House was in progress in Chicago and New York, a group of DJs in Detroit were developing their own forms of electronic dance music using early computers and synthesizers to create forms of 'technological music' – or 'techno' music as it came to be known. It is crucial to note, though, that a key influence for these Detroit DJs (the most well-known are DJs Derek May, Juan Atkins, and Derek Saunderson) was the German band *Kraftwerk*, whose early innovative technological music creations were central to the emergence of various forms of synthesizer music at the time and since. Kraftwerk were notorious for their ability to 'edit the soul out of modern music,' and (according to some analysts) to create 'pure music from their machines', 'music that demands to be listened to on its own terms, with its internal reference points and logic' – 'modernist music taken to its ultimate conclusion' (Sinker, 1996, p.94). Most significant for this chapter though, is that Kraftwerk themselves were also influenced by the early American punk bands that came out of Detroit and New York, in what Reynolds (1998) called 'one of those weird pop-historical loops'. Reynolds explained this intriguing relationship between Detroit, New York and Dusseldorf:

> The story of techno begins not in early-eighties, but in early-seventies Dusseldorf, where Kraftwerk built their KingKlang soundfactory and churned out pioneering synth and drum machine tracks like Autobahn...In New York, the German band almost single-handedly sired the electro movement...But while New York hip-hop soon abandoned electro's drum machines for seventies funk breakbeats, Kraftwerk had a more enduring impact on Detroit. Their music's Teutonic rigor and glacial grandeur plugged into the Europhine tastes of arty middle-class black youth and fired the imaginations of [the inventors of] Detroit techno. [At the same time], Kraftwerk were themselves influenced by Detroit – by the adrenalized insurgency of the MC5 and the Stooges...Kraftwerk were also influenced by the mantic minimalism and non-R & B rhythms of [New York's] Velvet Underground...Replacing guitars and drums with synthesizer pulses and programmed beats, Kraftwerk sublimated the Velvets' white light/white heat speed rush into the cruise-control serenity of motorik, a metronomic, regular-as-carburetor rhythm that was at once post-rock and proto-techno (1998, p.13-14).

Although the rave movement came to fruition in Britain, the roots (or perhaps we should say *routes*) of the movement can be traced back to Ibiza, Spain – an inexpensive holiday-sun location for bohemian British working class youth in the early 1980s (Collin, 1998; Eisner, 1994; Garratt, 1998; Reynolds, 1998). The influx of tourism to Ibiza at this time coincided with the import of American House music to the island's night clubs and the increasing availability of the drug Ecstasy (LSD, mescaline and cocaine were the stimulants of choice until this time), creating a stage for a radical adaptation of the American dance sound. The original 'pre-rave' parties were held at an Ibiza club named *Amnesia*, where DJ Alfredo Fiorello, 'a former journalist who'd fled the fascist rigors of his native Argentina for the laid-back bohemian idyll' began to 'spin' and 'mix' imported house music from New York and Chicago (Reynolds, 1998, p.58), thus gaining him a loyal audience of subaltern youth from London.

This following of young British youth included Paul Oakenfold, a British DJ who had been to *Paradise Garage*, one of the infamous early dance clubs in New York City, and had unsuccessfully attempted to open an Ibiza-style club in Britain in 1985. Inspired by his first Ecstasy drug experience in Ibiza 1987, Oakenfold and his business partner Ian St. Paul opened up an after-hours club called *the Project* where 'Ibiza veterans' would come sporting an 'Ibiza look and attitude' that was a 'weird mix of Mediterranean beach bum, hippie, and soccer hooligan – baggy trousers and T-shirts, paisley bandannas, dungarees, ponchos, Converse All-Stars sneakers – loose fitting because the Ecstasy and non-stop trance dancing made you sweat buckets' (Reynolds, 1998, pp.58-59). Following *the Project's* opening, a series of 'house music nights' at other locations – particularly in a club named *Shoom* – emerged and an exclusive 'pre-rave' scene now existed.

Despite its origins that supported a privileged 'in-crowd', rave culture (known also at this time as the 'acid house' culture) soon began to spread, as did the importing of the drug Ecstasy into Britain. Other 'acid house' nights began taking place and the scene was becoming almost too popular for the previously 'alternative' Ibiza originals. However, for the broader British youth population, the discovery of acid house music (along with the drug Ecstasy) led the rave movement to its peak in the summers of 1988 and 1989, when large-scale all-night raves attracting upwards of 10,000 ravers took place, often illegally, in various warehouses and countryside spaces.

According to most commentators, the end of the summer(s) of love was as abrupt as the beginning. As Redhead (1997a) argued, 'the summer of 1988 was over when, on 1 October, the *Sun* signaled the dawn of acid house as 'cool and groovy'' (p.57).[6] The over-exposure of the underground scene, combined with the attempts by the Conservative government of the day, to control and prohibit such large scale unlicensed music events, (evidenced in The Entertainment [Increased Penalties] Act, 1990), meant that by the mid 1990s, illegal raves on the scale seen in the late 1980s had largely disappeared. Moreover, another 'anti-rave law' was eventually passed (the infamous Criminal Justice Act of 1994) in reaction to the continuing mediated 'moral panics' about the rave scene (particularly around sensationalizing high profile Ecstasy-related deaths – see Thornton, 1994, 1995). This enabled twin processes of cultural regulation to emerge which sought to both incorporate elements of the rave scene into the leisure industries, whilst allowing greater sanctions to be taken against those collectives that still organized outside of the new legislative and regulatory framework. Dance music thus became a central part of mainstream youth experience and a number of commercially-oriented 'super-clubs', that could accommodate the numbers – if not quite the atmosphere – of the earlier 'raves' such as the *Ministry of Sound* and *Cream*, rose to prominence.

What evolved during the 1990s is what Thornton (1995) has called 'clubculture'.[7] This was a culture governed less by 'peace, love and togetherness' and more by a subcultural status system, marking the shift from unregulated cultural spaces of leisure participation to controlled, and therefore more easily commodified, forms of leisure consumption. According to clubbers (in Thornton's research), it is what you wear, how you dance and how you talk that *matters*. This 'evolved rave' was similar in some respects to the scene during the summers of 1988 and 1989 (e.g., dance, electronic music, and drugs-based). However, commentators argue that people's interpretations of rave-related activities in the late 1980s were radically different from the 'post-rave' scene in term of the ambience and moral life-world that structured the informal codes and value systems of the two moments in dance music's development (i.e., 'be free' in 1988 versus 'be cool' in the mid and late 1990s). This evolved scene is characterized by the fragmentation of dance music genres and the use of less 'friendly' drugs. As Reynolds (1997) explained:

> Each post-rave fragment seems to have preserved one aspect of rave culture at the expense of the others. House music, in its more song-ful, hands-in-the-air, handbag form, has reverted to mere disco...Progressive house and garage is just your pre-rave metropolitan clubland coked-out elitism back in full effect. Techno, ambient and electronica strip rave of its, well, raveyness, to fit a white student sensibility...Jungle...[is] the post-rave offshoot that has most thoroughly severed itself from rave's premises. You could call it 'gangsta rave', in so far as jungle has taken on hip-hop and reggae's ethos of masked self-containment and controlled dance moves, and shed rave's abandonment and demonstrativeness (Reynolds, 1997, p.103).

Embedded in this admittedly annotated history of the British rave scene are clear references to the borrowing and movement of dance music culture. Of course, with the worldwide coverage that the 'summer of love' received at the time, and the subsequent emergence of a highly commercialized global 'club culture', various countries were influenced by Britain – leading to the development of various rave scenes across the major cities of Europe and North America. In Toronto, Canada, for example, rave culture evolved out of a combination of an early 1980s gay dance club scene in the city (which was directly influenced by the New York City gay scene), and the import of the rave concept from Britain by renowned Canadian radio personality and DJ, Chris Shepperd. Shepperd explained how his time in Britain during the summer of 1988 influenced him and his business partner:

> After the 'Summer of Love' in 1988, Richard [Shepperd's business partner] and I wanted to create that vibe in Toronto. It was October 1988 that we threw our first party trying to create the 'love one another...be free carnival vibe' that was so apparent in this scene (quoted in Canadian rave zine *Klublife*; taken from Wilson, 1999, p.88).

Following Canada's first rave on October 23, 1988 in Toronto, a small number of rave promotion companies emerged in the city, most of them composed of individuals who had recently moved to Canada from Britain. In the early and mid 1990s, regular 'rave nights' began to occur in warehouse locations, and weekly raves started taking place in different locations, promoted more often by Toronto locals. In the late 1990s, the Toronto rave scene was becoming increasingly 'criminalized' as all-night parties were sometimes invaded by police concerned with media coverage about 'drugs, youth and dance culture'. For this reason, Toronto's rave scene was becoming more of a club scene, as the parties began moving into mainstream dance venues (Silcott, 1999). The scene also became fragmented according to age, drug preference, and most of all music preference.[8]

Although in many respects the development of this youth culture in Toronto paralleled that of Britain (with about a 3 year time lag), a key difference was that Toronto often used the British scene and music as a cultural reference point. British DJs (as well as various other foreign DJs) were sometimes flown to major Canadian events and interviewed on local radio stations and/or on *Muchmusic*, Canada's music-television station. Available in *Chapters*, Canada's major book mega-chain, is an array of largely Britain-based dance music magazines, such as *Mixmag*, *MUZIK*, and *DJ* that describe the most recent developments in the UK dance scene and provide interpretations/portrayals of other scenes around the world from the 'UK perspective'. It might be argued therefore that with these influences and aspirations, Toronto might be (or have been) 'more British than Britain ever was' (Wilson, 1999). Of course, this general analysis underplays the variations within the Toronto rave and club scene, and certainly the variety of scenes across Canada (e.g., Vancouver and Montreal have their own somewhat distinct styles and influences, in part reflecting their differing linguistic and ethnic communities). The underlying point is that there are several 'layers' of flows and influences is crucial background for approaching an understanding of youth cultural transmission.

Appadurai's 'scapes' are a useful guide for examining the global flows of dance music culture in this case. The brief history of rave and clubculture shows how travelers (within the ethnoscape) contributed to the transmission of dance music culture from America and Ibiza to Britain, and then, subsequently, from Britain to Canada. In the same way, young British immigrants who promoted raves in Canada influenced the Toronto scene. As noted in the introduction to this chapter, the 'post-rave tourist' has also emerged, as a clubber who travels to locations around the world with the explicit purpose of experiencing the club/rave culture of the area.[9] A recent lead article in *New York* magazine explained this phenomenon, referring in this case to the British invasion of New York City's clubs:

> Mello is at the Park View to pick up the 50 or so tourists he's taking to the Flatiron-district nightspot Cheetah for its weekly 'Great British House' party. None of his clients are the kind of tourists who come to New York for the Statue of Liberty or the art museums…Thanks to the global rise of D.J. culture, what's marginal about New York has become mainstream in Europe, especially England. Lured by breathless features about New York nightclubs like Twilo in magazines like *The Face*, tourists are arriving by the hundreds each weekend seeking dance floor transcendence, a glimpse of nightclub history, and an appropriately debauched evening they can brag about back home (Brown, 2000, p.58).

This excerpt is instructive and ironic on multiple levels. Not only does it illustrate the inextricable links between the ethnoscape (the tourist), the mediascape (the mass mediated promotion of dance music culture), and the financsape (the tourist industry), but this magazine article is itself part of 'the process' because it sensationalizes the global club phenomenon in mainstream media.

Of course, it is the economic underpinnings of the music industry alluded to above – the focal point of work by authors like Negus (1992, 1996) and Rowe (1995) – that are noteworthy here. Rowe (1995), for example, explains how:

> Various models of international musical exchange reflect, in different degrees, the ways in which popular music may be exportable in finished units, adaptable to local conditions, resistant to external influences, or amenable to unpredictable and innovative syntheses (Rowe, 1995, p.96).

Although Rowe (drawing on Robinson et al., 1991) goes on to describe a historically-informed 'mega-narrative…of the nature of cultural processes of contact and transmission' in the pop music industry, the key point for our purposes is that the most recent stage of evolution is one 'exemplified by increasing fragmentation in internationalized musical genres and smaller production units', a movement that reflects a worldwide shift toward a post-Fordist flexibly specialized economy (Robinson et al., 1991, p.262; Rowe, 1995, p.96). Central to this argument is that the corporate adaptations that are hallmarks of the post-Fordist shift 'do not so much signal the decline of cultural corporations and the rise of independents as indicate a dynamic redrawing of the boundaries between them' (Rowe, 1995, p.48; see also Negus, 1992).

This political economic argument can be extended to shed light on the cycle of media/music production through a (post-Fordist) analysis of the ways that youth (re)create and (re)distribute their own music. Although not a central aspect of this chapter's discussion of the British and Canadian club scenes, previous work has contributed some compelling insights into the ways that 'underground' music production and rave/club promotion are a central part of both scenes. Smith and Maughan (1998), for example, have argued for a 'political economy of dance culture' that is characterized by youth participation in independent record labels, in nightclub promotion, and in DJ culture (a culture of music mixing/selecting for performance and production). As the authors point out:

> The aesthetic of dance culture cannot be separated from the organization of the economy, nor can the economy be separated from the culture, given that there is a cultural imperative to engage in these cultural activities – an individual sets up a label because he/she loves the music but that label will not survive unless it sells...The availability of forms of technology has been vital to the formation of the aesthetic of dance music...[It has allowed] the costs of production to fall, this allowing micro-labels to survive free from the major labels. This 'white label' culture has been given a privileged place in the aesthetic of dance, especially as the 12-inch vinyl record remains the medium of choice by the DJ, and it is the pivotal position of the DJ as the cultural arbitrator supreme within dance culture that often gives the micros the edge over the majors...Most significant is the empirical reality that this is being done by young people themselves. They are using the technology, establishing their own labels, getting into distribution, organizing parties, becoming DJs. They are making the connections and linkages, they are establishing this social and economic structure separate from the major record companies, and often to a large extent separate from the formal economy itself...This makes young people the producers of culture by being *the producers* (Smith and Maughan, 1998, p.225-226).

In essence, this is an example of the way that dance culture flows through and beyond local scenes with the help of youth producers/redistributors. In a rudimentary way at least, this completes one description of the cycle of cultural transmission, interpretation, rearticulation, and retransmission in the context of dance music culture.

Departure Points and Conclusion

Our argument has been that existing work that examines the ways that youth create (locally distinct) music-related cultures in spite of the potential homogenizing effects of global economic forces, could be usefully extended to other research areas that focus on *the processual and relational ways that global influences impact these local cultures, and the way that global flows circulate through these cultures*. This means emphasizing not only the ways that youth use global resources, but also how youth interpret these resources (e.g., how they make sense of dance music magazines), how this influences their participation in dance music culture (c.f., Currie, 1999; McRobbie, 1994), and ultimately how their engagement with such music cultures help to frame their social identities more generally. This is a methodological call for implementing more focused 'audience research' along with critical ethnographies when studying the flows and determinates of culture.

In making this argument, we also emphasize the need to be attentive to the intertextuality of influences on youth cultural development (i.e., the way that traveling and travelers impact local scenes and the various exposures to media), as well considering the cultural, political and economic 'history' of these influences. While ethnographic research might unveil youths' experiences in negotiating these various influences, understanding the flows of culture also requires an understanding of the market practices of media/music producers through an examination of the placement of youth cultural images and the codes that guide these image placements (through a combined ethnographic, social semiotic and materialist approach).

Finally, and in addition to these more specific theoretical and methodological suggestions, we argue that there is a need for more reflexive cross-cultural analyses of youth (dance music) cultures. That is to say, research that concentrates on the flows of culture *between* various countries, as well as the processes of interpretation within each scene/setting, would provide a more comprehensive and compelling portrayal of a global culture. In this context we would agree with Featherstone when he points out that:

> It is not helpful to regard the global and local as dichotomies separated in space or time; it would seem that the processes of globalization and localization are inextricably bound together in the current phase (Featherstone, 1995, p.103).

In the present context, where the logic of late capitalism seemingly determines all aspects of social and cultural life, tracing the emergence, diffusion and incorporation of global cultures and their attendant communities is an important task for social scientists. As we have noted earlier, dance culture is arguably the most visible exemplar of an emergent global culture. It would be a mistake to simply read young people's consumption (and production) within this scene as an index of cultural manipulation. We would posit that there is a sense of agency in the ways in which young people, through their engagement with the dance scene, have developed a degree of skepticism around the truth claims made by the scientific knowledge industries. For example, the attempt to define dance cultures through a public health discourse, as inherently dangerous sites of unknown and indeterminate risk, have spectacularly failed to prevent young people from embracing, adapting and exploring the possibilities of dance culture. However this engagement with 'risk' is not based on a pragmatic or instrumentalist approach to 'managing' or reducing the risks involved – primarily filtered through the moralized discourse of the dangers of drug (ab)use. Instead risk is normalized, shorn of its bourgeois pretences, and dissipated as a necessary but unexceptional component of the dance experience itself. Hence why, despite the attempt of most Western governments to prohibit the consumption of narcotics especially amongst the 'vulnerable' young, rates of consumption of Ecstasy, amongst other drugs, have remained high. Indeed it could be argued that the dance scene, by the extent and degree of its normalization of drug use, has challenged the hegemony of the anti-drug discourse such that a number of governmental agencies and States are having to radically rethink the effectivity of the 'war on drugs' – Portugal's dramatic decriminalization of its drugs laws in 2001 being perhaps the clearest example of this.

The emphatically outer-national identifications and trans-local collectivities that dance culture promotes should not be dismissed too readily in a political climate where appeals to forms of ethnic absolutism and nationalistic belonging are gaining increased legitimacy in many parts of the post Cold-War world. Whilst talk of a dance music diaspora may be pushing the analytical categories too far, these grounded everyday encounters of cultural hybridity, exchange and dialogue may prove to be effective organic responses to the fundamentalist and regressive programs of essentialist identity politics that have emerged in the face of globalization's cosmopolitan impulses.

However, these potentially progressive manifestations need to be set alongside the inequalities and disjunctures that have inevitably arisen within global dance music cultures. The power geometry, as Massey (1994) puts it, of the uneven nature of cultural and economic flows between various regions of the world have to be kept constantly in mind. In this context we would concur with Rietveld's observations when she notes:

> In the global loops of music production and distribution, dance or club cultures are taking root from Sao Paolo to Tel Aviv across a wide political and cultural spectrum. Yet the spread has done little to shift uneven power distribution; Western global cities continue to dominate along with the five major record companies which control distribution and abide by the stubborn distinctions of gender and class. We cannot help but ask, "Is everybody equally welcome at this global party?" (Rietveld, 2000, p.30).

These final points reflect the underlying goal of this project, which is to work towards a more theoretically and methodologically integrated approach to studying global clubcultures in the hope that subsequent cross-cultural studies might be attentive to the flows between various local youth cultures as well to the distinctiveness of the cultures themselves. Such a standpoint, we believe, is vital if we are to understand the dialectical and potentially transcendent nature of popular culture, and what describing youth cultures as sites of resistance might actually mean in the twenty-first century.

Notes

1. The term 'clubcultures' refers to the youth cultural phenomenon that is associated with all-night dance parties at nightclubs or other venues, the production and consumption of various dance music genres (music 'mixed' or electronically created by DJs), and with the use of amphetamine drugs (particularly MDMA or 'Ecstasy') to enhance the dance/music experience. The culture's roots lie in the 1970s and early 1980s American dance music scenes of New York, Chicago and Detroit, and more recently in Britain where 'rave culture' emerged in 1988 during what came to be known as the 'second summer love'. In Britain in particular, the subsequent criminalization of the rave scene (a partial result of moral panics about rave-related drug use) and incorporation of the rave scene (by the mainstream music industry) led the culture to become grounded in 'nightclub' venues, and how ravers, in effect, became 'clubbers'.
2. This overview, while a useful summary for our purposes, does not capture the full complexity of the work conducted in America or Britain. For example, American work by Miller (1958) and Matza (1964) in some ways departed from traditional 'delinquency theory', with Miller arguing that traditional explanations of subcultural activity underestimated the link between working class culture and deviant youth

subcultures, and Matza highlighting the importance of 'chance' encounters and 'bad timing' in determining a youth's tendency to 'drift' into a delinquent lifestyle. At the CCCS, both Willis (1977) and McRobbie (1977) studied *un*spectacular groups and emphasized the ways that symbolic forms of resistance actually reinforce existing structures of class relations/inequality. There were also methodological differences in the work that emerged from the CCCS, where Willis (1977) and others privileged critical ethnographic methods while others, such as Hebdige, preferred social semiotics and textual analysis.
3. When these 'earlier times' were is unclear, although it would seem that the period up to and including the 1970s when the seminal work on youth culture was conducted, is some kind of marker.
4. This pessimistic analytic approach is consistent with work that has linked the globalizing trends of late modernity with the emergence of a 'risk' society. Although the notion of 'risk' has been developed elsewhere in this book, it is crucial to note here the ways that issues related to 'youth and the media' are positioned. For example, some commentators suggest that impressionable youth are more susceptible to the dangers of media exposure, while others emphasize the ways that youth are 'controlled' and 'censured' through the overemphasis on concerns about 'today's troubled and troubling' youth in the form of mediated 'moral panics' – Acland, 1995; Critcher, 2000; Furlong and Cartmel, 1997; McRobbie, 1994; McRobbie and Thornton, 1995; Miles, 2000; Tanner, 1996 amongst others discuss these issues drawing in part on S. Cohen's (1972) seminal work. For discussions on the nature of 'risk' and its relationship to aspects of everyday life and culture see Adam et al. (2000).
5. Or as Kobena Mercer puts it: 'The postmodern riddle of political subjectivity – what do a trade unionist, a Tory, a racist, a Christian, a wife-beater and consumer have in common? *They can all be the same person*' (1994, p.273).
6. In part, though, due to the media attention that 'acid house' raves received during the previous summer, 1989 was arguably as important a year at least in terms of the number and size of illegal raves that were held.
7. The term 'clubculture' has come to be more loosely defined, as its usage in this chapter shows.
8. In fact, a somewhat competing club *and* rave scene still exists in Toronto, with some raves still occurring in usually legal but still non-nightclub locations.
9. British satellite and terrestrial television companies continue to make programmes such as *Ibiza Uncovered* (BSkyB) and *Around the World in 80 Raves* (Channel 4) aimed at this newly found constituency of clubbing tourists, who can now enjoy the spectacle related to the post-rave tourist gaze without ever having to engage with the old modernist tradition of actually leaving their front rooms to experience the club sensation.

References

Acland, C. (1995), *Youth, Murder, Spectacle: The Cultural Politics of 'Youth in Crisis'*, Boulder, CO, Westview Press.

Adam, B., Beck, U. and Van Loon, J. (eds.) (2000), *The Risk Society and Beyond*, London, Sage.

Alasuutari, P. (ed) (1999), *Rethinking the Media Audience*, London, Sage.

Amit-Talai, V. and Wulff, H. (eds.) (1995), *Youth Cultures: A Cross-Cultural Perspective*, New York, Routledge.

Appadurai, A. (1990), 'Disjuncture and difference in the global cultural economy', in *Theory, Culture and Society*, vol.7, pp.295-310.
Bennett, A. (1999), 'Subcultures or neo-tribes? Rethinking the relationship between youth, style and musical taste', in *Sociology*, vol.33, no.3, pp.599-617.
Bennett, A. (2000), *Popular Music and Youth Culture: Music, Identity and Place*, New York, NY, St. Martin's Press.
Best, S. and Kellner, D. (1997), *The Postmodern Turn*, New York, NY, The Guilford Press.
Blumer, H. (1969), *Symbolic Interactionism: Perspective and Method*, Englewood Cliffs, N.J., Prentice-Hall.
Brake, M. (1985), *Comparative Youth Cultures*, London, Routledge and Kegan Paul.
Brown, E. (2000, Nov. 6), 'London Coming', in *New York*, vol.33, no.43, pp.58-59.
Buckingham, D. (ed.) (1993), *Reading Audiences: Young People and the Media*, Manchester, Manchester University Press.
Buckingham, D. (1997), 'Electronic child abuse? Rethinking the media's effects on children', in Parker, M. and Petley, J. (eds), *Ill effects: The Media/Violence Debate*, London, UK, Routledge.
Carrington, B., Andrews, D., Mazur, Z. and Jackson, S. (2001), 'Global Jordanscapes', in Andrews, D. (ed.), *Michael Jordan Inc: Corporate Sport and Media Culture*, Albany, NY, SUNY Press.
Chambers, I. (1994), *Migrancy, Culture, Identity*, London, Routledge.
Cohen, A. (1955), *Delinquent Boys: The Culture of the Gang*, New York, NY, Free Press.
Cohen, P. (1972), 'Subcultural conflict and working-class community', *Working Papers in Cultural Studies*, vol.2, pp.5-52.
Collin, M. (1998, 2nd ed.), *Altered State: The Story of Ecstasy Culture and Acid House*, London, UK, Serpents' Tail.
Cote, J. and Allahar, A. (1996), *Generation on Hold: Coming of Age in the Late Twentieth Century*, New York, NY, New York University Press.
Critcher, C. (2000), '"Still raving": Social reaction to Ecstasy', in *Leisure Studies*, vol.19, no.3, pp.145-162.
Currie, D. (1999), *Girl Talk: Adolescent Magazines and Their Readers*, Toronto, ON, University of Toronto Press.
De Certeau, M. (1984), *The Practice of Everyday Life*, Berkeley, CA, University of California Press.
Duncombe, S. (1997), *Notes from the Underground: Zines and the Politics of Alternative Culture*, New York, NY, Verso.
Eisner, B. (1994), *Ecstasy: The MDMA Story*, Berkeley, CA, Ronin Publishing.
Featherstone, M. (1995), *Undoing Culture: Globalization, Postmodernism and Identity*, London, Sage.
Fine, G. (1987), *With the Boys: Little League Baseball and Pre-Adolescent Culture*, Chicago, IL, University of Chicago Press.
Fine, G. and Mechling, J. (1993), 'Child saving and children's cultures at century's end', in Heath, S. and McLaughlin, M. (eds.), *Identity and Inner-City Youth*, New York, NY, Teacher's College Press.
Fish, S. (1979), *Is there a Text in this Class? The Authority of Interpretive Communities*, Cambridge, MA, Harvard University Press.
Furlong, A. and Cartmel, F. (1997), *Young People and Social Change*, Buckingham, Open University Press.
Garratt, S. (1998), *Adventures in Wonderland: A Decade of Club Culture*, London, UK, Headline Book Publishers.
Hafeneger, B., Stüwe, G. and Weigal, G. (1993), *Punks in der Großstadt Punks in der Provinz: Projektberichte aus der Jugendarbeit*, Opladen, Leske and Budrick.

Hall, S. and Jefferson, T (1976), *Resistance Through Rituals: Youth Subcultures in Post-War Britain*, London, UK, Hutchinson.
Hebdige, D. (1979), *Subculture: The Meaning of Style*, New York, NY, Methuen and Company.
Hebdige, D. (1987), *Cut 'n' Mix*, London, UK, Comedia.
Jackson, S. and Andrews, D. (1999), 'Between and beyond the global and the local', in *International Review for the Sociology of Sport*, vol.34, no.1, pp.31-42.
Kempster, C. (ed.) (1996), *History of House*, Kent, Staples of Rochester.
Kruse, H. (1993), 'Subcultural identity in alternative music culture', in *Popular Music*, vol.12, no.1, pp.31-43.
Laing, D. (1985), *One Chord Wonders: Power and Meaning in Punk Rock*, Milton Keynes, UK, Open University Press.
Lash, S. (1994), 'Reflexivity and its doubles: Structure, aesthetics, community', in Beck, U. Giddens, A. and Lash, S. (eds.), *Reflexive Modernization: Politics, Tradition and Aesthetics in the Modern Social Order*, Cambridge, UK, Polity Press.
Lash, S. and Urry, J. (1987), *The End of Organized Capital*, Madison, University of Wisconsin.
Lull, J. (2000), *Media, Communication, Culture: A Global Approach*, New York, NY, Columbia University Press.
Malbon, B. (1998), 'Clubbing: Consumption, identity and the spatial practices of every-night life', in Skelton, T. and Valentine, G. (eds.), *Cool Places: Geographies of Youth Cultures*, New York, NY, Routledge.
Malbon, B. (1999), *Clubbing: Dancing, Ecstasy and Vitality*, New York, NY, Routledge.
Massey, D. (1994), *Space, Place and Gender*, Cambridge, UK, Polity Press.
Matza, D. (1964), *Delinquency and Drift*, New York, NY, John Wiley and Sons.
McRobbie, A. (1977), *Working-Class Girls and the Culture of Femininity*, Unpublished MA thesis, Centre for Contemporary Cultural Studies, University of Birmingham, UK.
McRobbie, A. (1993), 'Shut up and dance: Youth culture and changing modes of femininity', in *Cultural Studies*, vol.7, no.3, pp.406-426.
McRobbie, A. (1994), *Postmodernism and Popular Culture*, London, UK, Routledge.
McRobbie, A. and Thornton, S. (1995), 'Rethinking "moral panic" for multi-mediated social worlds', in *The British Journal of Sociology*, vol.46, no.4, pp.559-574.
Melville, C. (2000), 'Mapping the meanings of dance music', in *Youth's Sonic Forces: The UNESCO courier*, July/August, pp.40-41.
Mercer, K. (1994), *Welcome to the Jungle: New Positions in Black Cultural Studies*, London, UK, Routledge.
Merton, R. (1938), 'Social structure and anomie', in *American Sociological Review*, vol.3, pp.672-682.
Miles, S. (2000), *Youth Lifestyles in a Changing World*, Philadelphia, PA, Open University Press.
Miller, W. (1958), 'Lower class culture as a generating milieu of gang delinquency', in *Journal of Social Issues*, vol.14, no.3, pp.5-14.
Mitchell, T. (1996), *Popular Music and Local Identity: Rock, Pop and Rap in Europe and Oceania*, New York, NY, Leicester University Press.
Morley, D. (1980) *The Nationwide Audience: Structure and Decoding*, BFI, London.
Muggleton, D. (1997), 'The post-subculturalist', in Redhead, S. (ed.), *The Clubcultures Reader: An Introduction to Popular Cultural Studies*, Malden, MA, Blackwell.
Muggleton, D. (2000), *Inside Subculture: The Postmodern Meaning of Style*, New York, NY, Berg.
Negus, K. (1992), *Producing Pop: Culture and Conflict in the Popular Music Industry*, London, UK, Edward Arnold.
Negus, K. (1996), *Popular Music in Theory: An Introduction*, Cambridge, UK, Polity Press.

Osgerby, B. (1998), *Youth in Britain since 1945*, Cambridge, UK, Blackwell.

Prus, R. (1996), 'Adolescent life-worlds and deviant involvement', in O'Bireck, G. (ed.), *Not a Kid Anymore: Canadian Youth, Crime, and Subcultures*, Toronto, ON: Nelson Canada.

Radway, J. (1984), *Reading the Romance: Women, Patriarchy and Popular Literature*, Chapel Hill, NC, University of North Carolina Press.

Redhead, S. (1990), *End of the Century Party: Youth and Pop Towards 2000*, New York, NY, St. Martin's Press.

Redhead, S. (1997), *Subcultures to Clubcultures: An Introduction to Popular Cultural Studies*, Malden, MA, Blackwell.

Reynolds, S. (1997), 'Rave culture: Living dream or living death', in Redhead, S. (ed.), *The Clubcultures Reader: Readings in Popular Cultural Studies*, Malden, MA, Blackwell Publishers.

Reynolds, S. (1998), *Generation Ecstasy: Into the World of Techno and Rave Culture*, Toronto, ON, Little, Brown and Company.

Rietveld, H. (1997), 'The House Sound of Chicago', in Redhead, S. (ed.), *The Clubcultures Reader: Readings in Popular Cultural Studies*, Malden, MA, Blackwell.

Rietveld, H. (1998), *This is Our House: House Music, Cultural Spaces and Technologies*, Aldershot, Ashgate.

Rietveld, H. (2000), 'The body and soul of club culture', in *Youth's Sonic Forces: The UNESCO courier*, July/August, pp.28-30.

Robinson, D., Buck, E. and Cuthbert, M. (1991), *Music at the Margins: Popular Music and Global Cultural Diversity*, Newbury Park, CA, Sage.

Rowe, D. (1995), *Popular Cultures: Rock Music, Sport and the Politics of Pleasure*, London, UK, Sage.

Shaw, C. and McKay, H. (1927), *Juvenile Delinquency and Urban Areas*, Chicago, IL, The University of Chicago Press.

Silcott, M. (1999), *Rave America: New School Dancescapes*, Toronto, ON, ECW Press.

Sinker, M. (1996), 'Electro kinetic', in Kempster, C. (ed.), *History of House*, Kent, Staples of Rochester.

Skelton, T. and Valentine, G. (1998), *Cool Places: Geographies of Youth Culture*, New York, NY, Routledge.

Slobin, M. (1993), *Subcultural Sounds: Micromusics of the West*, London, UK, Wesleyan University Press.

Smith, F. (1998), 'Between east and west: Sites of resistance in East German youth cultures', in Skelton, T. and Valentine, G. (eds.), *Cool Places: Geographies of Youth Cultures*, New York, NY, Routledge.

Smith, R. and Maughan, T. (1998) 'Youth culture and the making of the post-Fordist economy: Dance music in contemporary Britain', in *Journal of Youth Studies*, vol.1, no.2, pp.211-228.

Sutherland, E. (1947), *Principles of Criminology*, 3rd edition, Philadelphia, PA, Lippincott.

Szemere, A. (1992), 'The politics of marginality: A rock musical subculture in socialist Hungary in the early 1980s', in Garofalo, R. (ed.), *Rockin the Boat: Mass Music and Mass Movements*, Boston, MA, Southend Press.

Tanner, J. (1996), *Teenage Troubles: Youth and Deviance in Canada*, Toronto, ON, Nelson Canada.

The Guardian (2000, Nov. 4), Travel: Clubbing all over the world, pp.2-4.

Thornton, S. (1994), 'Moral panic, the media and British rave culture', in Ross, A. and Rose, T. (eds.), *Microphone Fiends: Youth Music, Youth Culture*, New York, NY, Routledge.

Thornton, S. (1995), *Club Cultures: Music, Media and Subcultural Capital*, Hanover, NH, Wesleyan University Press.

Tinning, R. and Fitzclarence, L. (1992), 'Postmodern youth culture and the crisis in Australian secondary school system', in *Quest*, vol.44, pp.287-303.

Willis, P. (1977), *Learning to Labour: How Working Class Kids Get Working Class Jobs*, New York, NY, Columbia University Press.

Willis, P. (1990), *Common Culture*, San Francisco, CA, Westview.

Wilson, B. (1999), *Empowering Communities or Delinquent Congregations? A study of complexity and contradiction in Canadian youth cultures and leisure spaces*, Unpublished doctoral dissertation, McMaster University, Hamilton, Ontario, Canada.

Wilson, B. and Sparks, R. (1996), '"It's gotta be the shoes": Youth, race and sneaker commercials', in *Sociology of Sport Journal*, vol.13, no.4, pp.398-427.

Young, K. and Craig, L. (1997), 'Beyond white pride: contradiction in the Canadian skinhead subculture', in *Canadian Review of Sociology and Anthropology*, vol.34, no.2, pp.175-206.

Chapter 6

Research on Youth Transitions: Some Critical Interventions

TRACEY SKELTON

Introduction

In this chapter I offer a range of critiques about the concept of *transition* in youth studies. I find that there are fundamental problems with the way transitions are often conceptualized and argue that some of the ways in which they are theorized provide exclusionary understandings of processes which young people are said to 'pass through'.

Similar problems have been faced by feminist theorists who have had difficulties with the conceptualization of 'woman' as a social, cultural and symbolic category defined within a patriarchal discourse. However, they have not been able to find an alternative concept that actually has meaning for people, especially for women, so the term and concept has remained but with ever increasing caveats of definition around its meaning. The monolithic construction of 'universal woman' of the early theorizing of the 1970s has been heavily critiqued and more nuanced and sophisticated understandings of 'woman' have developed. In a similar way the concept of 'transition' seems to remain highly influential in youth research. It is not something that we can discard (yet). However, this chapter argues that it is a concept which we have to handle carefully and that there needs to be an increasing layering of the meaning of the term.

The concept of transition, if it is to have any real explanatory power, has to take into account the greater diversity of youth experience and be re-thought to include young people who, I argue, have never really fitted with the conventional understandings of transition. This is not the fault of these particular groups of young people, rather it is the fault of the concept and those who have defined it in rather narrow terms over the past decades in which it has gained common acceptance. As I examine and critique the notion of *transition* I will draw upon research conducted with a group of young people who I will argue tend to be excluded in the common conceptualizations of transition just as they can face a marginalized and excluded youth experience. This group are young lesbians and gay men.[1]

Once I have offered my critiques of *transition as concept* I will suggest ways in which we can maintain the concept so that it allows youth studies to reflect the diversity of young people's lived experiences.

Critical Engagements with the Concept of 'Transition' in Youth Studies

Based on the reading of a range of youth theory texts, in particular several which aim to examine 'youth transitions', this chapter explores several facets of critical commentary about the concept of transition. Firstly it draws together some of the common place understandings of the term in order to establish a grounded interpretation of the concept. From there it identifies a series of critiques which can be made against the concept based on readings of contemporary literature (Bynner, Chisholm and Furlong, 1997; Coles, 1995, 1997a, 1997b; Kelly, 1999; Kerckhoff, 1990; MacDonald, 1998; Morrow and Richards, 1996a; Roche and Tucker, 1997; Wallace and Cross, 1990; Wyn and Dwyer, 1999).

Common Definitions of the Concept of Transition

There are a range of definitions of the term 'transition' within the youth studies literature but there are certain common elements. The transition to adulthood is invariably taken to involve the following: completion of full-time education; entry into the labour market; leaving the parental (or substituted) home; establishing an independent household; entry into marriage or cohabitation; and parenthood (Evans and Furlong, 1997; Kerckhoff, 1990; Morrow and Richards, 1996a). There is a sense of linearity, progression and development, indeed Allat (1997) talks of youth as a process of 'becoming'. Hence, from this definition, youth is a stage, a phase through which we pass in order to become adult, to mature, to grow up.

Much of the debates about transitions have focused on the school-to-work transition (Kelly, 1999; MacDonald, 1998). However, Coles discusses three status transitions: leaving full-time education and entering the labour market (school-to-work transition); attaining relative independence from families of origin and beginning family formation (domestic transition); and moving away from the parental home (housing transition), (1997b, p.98). There is the recognition that not all of these transitions happen at the same time, although there is a sense in which all of them should happen for there to have been a transition to adulthood. A young person is said to have become an adult when these shifts have taken place. Even with a wider definition of transition beyond that of school-to-work the concept of progress, arriving at some end point, passing through a stage, remain implicit and explicit.

Discussions of transition also state that the social variables of class, gender and race (and these are the three most commonly listed) are important in the ways they affect transitions and the possible outcomes of different adulthoods (Coles, 1997a, 1997b; Morrow and Richards, 1996a). There is also growing recognition of the influence of the family in young people's transitions (Allat, 1997). Hence, there are definite mentions of the ways in which youth transitions are mediated by social factors. It is worth noting here how infrequently the social variable of sexuality or sexual identity is mentioned and that, vice versa, a chapter specifically on young people's sexuality (Edwards, in Roche and Tucker, 1997) does not mention the concept of transition at all. I would argue that the experiences of young lesbians and gay men means that we have to question the notion of transition and critically engage with a literature on young people which still ignores significant groupings of young people within its definition of youth.

In their study of 'Transitions to Adulthood: a Family Matter?' Virginia Morrow and Martin Richards argue that, 'the transitions to adulthood involves a transition to mature sexuality' (1996a, p.64) but it is not clear what constitutes a 'mature sexuality'. In their third chapter entitled, 'The Transition to Adult Sexuality and Coupledom', they write, 'except where otherwise stated, this chapter discusses heterosexual development in the white community' (p.68). However, they do not explain this particular focus. We might infer from this statement that they feel that homosexuality cannot achieve a 'mature sexuality' status, and potentially that non-white youth cannot either. There is also the problem of interpreting 'mature sexuality' as something which is fixed. Research on sexuality demonstrates that this is far from the adult experience. While I appreciate that studies have to set boundaries to their research it could be argued that exclusions of homosexual young people from discussions about the 'sexual transition' means that representations of what is deemed as 'normal' and 'deviant' are perpetuated. There is also the implication that young lesbians and gay men do not experience 'sexual transitions'. Sexuality is therefore an important variable to be taken into account as part of the differential context for young people's experiences of transitions.

Having established that there are basic elements of the concept of transition to adulthood it is important to recognize that recent work on transitions offers more nuanced approaches to the subject. Bynner et al. argue that it is now harder for young people to make transitions into the labour market (1997, p.4). Wyn and Dwyer state that the 'ever lengthening time designated as youth' means there has to be a questioning around the idea of '*a* transition' (1999, p.16, my emphasis). Kelly suggests that the concept of youth as a transition process 'emerges as a truth which dominates government horizons' and hence determines the type of policy and planning made for young people even though reflexive modernization has rendered youth transitions ever more risky and unpredictable (1999, p.193). MacDonald (1998) investigates how social and economic change has recast school-to-work transitions for most young people, especially the most vulnerable, so that there transitions are very different to their parents. Craine (1997) talks of cyclical transitions with a specific focus on social exclusion and 'alternative' careers. Furthermore, Du Bois-Reymond (1998) draws upon empirical work with a youth project in the Netherlands and argues that 'status passages' have changed for young people and that the tendency is towards 'synchronicity instead of linearity and that transitions have become reversible' (p.63). Yet, while critiquing the notion of transition in a narrowly defined way, none of these authors actually abandon the concept altogether. Once the critique has been made there is a tendency to leave the concept of transition as central with some tweaking of the meaning.

Below I argue that perhaps we need to do more than expand the meaning of transition slightly, or discuss the ways in which contemporary transitions are different (more risky, less predictable). We need to acknowledge that there are some problematic implications in the term and urge that we are careful in how we use the concept and what its use might be taken to imply about young people. In many ways the discussion below closely interconnects, the sub-headings used to help the reader are effectively artificial boundaries.

Youth as a State of Becoming: Transitions as Passing Through

Allat argues that in many ways all young people are vulnerable, that is part of the very meaning of transition. The transition to adulthood is a marginal state, dangerous and risky (1997, p.90). Later she states that 'Youth...is a process of becoming' (p.94). This sense of youth being a transitory state, rather than a recognized stage in its own right with distinctive experiences and issues, sets up notions of, phases, passing through, emerging at the end as something better, improved, fully formed. It is a developmentalist approach (Evans and Furlong, 1997). Prout and James (1997b) argue that in research on children (defined to include those aged up to 18) 'development' still remains a resistant and influential concept. Hood et al. (1996) state:

> Most research on children has been profoundly influenced by developmental approaches. The goal has been largely positivist: an attempt to document how, in the light of which factors, they progress through certain stages towards adulthood (1996, p.118).

Morrow and Richards (1996b) discuss the work of Allison James (1995) which employs four ideal types of children, one of which is the developing child. Such an approach they suggest, undervalues children's competencies and points to the fact that even *if* children are listened to, then they are not taken seriously or trusted. As children (and young people) are growing up there is an obsession with their age and always the question from adults, 'what will you do when you grow up?' This questioning, James and Prout (1997b) argue, 'denies time present in the life of the child' (p.235). The importance of age in childhood is that it provides an indication of movement (progression) towards adulthood, always looking to the future. Childhood therefore is deemed only to be important in terms of a future period of life (p.239). In considering children's research alongside youth research we can begin to see where the concept of transition emerged from and why it holds such significance. We can also recognize its roots in developmental approaches. The problem with such approaches is that they assume common experiences, behaviours, decisions and so forth based upon age: 'By this age you should be thinking and feeling like this, planning to do this, have stopped doing that'. This then leads to the assumption that young people will all approach transitions in similar ways with the similar support, resources and aspirations. Hence differences between young people are minimized, although those who don't match the stages set for their ages are deemed to be 'behind' or 'failures' (Evans and Furlong, 1997).

I would argue that this notion of 'becoming', of developing into something else, or maturing, is somewhat at odds with recent work with young people and children which calls for the recognition that young people are social agents. James and Prout (1997b) argue that sociological studies of childhood (and we could easily extend this to youth studies) must recognize the present time-frame. They propose that children (and I would add young people) have, and experience, a time, and that it should not always be perceived as a process only towards adulthood (p.241). Recent research which focuses on the school-to-work transition, states that, increasingly, young people are showing considerable creativity in adapting to difficult social and economic circumstances. In many cases these are problems and obstacles not faced by the generations before.[2] Wyn and Dwyer argue:

> The established linear models of transitions to adulthood and future careers are increasingly inappropriate for the changed economic and social conditions of the later twentieth century (1999, p.5).

Drawing on Beck (1992), Kelly stresses that at times of increasing uncertainty, risk and insecurity young people have to become the makers of their own futures, their paths are no longer mapped out for them. Their futures, he argues, will be determined inevitably by the market but also by their own agency as they plan their desired biographies (1999). MacDonald shows that in Teesside teenagers and young people have borne the brunt of economic collapse with rising unemployment rates and enrolment on youth training schemes. However, he found considerable evidence of social and economic agency among these young people. He describes them as being 'remarkably persistent, enterprising and resilient in their search for work and attempts to establish new working lives' (1998, p.168, see also MacDonald et al., 2001).

What is clear therefore is that young people, even in the face of extremely difficult situations, do not see their time as young people as a stage, a process of development, a 'becoming'. Rather, they are agentic in achieving what they desire for their lives, they are forging new ways forward in socially and economically difficult circumstances. They are living their present and making the most of the time they have.

For young lesbians and gay men their later teenage years and early twenties are often seen as a time of arrival. For many it is the age in which they gain the confidence, or have to make the decision, to admit to themselves, and invariably to those close to them, that they are gay. For them youth is not necessarily a time of 'becoming', in terms of their identity, rather it is a time at which they recognize something of fundamental importance about themselves, a time of knowing.

> My first boyfriend was when I was at school, when I was 15, and we were going out together for about two and a half years, then he left school. I left and went into a job and that was that…it took me four years to come out on my own. I came out when I was 19 and made contact with [a range of gay organizations in Sheldon] (Barry, 24, unemployed).
>
> I kind of went through denial for at least sort of two years, and then sort of 14…I actually knew then, 100 per cent sure, definitely 100 per cent sure at 14 that I was gay. And then I started to panic, then sort of found out [more about

being gay] late 15/16, nowish, I'm kind of over the accepting bit and just getting on with everything (Terry, 16, student).

I remember when I was a younger teenager, say 13/14, I had ideas that I fancied men...[but]...I never talked to anybody about it. It wasn't until I came to university, at the end of my first year [aged 19] that I went along to this big debate between the Debating Society and the Anglican Society on 'Should Homosexuality be Accepted within the Church' and then I just thought, well, I need to stop kidding myself and you know a lot of people came up who were saying 'this is me' and I thought well it's about time I did that and so I did (Robbie, 22, health worker).

I think I was in denial for a long time because I did my slapper bit with men and whole thing...just to prove a point so that they [people at school] would shut their mouths basically and then me and Mary were friends for about two years and one day we just ended up kissing each other and then we went out with each other for nearly a year and a half...that's when I accepted it (Megan, 17, student).

Coming to terms with their sexual identity was clearly a process that troubled and disturbed these young people. Many of them tried to deny how they felt to themselves and, if asked, to those around them. However, often the relief of finally admitting their identity to themselves is marked as a significant time in their lives, at times both a starting point as well as an end to self-deception and pretending. However, as explored in Valentine et al. (forthcoming) coming out to others, in particular family, friends and colleagues can be extremely difficult and painful. It can result in homelessness, job loss and intense social isolation as families and friends may reject them. Negative reactions to the telling of sexual identity can result in forced housing transitions as young people are thrown out by their parents. It can also be something that interrupts planned transitions from education into work as gay students often leave courses early because of bullying or because being made homeless forces them to draw upon benefits or find paid work. Hence for lesbian and gay young people their transitions can be as much about their sexual identity as about their 'becoming' adults.

Adulthood as the Norm

In theorization about transitions, adulthood is established as the norm against which young people are measured. This critique clearly links strongly to that discussed above. Adulthood is the state to which young people should aspire, it is the correct social status to attain and there are expected behaviours, roles and responsibilities associated with being an adult. Adulthood is the age and stage of arrival, accomplishment and achievement. The *becoming* is over, once an adult, with all the social, cultural and economic trappings of the age, an individual can just *be*.

There are all sorts of problems associated with such assumptions that nevertheless are implicit within the concept of youth transitions. Here I discuss two central critiques which appear contradictory within youth research itself.

The first is the assumption of 'adulthood as norm'. It is adultist which puts it at odds with the shifts within research about children and young people which aims to deconstruct the ways in which adults define young people. Prout and James (1997) discuss the ways in which research with children needs to view children in a different way than has been the case in the past. This same argument can be made for research with young people:

> Childhood and children's [youth and young people's] social relationships and cultures are worthy of study in their own right, and not just in respect to their social construction by adults. This means that children [young people] must be seen as actively involved in the construction of their own social lives, the lives of those around them and of the societies in which they live (1997, p.4, my additions in brackets).

Secondly, just as reflexive modernization (Kelly, 1999) impacts upon young people it also affects adults. What it means to be an adult at the beginning of the twenty-first century is very different to what it meant through the 1970s and 1980s when the concept of youth transitions was gaining ground. Wyn and Dwyer (1999) state:

> The meaning of 'transition' has changed in ways that raise questions both about the links between social structures and individual agency and about new definitions of adulthood (Wyn and Dwyer, 1999, p.5).

Hence the enormous social and economic changes of the recent years means that not only should we be questioning the notion of 'transition' but also of 'adulthood'. The uncertainties, risk and insecurities facing people today are impacting on adults too (Kelly, 1999; Wyn and Dwyer, 1999) Hence, we have to ask transition to what? What is 'adulthood' at the start of this new century, what is the 'norm' to which young people are expected to progress into? What the past generations of adults have experienced is established as the 'norm' against which youth experiences are measured, but this assumes an adulthood unchanged and unchallenged. Reflexive modernity has not left adult experiences untouched and so people are having to redefine their adult identities. We have to question the usefulness of the 'adult norm' against which we measure and evaluate young people's lives and experiences.

In work with young lesbians and gay men their future view of so-called adulthood are very different and for some allow greater scope of self-definition and 'choice biographies' (Wyn and Dwyer, 1999), and 'DIY projects in process' (Kelly, 1999):

> One of the most brilliant things is the fact that you have many more choices in a way. I mean in terms of kind of expectations of rites of passage and things like that...this is a complete kind of stereotyped view of what it means to be heterosexual but I quite like it. You know this idea that at 30 you really should be settling down, finding yourself a nice man, getting married and having 2.2 children and all of that...by not being heterosexual...it is nice to be able to opt out of all that and have more flexibility (Lynne, 24, student).

However, there are risks for this group and so-called 'choices' may in fact be forced upon them. In some cases the 'coming out' time and telling parents may lead to a terrible breakdown in the relationship and can throw planned for futures out of synch. For some it means losing their home. This happened to Vinnie who was thrown out by his parents and spent time sleeping on friend's floors before eventually finding a place of his own. However, he felt that being thrown out of his home allowed him the space to establish a form of adulthood in the eyes of his parents when he re-established a relationship with them:

> I got kicked out of home...I was quite independent at home anyway...I've been really closer [to my parents] now than I ever was...'cos I go back and they see that I'm an adult and I can do my own thing and I can survive on my own. Like I used to do it at home anyway, do all my cooking, washing, ironing. So I was quite independent but now I'm actually doing it for myself instead of doing it there because I wanted to, I have to do it now (Vinnie, 18, unemployed).

Transition as the Norm

If the notion of transition which includes conceptualizations of passing through, becoming adult, progress, achievement and improvement is established as the norm then what happens to those many young people who do not/cannot follow the required trajectory? Establishing adulthood as the goal to be achieved through 'successful' transitions means that it is then possible to talk of 'failed' transitions (or 'broken' transitions [Craine, 1997]). This concept of failure combined with the emphasis on individualization of choice and Do It Yourself biographies means that young people who do not follow expected paths are blamed for their own failures (Beck, 1992; Evans and Furlong, 1997; Kelly, 1999; Wyn and Dwyer, 1999). Structural and social inequalities, social prejudices and discrimination, are not part of the explanation.

In a society which already denigrates young people and which excessively interferes with their lives through state policy (Wallace and Cross, 1990), the added concept of 'failed transitions' reinforces negative representations of young people. In many cases the focus on the young person's failure to make a successful transition obscures wider processes such as the actual failures of adults, systems and structures.

Bob Coles (1997a and 1997b) offers an excellent insight into the experiences of young people. He especially concentrates on highly vulnerable young people: young people in care/ being looked after; young people with disabilities and/or special education needs; and young people who go into 'alternative careers' often involving small scale criminal activity. I admire his work which has brought young people marginalized both by society and, to some extent, by youth research, into focus. However, there are problems with his discussion of 'failed transitions' (1997b, p.100). It is clear that these three groups of young people face particular difficulties but in an emerging discourse whereby the process of transition is an individualized process the designation of some young people as 'failing' to make the transition places the blame at the young person's feet. Finding work, moving to independent living, forging peer group relationships are increasingly difficult for young people. However, when this is named as a 'failed transition' within a context of youth research which claims that transitions are now individualized and open to 'choice', a DIY process, the failure is not about social and economic relations and structures but about the individual young person. This is yet another reason for interrogating what we mean by the concept of transition and for remembering the wider context in which the concept is defined, utilized and interpreted.

In practical, everyday living, with the day-to-day, face-to-face social interactions we all experience then the concept of 'transition' as a norm, almost as a rite of passage to adulthood, loses validity. The interesting thing is not whether young people make the supposedly successful transitions (to employment, own home and new family), but that they are all deemed as adult at some stage in terms of social expectations. However, if we consider particular moments of discourse around lesbian and gay sexuality, some are considered more adult than others.

Here we might recall the famous Spanner case where several men were imprisoned for consensual sado-masochistic sex among adult men in their own homes. There was direct intervention by the police, the courts and the state into what most heterosexual adults would assume was their right to private behaviour. Furthermore, the Conservative Government, as part of the family bill, enacted legislation which disallowed lesbians and gay men for consideration as adoptive parents. In an interview on BBC Radio Four at the time of the debate Teresa Gorman stated that there is, 'no room for ideology' in decisions about adoption, and that lesbian and gay adults were not considered suitable as adoptive parents. More recently the current Labour Government has experienced considerable opposition (led by Baroness Young in the House of Lords), to its efforts to reduce the age of consent for gay men to 16 years of age. This would make it equal with the age for heterosexual men. It appears that young straight men who are sexually active by the age of 16 are deemed to 'know themselves' (Edwards, 1997), gay men were not deemed to 'know themselves' and be sexually competent until they were 18. Young gay men were infantilized and adult gay men demonized by Baroness Young's arguments in ways which were not applied to their straight peers.

For Mark coming out to his parents (he was still living at home) at the age of 17 changed the way they treated him totally. One day he had considerable freedom to do as he wished in the house, to stay out all night with friends, return home as late as he wanted. He was attending college, had part-time work, was paying board to his parents and felt that he had a degree of autonomy in his life. However, he found the 'living a lie' increasingly difficult and as he felt close to his parents found it harder to deliberately deceive them about where he was spending his evenings and who his friends were. He first told his father, after some probing questioning, and received a very bad reaction: 'in the conversation he managed to call me a pervert, said that queer bashing was normal and that any normal father would throw his kid out on the street for being gay'. Mark's mother was much more sympathetic and understanding, although shocked. A few days after coming out however, Mark's home world was transformed:

> The really bad part came about a day or two later when for the first time ever in our family history, like what you often see in American TV shows, we had a family meeting. My dad called this family meeting for me, my mum and him to sit down and everything and rather than sit objectively and talk about it and let me explain how I felt and everything they basically sat me down and told me how I was going to live my life, you know, in the blink of an eye take away all my freedom, you know my freedom and liberties and everything, and you know I didn't get any say or negotiations on the matter because they just told me how it was gonna be. They laid down these five golden rules as I call them: I wasn't to flaunt my homosexuality in the house, I wasn't to talk about that side of my life, I wasn't to bring any boyfriends home, I wasn't to bring

any of my friends who were 'that way' home and I wasn't to tell anyone else... I knew that if I pushed the matter too far they would throw me out the house and you know they were saying to me that it seemed as though I wasn't their son anymore, that I'd been replaced by someone else, that I was a stranger to them...and the weird part was I felt the same as well, I mean I sat there looking and talking to these people and I didn't see my Mum and Dad anymore...I just saw these two strangers, these authoritarian people who in the blink of an eye took away all my freedom and liberty and human rights and everything (Mark, 19, employed).

Mark, before the admission of his sexuality, was deemed to be 'growing up,' to be forging his way through appropriate transitions. He was at college but also had part-time work. He was building up a peer group for more adult-style socializing. His father had often asked him whether he had a steady girlfriend. However, with the knowledge of his homosexuality Mark's parents chose to close down the space for discussion and effectively rendered him a child once again. He had rules of the household to obey, they structured the home as a heterosexual space and while they would tolerate him living there it was to be in state of denial of his identity. Mark was infantalized at an age when he should have been perceived as making good progress to adulthood.

Mark's parents, like much of the existing youth research, assumed certain types of transition to adulthood. His parents would have been delighted if he had taken his girlfriend home, happy to have talked about his new 'heterosexual' relationships to family and friends. Hence there is a difficulty with the concept of 'transition' as the norm and also with the assumptions behind the concept of 'normal transitions'. The assumptions about 'normal transitions' do much to exclude a range of youth experiences and continue a discourse of some young people as 'deviant'. In the next, and final section of this chapter, I consider ways in which the concept of transition needs to take a better account of difference if it is to remain a valid model with which we try to capture more of the complexities of lived youth experience.

Transitions and Difference: A Concept for Complex Youth Experiences?

Within the youth transitions literature there is discussion of the importance of difference and diversity which have an impact on young people's lives and experiences. However, while such differences are often mentioned as part of the broader discussion about the concept, they are often lost in the remaining discussion which can then lead to some of the problems identified above.

Let us consider work on sexuality as an illustrative example. Roche and Tucker (1997) argue that they want to capture the complexities of the transitions that young people go through, and indeed the chapters in their edited book offer varied analysis of different youth experience. However, within this same collection the one chapter which focuses on sexuality (Edwards, 1997) has no focus on what this might mean in the context of transition. As mentioned above, Morrow and Richards (1996a) explicitly exclude discussion of difference in the context of sexual identities stating that their discussion related to heterosexual, white young people. Kerckhoff's text 'Getting started: transition to adulthood in Great Britain'[3] (1990) has a very traditional view of what constitutes the transition to adulthood as identified in his chapter headings. Chapter 5 is titled: 'Becoming Independent: Leaving Home, Cohabitation, Marriage and Parenthood'. Its focus is on heterosexuality. There is no conceptualization of what might constitute 'becoming independent' for your lesbian and gay people. A valuable exception to this 'invisibility' of young lesbians and gay men is found in Heath's (1999) work on housing transitions.

However, while there are identifiable problems in the lack of inclusion of young lesbian and gay people in discussions about transitions to adulthood, there has been in more recent literature a recognition of the need to take diversity within youth experiences seriously.

Wyn and Dwyer (1999) provide a review of work with young people in Canada, the Netherlands, Britain and their own research project in Australia. In their discussion of new directions in research on youth transitions they demonstrate that in the case of the 'school-to-work transition' young people are making more diverse choices than professionals working with young people at this juncture of their lives think they are. They ask how researchers can grapple with this and claim that a starting point is to add in more trajectories to reflect actual experience. Hence broaden the concept of what possible, existing and desired transitions might be. Theoretical explanations of flexible modernization, the social and economic contexts of the twenty-first century, stress the importance of individualization and as I have shown above, this offers explanatory power in the context of youth research. Wyn and Dwyer stress:

> What is important here at the policy and research levels is that if this increasing emphasis on individualization implies an understanding of youth as an *active process*, rather than a stage of development, it also implies that for young people their own sense of agency carries a degree of personal investment that looks forward to – even insists on – positive outcomes (1999, p.14).

Therefore, the concept of a process rather than a stage to be passed through allows us to conceptualize transitions which happen at different times for different groups of young people. It allows the space to recognize that there are as many different transitionary processes as there are different groups of young people and that they are all valid processes, events and experiences. They are part of the learning curves, the acquiring of cultural capital which flexible modernity, a society with risks, uncertainties and insecurities means that we all have to go through. Just because we become adults does not mean the complexities are over, and if some young people do not cope well with the complexities it does not mean they have failed to become adults. They may have a different way through to adulthood and it might be much harder, but it is still part of the active process of growing up and growing older.

The recognition of diversity of experience and opportunity among young people is recognized by several authors (Coleman et al., 1997; Coles, 1997a, 1997b; Du Bois-Reymond, 1998; Edwards, 1997; French and Swain, 1997; MacDonald, 1998, MacDonald et al., 2001). Evans and Furlong (1997) argue:

> Analysis of the contemporary situation of young adults highlights an increasing fragmentation of opportunities and experience; the processes of youth are highly differentiated, reflecting and constructing social divisions in society in complex ways (1997, p.33).

If, as youth researchers, we can hold on to the complexities and differences within and between young people then we can begin to ask questions which will reveal more about complex transitions, or as I would prefer to say, processes, which affect young people as they grow older. It is important, if we continue to use the concept of 'transition' that we recognize its shortcomings and the critical commentaries levelled against it. It is important to always ask who is left out by the use of the concept and what kind of assumptions of privilege and normativity are we making in our use of the term.

The task of trying to capture and analyze the multitude of possibilities and complexities of what might be more meaningful definitions of transitions is not easy. However, as so much youth research demonstrates being a young person in the contemporary world is not easy either. It is important that youth researchers work as hard to actively and accurately represent young people's lives as young people work at living, surviving and achieving.

Acknowledgements

I would like to thank the young lesbians and gay men who agreed to give me an interview and who shared such intimate aspects of their lives with me. I was impressed by the ways they had come, and were coming to terms, with a whole range of difficulties imposed on them because they were lesbian and gay. Despite instances of harassment, bullying, explicit homophobia and rejection these young people were creating their own trajectories, 'getting on with it' as many of them put it and contributing to society in a range of ways.

Notes

1. Here I draw upon interviews I conducted with young gay men and lesbians in a city with the fictitious name of Sheldon which form part of an Economic and Social Research Council project (award no. L134 2 1032) called 'Living on the edge: understanding the marginalization and resistance of vulnerable youth'. The grant is held jointly between myself, Gill Valentine (Dept. of Geography, Sheffield University) and Ruth Butler (Faculty of Social Sciences, Hull University). The project focuses on two groups of 'vulnerable' young people: young lesbians and gay men and young D/deaf people.
2. It is important to note however, that in the context of sexual identities many young lesbians and gay men are facing very similar obstacles, difficulties and prejudices as those faced be previous generations of young homosexuals. Coming to terms with their sexual identity and for many the process of 'coming out' can be as painful and risky as it was for generations before them.
3. The title of this book offers an illustration of some of the critiques I have made above. The concept of 'getting started' assumes that youth is a period of life on hold, that adulthood is when life really begins. It also assumes a context of one transition and yet his chapter headings indicate that there are several. As I have stated above, there is a fundamental question about whether we can talk about *a* transition.

References

Allat, P. (1997), 'Conceptualising youth: transitions, risk, and the public and the private', in Bynner, J., Chisholm, L. and Furlong, A. (eds), *Youth, Citizenship and Social Change in a European Context*, Aldershot, Ashgate.

Bynner, J., Chisholm, L. and Furlong, A. (1997), 'A new agenda for youth research', in Bynner, J., Chisholm, L. and Furlong, A. (eds), *Youth, Citizenship and Social Change in a European Context*, Aldershot, Ashgate.

Bynner, J., Chisholm, L. and Furlong, A. (eds) (1997), *Youth, Citizenship and Social Change in a European Context*, Aldershot, Ashgate.

Coleman, J., Catan, L. and Dennison, C. (1997), 'You're the last person I'd talk to', in Roche, J. and Tucker, S. (eds), *Youth in Society: Contemporary Theory, Policy and Practice*, London, Sage.

Coles, B. (1995), *Youth and Social Policy*, London, UCL Press.

Coles, B. (1997a), 'Vulnerable youth and processes of social exclusion: a theoretical framework, a review of recent research and suggestions for a future research agenda', in Bynner, J., Chisholm, L. and Furlong, A. (eds) (1997), *Youth, Citizenship and Social Change in a European Context*, Aldershot, Ashgate.

Coles, B. (1997b), 'Welfare services for young people', in Roche, J. and Tucker, S. (eds), *Youth in Society: Contemporary Theory, Policy and Practice*, London, Sage.
Craine, S. (1997), 'The "Black Magic Roundabout": Cyclical transitions, social exclusion and alternative careers', in MacDonald, R. (ed), *Youth, the "Underclass" and Social Exclusion*, London, Routledge.
Du Bois-Reymond, M. (1998) 'I don't want to commit myself yet': young people's life concepts', in *Journal of Youth Studies*, vol.1, no.1, pp.63-79.
Edwards, T. (1997), 'Sexuality', in Roche, J. and Tucker, S. (eds), *Youth in Society: Contemporary Theory, Policy and Practice*, London, Sage.
Evans, K. and Furlong, A. (1997) 'Metaphors of youth transitions: niches, pathways, trajectories or navigations', in Bynner, J., Chisholm, L. and Furlong, A. (eds) (1997), *Youth, Citizenship and Social Change in a European Context*, Aldershot, Ashgate.
French, S. and Swain, J. (1997), 'Young disabled people', in Roche, J. and Tucker, S. (eds) *Youth in Society: Contemporary Theory, Policy and Practice*, London, Sage.
Heath, S. (1999), 'Young adults and household formation in the 1990s', in *British Journal of Sociology of Education*, vol.20, no.4, pp.545-561.
Hood, S., Kelly, P. and Mayall, B. (1996), 'Children as research subjects: a risky enterprise', in *Children and Society*, vol.10, no.2, pp.117-128.
James, A. and Prout, A. (eds) (1997a), *Constructing and Reconstructing Childhood: Contemporary Issues in the Sociological Study of Childhood*, London, Falmer Press.
James, A. and Prout, A. (1997b), 'Re-presenting childhood: time and transition in the study of childhood', in *Constructing and Reconstructing Childhood: Contemporary Issues in the Sociological Study of Childhood*, London, Falmer Press.
Kelly, P. (1999), 'Wild and tame zones: regulating the transitions of youth at risk', in *Journal of Youth Studies*, vol. 2, no.2, pp.193-211.
Kerckhoff, A.C. (1990), *Getting Started: Transition to Adulthood in Comparative Perspective*, London, Routledge.
MacDonald, R. (1998), 'Youth, transitions and social exclusion: some issues for youth research in the UK', in *Journal of Youth Studies*, vol.1, no.2, pp.163-176.
MacDonald, R., Mason, P., Shildrick, T., Webster, C., Johnston, L. and Ridley, L. (2001), 'Snakes & ladders: in defence of studies of youth transition', in *Sociological Research Online*, vol.5, Issue 4, February.
Marshall, H. and Stenner, P. (1997), 'Friends and lovers', in Roche, J. and Tucker, S. (eds), *Youth in Society: Contemporary Theory, Policy and Practice*, London, Sage.
Morrow, V. and Richards, M. (1996a), *Transitions to Adulthood: A Family Matter?*, York, Joseph Rowntree Foundation and YPS.
Morrow, V. and Richards, M. (1996b), 'The ethics of social research with children: an overview', in *Children and Society*, vol.10, no.2, pp.90-105.
Prout, A. and James, A. (1997), 'A new paradigm for the sociology of childhood? provenance, promise and problems', in James, A. and Prout, A. (eds), *Constructing and Reconstructing Childhood: Contemporary Issues in the Sociological Study of Childhood*, London, Falmer Press.
Roche, J. and Tucker, S. (eds) (1997), *Youth in Society: Contemporary Theory, Policy and Practice*, London, Sage.
Roche, J. and Tucker, S. (1997), 'Youth in society: contemporary theory, policy and practice', in Roche, J. and Tucker, S. (eds) *Youth in Society: Contemporary Theory, Policy and Practice*, London, Sage.
Valentine, G., McNamee, S., Butler, R. and Skelton, T. (forthcoming), *Negotiating Difference: Lesbian and Gay Transitions to Adulthood*.
Wallace, C. and Cross, M. (eds) (1990), *Youth in Transition: The Sociology of Youth and Youth Policy*, London, Falmer Press.

Wyn, J. and Dwyer, P. (1999), 'New directions in research on youth in transition', in *Journal of Youth Studies*, vol.2, no.1, pp.5-21.

Chapter 7

New Deal or Raw Deal? Dilemmas and Paradoxes of State Interventions into the Youth Labour Market

BARRY PERCY-SMITH and SUSAN WEIL

Introduction

New Deal 18-24 (NDYP) is the latest in a long line of youth training and employment 'New Deals' designed to tackle problems of youth unemployment. In their 1997 election manifesto Labour stated their intention of getting 250,000 young people aged 18-24 off benefit and into work, education and training by 2002 as part of their welfare to work programme. It is claimed to be distinctive in reflecting the current British government's Third Way approach to policy-making which aims to recast the relationship between the state and young citizen whilst at the same time promoting economic growth and tackling social exclusion. The development of the Third Way, and New Deal in particular, is the government's response to wider economic and cultural changes associated with late modernity and a risk society. These have led not only to the restructuring of youth transitions, but also youth cultures and identities in contemporary societies, posing significant challenges for intervention practices. This analysis of education, training and guidance (ETG) interventions for unemployed young adults thus offers insights into the dilemmas, paradoxes and contradictions of Third Way politics and social policy.

New Deal was heralded in government circles as having the potential to make a real difference to youth unemployment (Labour Party, 1997) yet data suggests it has fallen short of its original aims. These concerns have led to a stepping up of targets and a move away from the client-centred approach that was originally intended. This shift raises questions about whose agenda New Deal is really working for, about the effectiveness of mainstream interventions such as New Deal, and the ambiguity of the state's commitment to socially excluded young people and the achievement of an inclusive stakeholder society.

This chapter is based on a case study exploration of New Deal as an example of a mainstream intervention into post-compulsory ETG for the young unemployed. The objective of the study was to learn from New Deal about what it means for interventions to effectively enhance the social and economic participation of unemployed young people. One of the key insights is how competing agendas at play give rise to tensions between the interests of clients, advisors and government ministers which can undermine the effectiveness of interventions. Despite official interpretations of New Deal as a success (Midgely, 1999), closer investigation suggests that long-term benefits of New Deal may be limited due to the predominance of professional rather than young people's interests. This study therefore argues that to improve initiatives such as New Deal, they should be sufficiently client-focused and flexible to accommodate the complex biographies of disadvantaged young people.

New Labour, New Deal

New Deal is the flagship of Labour's welfare-to-work strategy. The programme aimed at 18-24 year olds will cost £2.6bn over the 4 years between 1998 and 2002. After six months of unemployment the young person meets with a New Deal Personal Advisor (NDPA). Each individual receives personalized support and guidance during the initial four month Gateway period. If after four months the young person is still unwaged they are expected to participate in one of four options: full-time education and training (FTET), subsidized employment with at least one day a week training, work in the Voluntary Sector (VS) or Environmental Task Force (ETF) options, with at least one day a week training.

The ETF and the Voluntary Sector provide an allowance equivalent to the rate of unemployment benefit plus an extra £15 per week. The FTET option offers an allowance equivalent to benefit plus expenses, although there is the possibility of accessing a discretionary grant in exceptional circumstances. The maximum duration for the options stage is 12 months. It is stressed there would be 'no fifth option of life on full benefit' (Brown, 1997). Finally, the third stage offers a 'Follow-Through' period in which the client receives continuing support after their option, to help them find work. Sanctions, in the form of cutting benefit, are applied to individuals who consistently do not attend appointments or who fail to co-operate with New Deal procedures.

After the initial piloting of New Deal, responses from young people were generally positive (Hill and Stern, 1998). Even the most cynical were positive about the programme's ability to help young people find the kind of work they want to do, rather than employment of any kind (Legard et al., 1998). However, given the investment in New Deal, initial soundings suggest that New Deal is less effective than originally intended. Of particular interest in this study is why, given the espoused commitment to tackling social exclusion and the apparent radical nature of New Deal, so many young people are failing to reap the intended benefits? For example, figures from the Department for Education and Employment (2001) suggests that by the end of Apr 2001 out of 641,600 starting on New Deal 546,800 had left. Of those leaving, 39 per cent have entered sustained unsubsidized jobs, 11 per cent have transferred to other benefits, 20 per cent have left for other known reasons and 30 per cent have left for unknown reasons.

These patterns suggest that at best, less than half of those eligible for New Deal are gaining any tangible benefits. In spite of the governments claim that youth unemployment is down by 40 per cent, it could be argued that individuals are simply being relocated within the unemployment system, for example, transferring onto other benefits or onto one of New Deal's three non-employment options (File on 4, 20/6/99). Sykes (cited in Milne, 1998) also suggests that approximately 40 per cent of those going through New Deal are likely to find work, education or training anyway. It is also not clear how many of those that leave and go into employment are any better off than they were previously. There is little evidence to demonstrate whether these individuals stay in work, whether the work is permanent or provides adequate conditions and prospects to sustain employment for that person in the future. This suggests that there are either inadequate employment opportunities for young people or that employers are reluctant to make a commitment to New Deal. A key concern therefore, is that for these young people New Deal may actually be having a negative impact on their transition into full-time waged employment.

The Social and Political Context of New Deal

Underpinning New Deal as Labour's flagship welfare-to-work initiative are three political imperatives: tackling social exclusion, lifelong learning and labour's 'moral crusade'. The setting up of the Social Exclusion Unit symbolized a commitment from the New Labour administration to tackle problems of social inequality, poverty and exclusion. The chancellor Gordon Brown declared the need for a 'national crusade against unemployment and poverty' (Brown, 1997). Some observers, however, have criticized New Deal as being a coercive measure to reduce the benefit burden (Lister, 1998; File on Four, 20/6/99; Dwyer, 1998; Player, 1999), which Tonge (1999) highlights as the second highest social security bill amounting to £8bn, whilst offering few real opportunities (Jeffs and Spence, 2000). Nonetheless NDYP, through the provision of training and employment subsidies, was looked to as the means for getting unemployed young people into work and training and therefore for addressing problems of social exclusion. There is a concern however, that focusing on New Deal and employability obscures the wider structural issues of providing quality employment and reducing inequality (Lister, 1998; Stepney et al., 1999; Jeffs and Spence, 2000).

The second political imperative involves the lifelong learning agenda. Partly in response to changing labour market opportunities and the consequent lengthening of youth transitions, but also because of the need to ensure a flexible and skilled labour force, increasing emphasis has been placed on education and training for youth. It is envisaged that by 2010, 50 per cent of young people will be in higher education. But it remains to be seen how relevant lifelong learning is for those young people who have already become disaffected from education and learning and excluded from mainstream social and economic participation. The third imperative is Labour's moral crusade which emphasizes individual responsibilities. This has been informed by the notion of 'communitarianism' (Dwyer and Martell, 1997) as well as recent Third Way theorizing (Giddens, 1997, 2000). Le Grand (1998) highlights the elements of this philosophy as: community, opportunity, responsibility and accountability. The aim is to (re)create a new relationship between citizens and the state where welfare rights are only provided if individuals also fulfill their responsibilities by, for example, actively seeking waged employment (Heron and Dwyer, 1999).

New Deal embodies many of the elements of the Third Way approach to policy-making. In particular the key principles underpinning New Deal are:

1. Partnership. New Deal is founded on local partnerships with employers, voluntary organizations, education and training providers and career services.
2. Individual focus. New Deal is tailored to individual job seekers.
3. Quality. It provides high quality support from New Deal Personal Advisors and access to a wide range of high-quality training and job opportunities.

4. Resources. It is backed by £2.6 billion pounds over four years financed by the Treasury through a hypothecated tax.

(Employment Service, 1998)

New Deal is based on 'workfare' rather than welfare principles (Player, 1999), as unemployment benefit is conditional on individuals accepting personal responsibility to find employment – the Third Way principle of 'active citizenship' (Giddens, 1997). Only by entering into such a contract will unemployed individuals be guaranteed a basic level of income, specific training, assistance in job searching and career decision-making. However, commentators suggest the emphasis on fostering individual responsibility within New Deal through compulsion and the use of sanctions, raises questions about the conditionality being attached to the social rights of citizenship (Dwyer, 1998; Lister, 1998; Stepney et al., 1999). Lister for example argues that the emphasis on social inclusion and individual responsibility has been promoted at the expense of equality and social rights. What she argues is that instead of 'good quality work as a right' emphasis is now on integration into an unequal labour market.

Furthermore, given the collapse of youth labour markets in many parts of the country critics have argued that the emphasis on supply side employment policy, with little emphasis placed on investment in labour market opportunities, is unlikely to give rise to long term successes. For example Campbell et al. (1998) highlight the changing nature of local labour market opportunities for youth and argue the need for policy to be more responsive to local conditions. Furthermore, Sykes (cited in Milne, 1998) suggests that in areas where there is an acute shortage of jobs, New Deal will create 'a pool of people qualified to work but unable to find employment.'

Young People's Experiences of Guidance, Training and Employment

The emphasis of current policy on increasing the employability of unemployed youth reflects an underlying assumption that the problem rests more with the 'individual', rather than their inter-relationship with the economy and society or the quality of opportunities provided. Numerous studies, however, show that training opportunities are not always attractive to young people (Mizen, 1995; Williamson, 1997; Hocking, 1998; MacDonald, 1998; Lloyd, 1999). Even when they are, they do not always lead to tangible employment opportunities. Tonge (1999) suggests three broad sets of criticisms of previous training policy. First, that schemes amount to a form of cheap labour. Second, that the schemes have provided inadequate training. Third, that large numbers of individuals who complete training return to unemployment. As a result, writers such as Sutherland (1998) reiterate the need to ensure quality placements in the current New Deal programme on the basis that young adults who are put off training once are unlikely to accept a further option. What young people seek is not just training but employment with training opportunities (Evans et al., 1997; Gardiner, 1998; Sutherland, 1998). However, by concentrating on predetermined trajectories the complexity and diversity of individual transitions may remain hidden (Pollock, 1997).

New Deal seeks to succeed where previous policies have failed by offering a 'Gateway' period for young people providing careers assistance and a range of training and employment options. Yet, as Hodkinson and Sparkes (1997) and Dwyer (1998) highlight, there is a challenge to intervention practices in that young people often make decisions which appear irrational or irresponsible to policy-makers and welfare professionals but are none the less rational for the young people concerned. The authors also suggest young people make decisions which are often pragmatic, rather than systematic, context-related and based on partial information located in the familiar and the known. They concluded that career decisions could 'only be understood in terms of the life histories of those who make them' (Hodkinson and Sparkes, 1997 p.33). This echoes previous research which stresses the significance of the 'biographization' of the lifecourse in youth transitions (Buchner, 1990; Du Bois-Reymond, 1995).

Understanding Youth Transitions

The impact of globalization and detraditionalization on young people's lives has given rise to calls for new ways of understanding youth transitions, cultures and identities (Bynner et al., 1997). In particular there have been calls for a 'more interactive research process that enables the participants to articulate their own meanings and experiences' (Wyn and Dwyer, 1999, p.5), thus foregrounding the importance of individual biographies and agency in the construction of the lifecourse (Chisholm et al., 1990; Evans and Heinz, 1995; Evans and Furlong, 1997; Roberts, 1997; Wyn and White, 1997; Looker and Dwyer, 1998; Rudd and Evans, 1998; Wyn and Dwyer, 1999). In the search for new models of youth transitions some writers have drawn on discourses of social change in which youth transitions are seen to involve a process of individualization as young people negotiate the risks and uncertainty which characterize late modernity (Furlong and Cartmel, 1997). Yet Furlong and Cartmel also argue that whilst transitions are no longer predictable, lifechances are still structurally differentiated in terms of race, class and gender. Hence many now talk of a process of 'structured individualization' (Rudd and Evans, 1998) in which transitions are understood in terms of individual actions and choices as young people navigate their way through, 'a sea of manufactured uncertainty' (Evans and Furlong, 1997).

In spite of the reflective stance of youth researchers, discourses of youth and youth transitions in late modernity, and the changing nature of the youth labour market, policy responses have been slow in embracing these changing agenda. Yet in the space between theory and policy professionals struggle to mediate the disjunctions between policy intentions and the lived realities of young people. At the same time, young people live out their own lives but often in ways which are 'worlds apart' from the lives of professional policy-makers (Percy-Smith, 1999). In studying New Deal this chapter explores further some of these contradictions and paradoxes between policy rhetoric and the lived realities of young people.

Background to the Study

This chapter is based on research undertaken as part of a collaborative, cross-European research programme exploring professional interventions into youth transitions to the labour market. The research programme aimed to examine what constitutes effective provision in post-school ETG for unemployed youth. The project featured cycles of collaborative action inquiry with professionals and young people using narratives, metaphors, critical incidents, case histories, participant observation, informal interviews, video and inquiry groups. The research involved working simultaneously on different levels. At the outset a collaborative inquiry group with NDPAs, drawn from across the county, was undertaken to draw out and explore critical issues and concerns. Participant observations were undertaken of the encounters between NDPAs and clients in Employment Service offices, followed by individual interviews with young people and NDPAs.

The aim was to seek out a diversity of experiences at different stages in the New Deal process. We included young people currently going through Gateway, participating on New Deal options, as well as some who had completed New Deal, had chosen to opt out of New Deal or who, despite being eligible, had as yet remained beyond the reach of New Deal. In all a total of seventeen interviews were conducted with New Deal clients. Many informal conversations were also undertaken with young people in training settings, in work placements and with homeless young people in the YMCA. Eleven formal interviews and numerous informal conversations were conducted with training providers, employers, guidance professionals and other youth workers. Emerging issues were then explored further in ongoing collaborative inquiry groups of professionals, New Deal Advisors and young people.

The Strengths and Weaknesses of New Deal: Navigating Between Policy Targets and the Needs of Young People?

Competing Agendas

Those involved in New Deal all have very different agenda. There are tensions and contradictions between the rhetoric of New Deal as client-centred and the reality of pressures on NDPAs to meet targets; between the political priorities of getting young people off benefit and into work and the broader social and biographical concerns of young people; and between the 'respectable passions' of New Deal Advisors and the possibilities of practice. Empirical data suggests that young people were concerned to find 'quality employment' which was meaningful in terms of providing a sense of self-worth and relevant to their own biographies. But such jobs were rarely available. At the same time, advisors expressed a commitment to making a difference to the lives of unemployed young people. For advisors, doing a 'good job' meant:

- Helping someone get what they want out of life.
- Making a difference with that client.
- That the young person is happy with the end result.
- Seeing them increase in confidence and motivation.
- Placing the young person in the job most suitable and desirable for them.
- Helping a client in a way the Department or Employment Service doesn't particularly count as a 'result' but the client benefits from and can more forward.

(Comments from NDPAs, Inquiry group, 27/4/99).

In spite of this espoused client-centredness, contradictions emerged in practice with some young people who related stories of having to do things they did not want to do. One client was told by her advisor "Well maybe you can't do what you want to do". The data in this study suggests that young people viewed New Deal as successful only if it matched their needs and interests. Advisors, driven by targets, tend to be more concerned with getting young people into any work rather than work that was appropriate for the young person. NDPAs often expected unemployed, young people with few qualifications to accept and even be grateful for menial work. However, even those who were unsure about what they wanted to do, knew that they did not want to do boring, menial jobs. As one young claimant suggested:

> The worst thing is to get a warehouse job...I'm not going to be stuck in that that...just shuts off your mind really...become a robot...You get disheartened a bit really (Paul, age unknown, New Deal Office, 26/6/99).

As NDPAs expected young people to accept and remain committed to poor quality jobs it seemed that a key role of professionals was to manage or 'cool out' the career expectations of young people, based partly on an assumption that as a guidance professional 'they know what's best for young people'. This was problematic for many young people who were struggling to retain the right to self-determination in their life. It also suggests that 'social responsibility' is being imposed rather than nurtured. If New Deal and Third Way policy is supposedly tailored to life in a risk society it should be about empowering young people to develop the skills and capacities to negotiate and survive uncertainty and make informed choices.

A further dilemma is that taking menial jobs can distract young people from making more appropriate long-term career choices. For example, Kristine had done menial jobs before but now wanted to, 'do something with her life':

> I've signed on before and been stuck in jobs I don't want to be in...and could've done factory work...but I actually wanted to find something I was interested in...so I wouldn't be back here in 6 months...I don't want to go into a job I don't want...you've got to be happy in the job you've got...I mean I was doing an office job for a year...and I'd just see people that have been there 25 years and thought, they're happy with their little life, but I couldn't do this...until I find a job that...I'm interested in (Kristine, age 20, New Deal Office, 30/6/99).

Sheila's story also echoes this finding. Despite a clear career orientation towards work in the caring professions, the NDPA decided she should be placed in the voluntary sector:

> They were going to bung me in a charity shop and OK...I like working with people, but not in a charity shop. No way...Just seems like they've got nobody else. All the people who are unemployed – or the 'dolies' as we used to call them – and we're bunged into things we don't want to do, like charity shops, and making paving slabs...we're pushed into them because we're unemployed as if it's our fault. It's like the thing for me is for your self-worth because you're worth better than that...If they bunged me into a charity shop...It wouldn't be taking into account what qualifications I've done, what experience I've got, and it would send me backwards (Shiela, age 24, New Deal Office, 24/6/99).

There are other cases where appropriate choices were made, but these tended to involve less risky transitions. However, for young people for whom the education system has already failed and for whom gaining meaningful and sufficiently paid employment is problematic the only options left in New Deal are voluntary work (normally in care or retail) or work with the ETF. Moreover, if a client fails to choose an option by the third month of the Gateway Period advisors have to refer them to either the VS or ETF options. However, whereas employers, trainers and educators and voluntary placements can all choose who they are recruiting, the ETF is obliged to accept any referrals. What happens is that ETF seems to become a dumping ground for 'problematic young people'. Whilst advisors argue that a mandatory referral is only used in extreme cases, in reality, it appears that young people are frequently obliged to accept a placement on ETF even though they may have no commitment to that type of work.

> I want to get into the working world – and there's this (ETF) option and I don't want to do it – but I've got no choice...it's not what I want to do...it's nothing to do with what I want to do. They say to me 'It'll give you experience and it'll give you skills...' But it doesn't matter because that experience ain't going to be nothing to do with what my life's about (Sean, age 21, New Deal Office, 30/6/99).

The paradox of New Deal in this case is exemplified by the illusion of choice and the charade of opportunity. Whilst there may be benefit in providing an opportunity to gain transferable skills, this appears only to be worthwhile if matched by individual choice and commitment. Instrumental measures are only likely to be effective if they also take account of social and biographical considerations. Many New Deal Advisors acknowledge the fallibility of the process of referring young adults onto ETF who don't want to be there, but are apparently given no alternatives. The inflexibility of the 'no fifth option' and the failure to take sufficient account of young people's contexts and concerns produce the unintended effect of undermining the original policy intention. If young people were provided with support rather than conditions and accountability there appears more likelihood of achieving positive outcomes which would be beneficial to both the state and the individual.

However, for many, finding what they want, making choices and taking action may not be so easy, especially since many of the unemployed have already been failed by the system. Many appeared to be frozen in a state of unknowing or inaction, or what Blackman (1997) refers to as a 'fear of the fall', as a result of low self-esteem, emotional disturbance or difficulties coping in the face of multiple disadvantage.

Evidence here suggests the New Deal's focus on trying to get young people into work may in itself not be sufficient if long-term unemployment is to be addressed. This approach may well meet the short-term political agenda of getting young people off benefit and into work, but may be ineffective in harnessing young people's commitment and abilities. If young people are to find little more than low paid, temporary, unskilled work then there is little incentive for them to cooperate with New Deal. For example on one ETF 'induction day' only 6 of the expected 28 individuals attended. During a group interview with the 6 young males they all stated that they did not want to be there, with some expressing anger and frustration at why they had been sent there at all:

> I only got two choices – the voluntary sector and this one. They should give us like four, five – six maybe – it gives us more opportunity to get out and learn what we need to learn. They said I was too old for college schemes. I'm 21 and I'm too old for college! I feel like I'm back at school now (Group interview, ETF placement, 23/8/99).

Being too old for college is indeed ironic given Labour's commitment to lifelong learning and the development of a 'learning society'. When asked whether they will stay with ETF to gain whatever experience they can, the group of 6 responded that they would not stay on but would have to try and find a job somehow. Instead of helping young people, ETF in this case was making their situation even more difficult. They were not only being forced onto options they didn't want to do, but at the same time faced sanctions if they quit. What they really wanted was a genuine opportunity to earn money and a skill or trade which would improve their chances of sustained employability, an objective apparently shared by New Deal. In spite of the supposed ethos of client-centredness and the objective of achieving a competitive and skilled labour force, there appears to be more emphasis on directing young people into an uncertain labour market than enhancing their capacity for sustainable social and economic participation.

There appears to be a gap in the New Deal options that could be filled by a craft apprenticeship type scheme. There is ample evidence which highlights the potential value of work-based learning, as an effective way of facilitating young persons transition from learning to work (Evans et al., 1997). For example, the VIP scheme for supporting 16-18 year olds in undertaking a national traineeship or modern apprenticeship, is achieving considerable success. Yet, despite New Deal's emphasis on partnerships, there is no coherent programme for work-based learning provided through New Deal for the 18-24 year old age group. We suggest that this is a fundamental weakness which, if addressed, could provide positive opportunities for many long-term unemployed youth.

There are real problems facing policy-makers and professionals who seek to 'bridge the gap' between policy intentions and young people's lifeworlds through programmes such as New Deal. The most obvious is that the day-to-day lives, values and experiences of many young people are so often at odds with those of politicians and welfare professionals, as Hodkinson and Sparkes (1997) cited above suggest. There appears to be a need for a new approach to ETG which accommodates and respects young people's values, visions and 'ways of being' – particularly around meaningful career choices – rather than being driven by the short-term pursuit of state objectives. The paradox here is that failure to take account of young people's agendas results in them quitting options and coming back into the system, which fails to benefit young people and undermines the chances of NDPAs reaching targets. A fundamental question for youth policy interventions such as New Deal therefore is, 'How relevant are the opportunities to young people and to what extent do the processes, choices and options empower or disempower these youth?

Compulsion and Commitment: Sanctions and Injustices

The low level of success achieved through ETF suggests that compulsory attendance is ineffective. One outcome is that young people are unlikely to continue on the programme with the result that they rebound back into the system, are sanctioned and create a logjam for advisors. These situations seem to increase frustration for advisors and young people alike. Rather than serving as a 'kick start', sanctions act as a disincentive for positive action, as they hit those who are least able to deal with them and further compound the difficulties they already face.

New Deal operates within a culture which treats lack of commitment or misunderstandings as punishable offences rather than opportunities for learning and development. They appear to be based on a 'cultural deficit' paradigm – namely the use of stereotypes and misguided assumptions about the attitudes, motivations and orientation of unemployed youth, as the following story illustrates:

Sheila was due to start an option. It fell through, though apparently not as a result of her own doing. Yet, because she did not start the option and did not inform her advisor, she was sanctioned.

> My New Deal Advisor was very good...I found her very approachable. But I have seen another advisor while she was away and was given a real hard time. I was due to start this voluntary placement...and that fell through. I was told not to see my advisor anymore as I was on this option. Well I never signed last Thursday and of course I had no money going into my bank, I didn't realize I had to sign...So they had to send it to adjudication to decide. The advisor was horrible to me. I felt really really tiny and it wasn't my fault. I was nearly in tears. Then because I was arranging this new voluntary thing myself, she changed her tune...I think she thought I was just bumming around...but because I'd made the effort to go and...get an interview...it was alright, because if I was a no-hoper I wouldn't have done that would I? I had been categorized as a no-hoper... (New Deal Office, 24/6/99).

This story illustrates how Sheila had to fight for the right to be treated with respect. It also reveals how good relationships between advisor and client can be undermined because of the stereotypical views advisors may hold about young people. Given inappropriate interventions into young people's lives, it is no surprise that young people get frustrated and agitated with the system. In situations such as this young people express feelings of disempowerment rather than empowerment in their choices and actions. They can, as Sutherland (1998) suggests, undermine young people's integrity as social actors, distract them from finding an appropriate course of action and may risk further alienating an already vulnerable group in society. Yet NDPAs similarly talk of feeling frustrated and disempowered by the system.

Empowering and Disempowering Young People in Their Choices and Actions: The Critical Role of the Professional Relationship

Conversations with young people revealed how sensitive many felt towards issues of self, identity and power. The vulnerability of many on New Deal mean that effective interventions are crucial to enabling young people's successful transitions into the labour market. As Sutherland (1998) shows, all the evidence suggests that those who have had negative experiences of schemes in the past are less likely to accept further placements. This suggests that New Deal needs to ensure that initial placements are of relevance to young people and of the highest quality. Yet as has been shown in this paper, despite New Deal being marketed as client-centred, young people are often constrained in their ability to make their own decisions, as the following experiences from young people suggest:

> They kept trying to send me to Link Training and I didn't really want to go to them, but if I didn't go they were going to stop my money, and it's like, they're trying to tell me what to do, I don't want this...You don't really want to be told that you *have* to go there...it's like they're dictating to you,...it's like being told by your parents to go and tidy your room...But I was quite happy going into full-time education because that was my thought if I couldn't get a job with training, it was actually my choice...You can't expect someone to go along with a decision that's not theirs (Teresa, age unknown, local college, 25/5/99).

> It was their attitude...they don't give you the time to explain yourself. They treat you as if you're a kid...didn't like it at all...I'd like to be treated with respect. As adults not kids...instead of thinking they know our needs, they need to take time to listen to people (Martin, age 19, YMCA video, Aug 99).[1]

These comments raise questions about the sort of role advisors should take. Whilst advisors have expertise and knowledge of training and job opportunities, interventions appear to be most effective when young people are empowered to make an informed decision, rather than advisors acting in young people's 'best interests'. In situations where decisions are not clear, the tendency is for advisors to make a decision for young people in order to move them through the system. Instead, it may be beneficial to help young people achieve a situation where they are ready and able to make an informed and appropriate decision on their own terms.

One outcome of this study has been the construction of new models of professional practice in terms of the 'co-inquiring professional' (Janssens et al., 2000). They make the distinction between the 'expert professional' (who, by virtue of the authority invested in them, seek to *direct* decisions and courses of action) and the 'interpretive' or 'co-inquiring professional' (who works *with* the young people to better understand their situation and reach their own decisions for action rooted in the individuals lifeworld). There is the need therefore for personal advisors to shift the emphasis from directive approaches to more facilitative (or interpretive) roles in which the advisor becomes a supportive guide rather than an instructor. Having a supportive and empathic advisor makes a real difference for many young people, as Teresa related:

> She was really interested in how I was getting on with the course and everything...so she was fairly helpful in that way...She wanted to make sure that I'd made the right decision in the right course that I wanted to go on... When I started full-time employment she actually rang me up on my first day

to congratulate me. It's important really...nice to think you're not just a statistic to them, but...a human being...If they ring up...to see how you're doing on the course...and not just say...you haven't been to your work placement...it makes you feel better about yourself, about doing the course...I think that's a nice touch (Teresa, age unknown, local college, 25/5/99).

However, even if advisors do listen more carefully to young people the solution to many of the difficulties they may confront are likely to lie beyond what is possible within New Deal, in particular in dealing with problems of multiple social disadvantage.

Beyond New Deal: Dealing with Disadvantage

For many unemployed young people their lives are very complex and the success of programmes such as New Deal are dependent on how well they work with social and biographical issues. The example of Mike who was homeless illustrates the challenges that NDPAs face:

It was their attitude...I mean I'd just been made homeless and they expected me to continue doing ETF...and they didn't give me any time off what so ever. They said...'I'm sorry Mr. Dobson, you've still got to do it.'...Put me under a lot of stress, nearly had a nervous breakdown...cos I was constantly reminded I had to go to this option rather than sort out my life. I don't know why they call it the New Deal, might as well just call it the 'nervous breakdown' (Mike, age 23, YMCA, Aug 1999).

Advisors acknowledge the broader issues many youth face, but in reality can feel as powerless as young people in responding to them. Although the Gateway period was designed to get young people 'work ready', in many cases it is insufficient for addressing the many deep-seated problems that some young people experience. Moreover, enforcing commitment to New Deal procedures can have detrimental affects on other aspects of their lives. For example, one young male on the ETF option was frustrated as he really wanted to be working and earning a living:

They stopped my claim before cos I was supposed to come in before and start here...and I owe 600 quid on my rent...You've got no choice really you've got to pick something or you lose your money. I wanna job...I've got to support my family somehow, I can't wait for six months while I'm sitting in a classroom. The thing is, cos I've got my own flat and I've got a missus and my little girl and everything and my little wages come in and it's not enough to pay my rent, and Council Tax and things like that...I just can't afford to do that unless I get a decent wage (Group interview, ETF placement, 23/8/99).

In response to this type of situation many advisors alert young people to the possibilities of getting extra financial assistance, but this is not guaranteed. Besides, applying for yet another benefit tends to constitute another burden for many young people. The problem advisors face is how to help their clients find employment which allows them to earn enough money to cover their bills, when many have no qualifications. What advisors are dealing with here is not so much a problem with young people, rather a problem of labour market disadvantage, which is in turn part of a broader problem of social disadvantage. Yet NDPAs are, by implication, expected to deal with such problems. There is a growing tension here in Third Way government policy of trying to balance commitment to economic priorities with issues of social inclusion, social justice and individual choice.

New Labour's focus on individual responsibility means that programmes such as New Deal are unable to cope with the impact of social disadvantage on labour market transitions. A dilemma faced by many advisors is how to deal with those labelled as the 'hard to help'. NDPAs repeatedly expressed frustration with clients who fail to start an option, who don't attend interviews or who find it difficult to make a decision about what they should do. Our evidence suggests that some individuals lack confidence, are anxious about new situations or are overwhelmed by broader problems of social disadvantage such as: homelessness, few qualifications, low self-esteem, criminal records, emotional disturbance or substance misuse. In these cases there is a danger that the punitive effect of sanctions exacerbate marginalization and exclusion, deepen sense of low self-worth and further reinforce the histories and disadvantages that have contributed to their unemployment in the first place. If New Deal is to truly help all young people then measures need to be provided to enable individuals to transcend these barriers to social and economic participation.

Despite the policy rhetoric around New Deal there is a need to balance the demands of meeting performance targets with the needs of young people and in particular to take account of their individual capacities, life stories and social situations. Despite Tony Blair's categorical insistence that there would be no 'fifth option' (of staying at home on the dole), many advisors spoke of the need to reconsider the merits of an alternative fifth option, to release the log jam of hard-to-help young people who remain in the system. As one advisor said: "New Deal needs to be reviewed for those people with problems which can't be solved with a 4 month Gateway period." In light of the time and resources spent on these young people trapped in the system, it may be more cost effective to provide a referral system in which young people are supported in addressing difficulties through counselling and capacity building whilst still claiming benefit.

Conclusion: Lessons from New Deal

This chapter has shown that despite the commitment of advisors to 'making a difference', systemic factors and inflexibility in policy implementation can undermine the successful working of New Deal. Moreover, recent tightening up of New Deal practice in order to achieve policy targets is likely to exacerbate the alienation of unemployed young people and further hinder their labour market transitions. In so doing the original policy intention of widening choices and options for young people is compromised. This chapter suggests a number of ways in which New Deal and similar programmes could be improved.

Firstly, there is the need to develop a genuinely more client-centred and less bureaucratic service, in which social and biographical considerations central to young people's lifeworlds can be balanced with youth policy objectives. This requires a built-in critical reflexivity to enable continuous practice learning and development in the system itself (Weil, 1998; Percy-Smith and Weil, 2000). Secondly, interventions need to become more responsive to the problems of disaffection and multiple disadvantage that many unemployed young people experience, but which currently remain untouched by New Deal. Thirdly, because of options often being seen as inappropriate or unattractive, there is a need to broaden the range of opportunities to better meet the career aspirations of all young people. For instance by providing work-based training in mechanics, welding, plumbing, hairdressing, catering and leisure services and which offer a genuine commitment from employers in terms of pay, conditions, training and security. Finally, inter-personal relationships between advisor and client are crucial to whether interventions are successful in making a difference to young people's capacity for social and economic participation. There is therefore a need to provide a space for empowerment in which young people have a greater degree of autonomy in choice-making and choice-taking on programmes such as New Deal. This requires new approaches to professional intervention practices.

Note

1. Young people at the YMCA undertook a video project organized by themselves according to their own criteria and experiences of New Deal and being unemployed.

References

Blackman, S.J. (1997), '"Destructing a giro": a critical and ethnographic study of the youth "underclass"', in MacDonald, R. (ed.), *Youth, the 'Underclass' and Social Exclusion*, London, Routledge.

Brown, G. (1997), *Budget Statement*, 2nd July.

Buchner, P. (1990), 'Growing up in the eighties: changes in the social biography of childhood in the FRG', in Chisholm, L. et al. (eds), *Childhood, Youth and Social Change: a Comparative Perspective*, Basingstoke, Falmer.

Bynner, J., Chisholm, L. and Furlong, A. (eds) (1997), *Youth Citizenship and Social Change in a European Context*, Aldershot, Ashgate.

Campbell, M. with Sanderson, I. and Walton, F. (1998), *Local Response to Long-Term Unemployment*, York, Joseph Rowntree Foundation/York Publishing Services.

Chisholm, L., Buchner, P., Kruger, H-H. and Brown, P. (eds) (1990), *Childhood,Youth and Social Change: A Comparative Perspective*, Basingstoke, Falmer.

Department for Education and Employment (2001), *Statistical release*, SFR29/2001, 28th June, London, Department for Work and Pensions.

Du Bois-Reymond, M. (1995), 'Future orientations of Dutch youth: the emergence of a choice biography', in Cavalli, A. and Galland, O. (eds), *Youth in Europe*, London, Pinter Press.

Dwyer, P. (1998), 'Conditional Citizens? Welfare Rights and Responsibilities in the Late 1990s', in *Critical Social Policy*, 57, vol.18, no.4, pp.493-517.

Driver, S. and Martell, L. (1997), 'New Labour's communitarianisms', in *Critical Social Policy*, vol.17, no.3, pp.27-46.

Employment Service (1998), *What is New Deal?*, New Deal Booklet, NDL 6.

Evans, K. and Heinz, W. (1995), 'Flexibility, learning and risk: work, training and early careers in England and Germany', in *Education and Training*, vol.37, no.5, pp.3-11.

Evans, K. et al. (1997), 'Working to learn: a work-based route to learning for young people', in *Issues in People Management*, no.18, Institute of Personnel and Development.

Evans, K. and Furlong, A. (1997), 'Metaphors of youth transitions: niches, pathways, trajectories or navigations', in Bynner, J. et al. (eds), *Youth, Citizenship and Social Change in a European Context*, Aldershot, Ashgate Publishing.

Fairley, J. (1998), 'Labour's New Deal in Scotland', in *Scottish Affairs*, no.25, autumn, pp.90-109.

File on Four (20/6/99), *New Deal*.

Furlong, A. and Cartmel, F. (1997), *Young People and Social Change: Individualisation and Risk in Late Modernity*, Buckingham, Open University Press.

Gardiner, J. (1998), 'Learning, education and skills: young people's views', in *Education and Training*, vol.40, no.5, pp.202-205.

Giddens, A. (1997), *The Third Way*, Cambridge, Polity Press.

Giddens, A. (2000), *The Third Way and Its Critics*, Cambridge, Policy Press.

Heron, E. and Dwyer, P. (1999), 'Doing the right thing: Labour's attempt to forge a New Welfare Deal Between the Individual and the State', in *Social Policy and Administration*, vol.33, no.1, March, pp.91-104.

Hills, J. and Stern, E. (1998), 'New Deal for young unemployed people: case studies of delivery and impact in Pathfinder Areas', *Employment Service research and Development Report*, Ref: ESR7, December 1998.

Hocking, A. (1998), *Great Expectations? Young People's Perception of Work and Training*, Birmingham, West Midlands Low Pay Unit.

Hodkinson, P. and Sparkes, C. (1997), 'Careership: A sociological theory of career decision making,' in *British Journal of Sociology of Education*, vol.18, no.1, pp.29-44.

Janssens, C., Jans, M., Percy-Smith, B. and Wildemeersch, D. (2000), 'Towards an interpretive education, training and guidance professional', in *Balancing Competencies: Enhancing the Participation of Young Adults in Economic and Social Processes*, Final Report, European Commission, Targeted Social and Economic Research.

Jeffs, T. and Spence, J. (2000), 'New Deal for Young People: good deal or poor deal?', in *Youth and Policy*, no.66, pp.34-61.

Labour Party (1997), *New Labour: Because Britain Deserves Better*, Labour Party election Manifesto.

Le Grand, J (1998), 'The Third Way begins with Cora', in *New Statesman*, 3, April.

Legard, R., Ritchie, J., Keegan, J. and Turner, R. (1998), 'New Deal for Young Unemployed People: The Gateway', *Employment Service Research and Development Report*, Ref: ESR8, Dec 1998.

Lister, R. (1998), 'From equality to social inclusion: New Labour and the welfare state', in *Critical Social Policy* 55, vol.18, no 2, pp.215-225.

Lloyd, T. (1999), *Young Men, the Job Market and Gendered Work*, York, Joseph Rowntree Foundation/York Publishing Services.

Looker, E.D. and Dwyer, P. (1998), 'Education and negotiated reality: complexities facing rural youth in the 1990s', in *Journal of Youth Studies*, vol.1, no.1, pp.5-22.

MacDonald, R. (1998), 'Youth, transitions and social exclusion: some issues for youth research in the UK,' in *Journal of Youth Studies*, vol.1, no.2, pp.163-176.

Milne, K. (1998), 'Meet Mr Smith, minister for new deals and new dawns', in *New Statesman*, 3 April, pp.52-58.

Mizen, P. (1995), *The State, Young People and Youth Training: In and Against the Training State*, London, Mansell.

Percy-Smith, B. (1999), *Multiple Childhood Geographies: Giving Voice to Young People's Experience of Place*, Unpublished doctoral thesis, University College, Northampton.

Percy-Smith, B. and Weil, S. (2000), 'Empowering youth in research and social processes using critically reflexive action research: learning from practice', Paper presented to the *Researching Youth: Issues, Controversies and Dilemmas Conference*, University of Surrey, July 11th/12th.

Player, J. (1999), 'New Deal or Workfare Regime?', *Youth and Policy*, No.64, Summer, pp.15-27

Pollock, G. (1997), 'Uncertain futures: young people in and out of employment since 1940', in *Work Employment and Society*, vol.11, no.4, pp.615-38.

Roberts, K. (1997), 'Structure and agency: the new youth research agenda', in Bynner, J. et al. (eds), *Youth, Citizenship and Social Change in a European Context*, Aldershot, Ashgate Publishing.

Rudd, P. and Evans, K. (1998), 'Structure and agency in youth transitions: student experiences of vocational further education', in *Journal of Youth Studies*, vol.1, no.1, pp.39-62.

Stepney, P. Lynch, R. Jordan, B. (1999), 'Poverty, exclusion and new labour', in *Critical Social Policy*, vol.19, no.1, pp.109-127.

Sutherland, J. (1998), 'Youth Training: a New Deal?', in *Regional Studies*, vol.32, no.6, pp.572-577.

Tonge, J. (1999), 'New packaging, old deal? New Labour and employment policy innovation', in *Critical Social Policy*, vol.59, no.2, pp.217-232.

Weil, S. (1998) 'Rhetorics and realities in public service organisations: systemic practice and organisational learning as critically reflexive action research (CRAR)', in *Systemic Practice and Action Research*, vol.11, no.1, pp.37-62.

Williamson, H. (1997), *Youth and Policy: Contexts and Consequences*, Aldershot, Ashgate.

Wyn, J. and White, R. (1997), *Rethinking Youth*, London, Sage.
Wyn, J. and Dwyer, P. (1999), 'New directions in research on youth in transition', in *Journal of Youth Studies*, vol.2, no.1, pp.5-21.

Chapter 8

Domestic and Housing Transitions and the Negotiation of Intimacy

SUE HEATH

Introduction

The term 'domestic transition' is most commonly used to embrace the notion of a transition from a family of origin to a family of one's own (Coles, 1995), usually implying the eventual formation of a couple household. Youth researchers commonly draw a distinction between *domestic* transitions on the one hand and *housing* transitions – moving from the parental home to a home of one's own – on the other, yet in practice these key transitions are often interconnected and hard to disentangle in young people's lives. For example, many young people move in and out of particular households in order to marry or cohabit, with demographers and youth researchers often pointing to crucial differences in the housing and domestic trajectories of those who first leave home for these reasons and those who leave for reasons other than couple formation (see for example, Berrington and Murphy, 1994; Ermisch et al., 1995; Holdsworth, 1999). However, by establishing the couple household as the desirable end goal of the transitional process, the term 'domestic transition' not only carries with it an expectation of linearity in young people's patterns of household formation, but also plays down the importance of other intimate relationships in their lives. This is particularly problematic for the increasing numbers of young people who are either choosing to form couple households, if at all, at a later age, or who, having formed a couple household, subsequently experience its disintegration (McRae, 1999). If coupledom is positioned as the final point on the 'adult' end of the transitional scale, then where does that leave those not in couple households?

A broader definition of 'domestic transition' is needed, then, one which embraces the multiplicity of domestic arrangements commonly – and increasingly – adopted by young adults and which does not privilege couple formation. This is not to argue that couple relationships are unimportant to young adults, nor that most do not attach special status to couple households: far from it. Rather, it is to highlight the different degrees of independence and freedom achieved across a variety of different household forms, in relation to young people's changing status within a wide range of relationships – with parents, siblings, friends and co-residents, as well as with partners, and to point out that a sense of being a fully independent adult is not necessarily contingent on living with a partner. Shifting the focus in this way foregrounds the embedded nature of negotiations of intimacy within wider processes of household formation: whilst negotiations surrounding intimate personal relationships may not necessarily be the *cause* of every housing move – although they often are – they almost inevitably follow as one of the *consequences*. Leaving home for the first time, for example, results in an unavoidable shake-up of relationships with both parents and siblings. Living away from the parental gaze in turn opens up new opportunities for forming casual or more longstanding relationships, both platonic and sexual. At the same time, existing relationships may be consolidated or undermined by each move.

My aim here is to explore domestic transitions in this broader relational sense, through focusing on negotiations of intimacy amongst single young people in their twenties and early thirties. The chapter firstly considers current debates on the transformation of intimacy in the context of 'the second demographic shift'. I draw on the work of Beck and Giddens, whose writings on risk and individualisation have been widely debated within the context of transitions from school-to-work (for example, Furlong and Cartmel, 1997; Ahier and Moore, 1999). However, their work also sheds light on changing patterns of household formation and the relative importance of partners, friends and family during a period when normative scripts concerning leaving home and 'settling down' are being rewritten. The second part of the paper then adopts a case study approach to focus on the networks of intimacy of a group of single young people whose status as independent adults is often perceived as being particularly ambiguous: residents of shared households. The case studies consider the connections between a young person's specific living arrangements and the negotiation of a range of intimate relationships. Following Jamieson, I use the term 'intimate relationships' to describe relationships characterized by a level of disclosure: 'an intimacy of the self rather than an intimacy of the body, although the completeness of intimacy of the self may be enhanced by bodily intimacy' (Jamieson, 1998, p.1). Such relationships include those with parents and siblings, with friends, and with partners, and the phrase *'networks of intimacy' is* used to refer to the full range of intimate relationships embraced by any one person.

The Transformation of Intimacy?

During the late twentieth century, patterns of household formation unfolded in the shadow of what has been termed 'the second demographic transition'. This term distinguishes between the demographic shifts that have occurred since 1960 across many western industrialized nations, and those that took place in the first half of the twentieth century (Scott, 1999). These shifts, often associated with the rise during this period of social movements that challenged traditional sexual and domestic relations, have included the rise in divorce, a marked increase in cohabitation and lone parenthood, later childbirth and marriage, the growth of single person households, and the greater acceptability of gay and lesbian relationships (McRae, 1999; Berthoud and Gershuny, 2000). The smooth transitions from family of origin to family of destination which were the hallmark of the 1950s and early 1960s, when the age of first leaving home served as a reliable proxy for the age of first marriage (Kiernan, 1985), are no longer with us. Instead, frequent and complex movements back and forth between living alone or with parents, friends and partners are now increasingly common amongst young adults, removing any sense of a common linear transition.

Elsewhere, I have explored the dominant sociological explanations for these changing patterns of household formation amongst contemporary youth (Heath, 1999). Much existing research has emphasized the impact of fractured labour market transitions, through studying relatively disadvantaged young people. However, whilst economic factors have undoubtedly acted as powerful catalysts for recent demographic trends, by no means all young people have been negatively affected. Youth researchers need also to consider growing evidence of changing attitudes towards intimacy and commitment prevalent amongst contemporary youth, particularly amongst relatively affluent young people of graduate and/or professional and managerial status – Du Bois-Reymond's (1998) 'post-adolescent cultural elite'. Many young people now expect, for example, in contrast to earlier periods, to form a couple household later rather than sooner, after a protracted period of independence (Wilkinson, 1994; Wilkinson and Mulgan, 1995). As a consequence, both single person and shared households are becoming increasingly common living arrangements, particularly amongst young people of graduate and/or professional and managerial status (Hall et al., 1997 and 1999; Bynner et al., 1997; Bell and Jones, 1999; Heath and Kenyon, 2001). These changing attitudes, then, have implications for the current attractiveness of traditional forms of household and family living, particularly with respect to their desired timing. Whilst most young people continue to aspire to cohabitation or marriage at some point, many are in no immediate hurry to do so (Jamieson et al., 2000; Ermisch, 2000; Kenyon and Heath, forthcoming).

Giddens (1991) ascribes these shifts to the 'transformation of intimacy' in late modernity, driven by a sexual revolution in which women increasingly seek equality with men in both the public and the private spheres, 'implying a wholesale democratizing of the interpersonal domain' (p.3). The realm of intimate relationships, he argues, has become a key area for self-reflexivity, resulting in the emergence of:

> The pure relationship, one in which external criteria have become dissolved; the relationship exists solely for whatever rewards that relationship as such can deliver (Giddens, 1991, p.6).

In other words, the relationship is sought only for what it can give to the partners involved, and will disintegrate once it ceases to be mutually beneficial. Wilkinson and Mulgan (1995) have argued that contemporary youth do indeed place a high value on emotional intimacy, mutual affection and sexual satisfaction within their sexual relationships. However, this may be more of an ideal than something that is achievable in practice; most research on young people's sexual relationships suggests that heterosexual couple relationships continue to be based on unequal power relations (Holland et al., 1998), although Morris and Fuller (1999) offer a more optimistic account. Nonetheless, as Jamieson has argued, 'the creative energies of many actors are still engaged in coping with or actively sustaining old inequalities rather than transforming them' (Jamieson, 1999, p.491).

Beck and Beck-Gernscheim suggest that it is precisely these tensions between the desirability of egalitarian 'pure' relationships and the increasing impossibility of achieving them that have led to the growth of the single lifestyle (Beck, 1992; Beck and Beck-Gernscheim, 1995). They point to growing tensions between the maintenance of personal relationships in the private domestic sphere and the incompatible demands of employers in the public sphere, tensions which are most keenly felt by young adults seeking to carve out their careers under the demands of unconditional commitment and loyalty to employers. Employers increasingly expect geographical and temporal flexibility from their workers, placing a particular stress on couple relationships between individuals who are equally committed to the labour market (Heath and Kenyon, 2001). To commit to another individual under such conditions almost inevitably results in at least one of the partners having to make some form of career sacrifice: within heterosexual partnerships, this is most usually the woman. Consequently, it may be easier to maintain a degree of distance in relationships with partners until both feel established in their careers, or a career opportunity of equal status becomes available.

If partnerships are increasingly fragile and carry with them the risk of undesirable compromise, young adults may look to other personal relationships to meet their immediate need for intimacy. One view is that platonic friendships now take on increased importance in the lives of single young adults. Beck, for example, has argued that as a form of protection against the 'built-in hazards' of being single, 'an intensification of the friendship network remains indispensable' whilst 'it is also the pleasure offered by the single life' (Beck, 1992, p.122). Thus, as partnerships and family life become either less desirable or more difficult to attain, non-familial and non-sexual social networks will begin to provide the support structures more traditionally associated with family and a partner. This idea has been reflected within the media in recent years, with a notable emphasis on the attractiveness of platonic friendship amongst young people in popular sitcoms such as *This Life*, *Friends* and *Ally McBeal* (although even most of the characters in *Friends* have now paired off either with each other or with outsiders).

Giddens (1991 and 1992) also sees platonic friendships as being of increasing importance. He argues further that close platonic friendships are the prototype of 'the pure relationship' between sexual partners, voluntarily entered into and no longer dependent on external criteria – the marriage certificate, societal approval – for their continuance. Beck (1992), however, contends that the development of strong platonic friendships may actually inhibit one's ability to form partner relationships, particularly those based on equality and mutual disclosure:

> In the single life, the longing for the other grows just as much as the impossibility of integrating that person into the architecture of a life that now really is 'one's own'. That life was fulfilled with the non-presence of the other. Now there is no space left for him or her (pp.122-123).

Nonetheless, whilst *living* with a partner may now be less desirable or attainable, there is little contemporary evidence to suggest that young adults are rejecting the pursuit of partnerships *per se*. Analysis of the *1998 British Household Panel Study* reveals, for example, that 26 per cent of never married, childless men aged under 35, and 33 per cent of their female peers, were involved in a non-resident partnership of at least six months duration, with around two fifths of these relationships having lasted for at least two years (Ermisch, 2000). Indeed, Jamieson (1998) has argued that the rather optimistic idea that 'good friends are all you need' is:

> A philosophical ideal which has become a pervasive public story rather than an everyday lived reality...Given that friendship is culturally defined as a non-sexual relationship, and a pervasive public story is that adults need a sex life, then friendship is not all you need (p.105).

Rather, relationships with close platonic friends and sexual partners are more often nurtured in parallel, albeit on occasions resulting in conflict. It is also entirely possible that many young people will enjoy an active sex life whilst prioritizing the emotional bonds of platonic relationships over those associated with their sexual relationships. Jamieson et al.'s (2000) own research hints at this possibility. Amongst a sample of 110 Scottish young people in their early twenties, 25 of the 62 who were involved in sexual relationships said that they neither felt any emotional ties or commitment to that person, nor did they think of that person as their partner.

Where do parent-child relationships fit into this account? Beck's writings suggest that time-pressured young people will attach less importance to traditional family ties, not least because of the increased likelihood that these relationships will be conducted at a geographical distance, and will instead place greater faith in the support of their locally-based friends. There is some evidence available to support Beck's claim of a weakening of family connections. McGlone et al. (1999), for example, found that visits between parents and children became less frequent between the mid-1980s and the mid-1990s, attributing this shift to greater geographical mobility and the pressures of work, although they do not state whether there is a specific generational effect. In contrast, Scott (1997) has argued that in general terms the family remains the primary concern in most people's lives, although younger people nonetheless make fewer references to family events than older people. Again, a question mark remains as to whether this is a generational or life-stage difference. However, other research suggests that family members remain an extremely importance source of financial, material and emotional support to most young people, particularly in the process of leaving home and during the first few years after first leaving (Jones, 1995a; 1995b).

Parent-child relationships also undergo an inevitable change as young people gain greater degrees of independence. Giddens (1991) argues that parent-child relationships 'stay partly distinct from the purview of the pure relationship' (p.98) because of the unequal power relations that exist between children and their parents. However, he states that as children get older there is an increased possibility that the features associated with the pure relationship may emerge:

A person who has left home may keep in constant touch with his parents (*sic*), as a matter of obligation; but reflexively ordered trust must be developed, involving mutually accepted commitment, if the relationship is to be deepened (Giddens, 1991, p.98).

Certainly, leaving home often triggers a relative improvement in the quality of relationships between young people and their parents, yet whether these relationships ever become truly equal and free from a sense of obligation on either side is questionable. As we shall see, old patterns of behaviour are hard to break, even where parent-child relationships are based on strong foundations.

Networks of intimacy embracing partners, friends and family members, then, appear to remain of considerable importance in the lives of most young adults, and the nature and importance of these intimate relationships cannot be divorced from young people's specific living arrangements. In the remaining sections of this chapter, this point is illustrated by exploring the housing experiences of four single young people, all of whom were involved in recent research on non-student shared household living. All had previous experience of a variety of other living arrangements and were able, then, to reflect on how their relationships had changed from household to household. The specifics of their living arrangements are also crucial in understanding their own unfolding sense of independence and adulthood. Their domestic and housing transitions are thus presented in a *relational* sense, thus demonstrating the embedded nature of negotiations of intimacy within processes of contemporary household formation.

Negotiating Intimacy in Different Household Settings

The Sample

The case studies presented here are taken from interview material collected as part of the ESRC-funded *Young Adults and Shared Household Living* project, conducted in conjunction with Liz Kenyon between 1998 and 2000. The project focused on the experiences of 18 to 35 year old single adults living in *non*-student shared households. In addition to establishing the socio-economic characteristics of sharers and of their households through secondary analysis of individual-level data from the *1991 Census of Population*, the routine operation of shared living has been explored through group interviews with 25 shared households based within a southern English city, involving 77 of the 81 residents (36 men and 41 women). The research has also examined young adults' motivations for living communally through conducting individual biographical interviews with 63 of the household members, allowing them to narrate their full housing histories on their own terms. In both sets of interviews the negotiation of intimate relationships with parents, friends and partners emerged as a key theme.

Overall, the 77 sample members are well qualified, with 58 per cent having highest qualifications of degree level or above. All but ten were in employment at the point of first contact (although one young man became unemployed by the time of the second interview). Of those in employment, 82 per cent were located in Social Classes I and II. To a large extent, then, this is a sample of relatively affluent young people, reflecting our particular interest in the growing association between shared living and social privilege, but also our concern to contribute to a redressing of the relative neglect of middle class young people within most youth research. If youth researchers are to explore the full implications of processes of individualisation and risk within contemporary society, including the growing polarisation between different social groups, then it is essential that the strategies and experiences of socially advantaged young people are explored alongside those of their less advantaged peers. As for other characteristics of the sample, the mean age amongst the respondents is 25.5: 26.9 for men and 24.3 for women, 36 six have a partner, 26 of whom live within a 30 mile radius. Seven households are all-female and five all-male. Household size ranges from two to six residents. In eight households, at least two residents have lived together since being students, whilst a further four households include at least two members with even longer-standing friendships. 17 households are located in privately rented properties, whilst the other eight are based in houses being bought by at least one of the residents.

The experiences of the four young people discussed below – Natalie, James, Carol and Nathan – are diverse, yet broadly representative of the range of housing experiences across the full sample. Neither are their stories examples of extreme cases, but are fairly typical of the stories we have been told by the majority of respondents. Between them, the four have experience of living in a variety of different households: with one or both parents, with partners, alone, in hostels, in student and non-student shared households. All four are currently in non-resident heterosexual relationships, and all are in employment. Notwithstanding my comment above concerning the relative affluence of the sample, for the purposes of this paper the case studies have been chosen to represent the *range* of social class backgrounds within the sample. Carol and James are graduates from middle class family backgrounds who first moved to the area for work and study reasons respectively, Natalie left school at 16 with several GCSE passes and comes from a lower middle class background, whilst Nathan left school at 18 after dropping out of his A levels and comes from a working class background. Both Natalie and Nathan have lived in the area for all of their lives. The following accounts foreground their changing relationships with parents, partners and friends over the different households in which they have lived, and illustrate the extent to which negotiations of intimacy are embedded within processes of household formation and change.

The Case Studies

Natalie is a 25 year old sales consultant, living with a friend in a two bedroom flat. She first left home at 21 in order to travel in India. On her return, she found life in the parental home 'claustrophobic', and was pleased when a former work mate, Paula, asked her to consider a flat share. This worked out well at first, although Paula spent an increasing amount of time visiting her boyfriend: 'towards the end I got really lonely...' They were eventually evicted for being too noisy, and subsequently moved together to a three bedroom house. A third tenant, whom they had found by placing an advert, had initially seemed 'lovely', but had 'turned weird', and had left owing them both money. Paula then moved in with her boyfriend, leaving Natalie having to find accommodation at short notice. Preferring company to the loneliness of a bedsit, she moved into the house of an old friend, Jane. However,

> ...it was hideous, absolutely the most miserable time in my life...She's one of my best friends, just didn't work living together...I was drunk when I asked her and she was drunk when she said yes. And all our friends that knew us both mutually said, you know, so stupid, it's not going to work... .

One particular bone of contention was Jane's attitude towards Natalie's then boyfriend:

> Right at the beginning she said I don't want to come home from work and find you sprawled out on the sofa with him watching a video or something...And it put huge pressure on me and I basically never stayed there...I used to spend all the time at his flat because I just felt like I couldn't have him round.

Natalie was so miserable that after eight months she asked her mother's permission to move back into the parental home: 'I really didn't want to go home, but I felt I had no choice'. This had a particularly negative effect on her relationship with her mother, resulting in arguments, tension and a sense of 'being a child again'. The situation was eased by spending weekends at her new boyfriend's house, but after a year she moved out, into her current flat. Initially, she shared with the sitting tenant, Kate, and although she was a stranger they got on 'absolutely brilliantly... it was fantastic, really, really good'.

Kate eventually moved in with her boyfriend, so Natalie invited her friend Tanya, still living at home, to move in. However, whereas previously they had socialized together frequently, they now rarely went out, and were beginning to annoy each other. Both felt that things would improve once they were no longer living together: Tanya was about to return to her parental home, whilst Natalie had just had an offer accepted on a two bedroom flat. Natalie was adamant that this time she would live alone, and was particularly insistent that her boyfriend should not move in with her, at least not in the short term:

> If my boyfriend said why don't we get a joint mortgage, I wouldn't. No way, I'd do this on my own...I mean it will get to a point where I probably do want a joint mortgage. Settle down with a bloke. But at the moment I'm settling down on my own.

She was also aware of a sense of progression amongst her friendship group that was very much linked to living alone, and felt that she would be left behind if she didn't move out soon:

> (My friends) are all single, I mean living on their own and I can see how happy they are and it's nice and it's sort of progressed to the next stage now, we're going round to each other's houses for dinner and things like that. Whereas before it's like 'what are you doing this Friday night? I'll meet you at the pub or whatever'... .

As for the various people she had lived with previously, she remained on good terms with them. Paula, her first flatmate, is 'one of my best friends now', and even her friendship with Jane has been retrieved, although 'it sort of fizzled out a bit after I moved out as well... I think it took a bit of time, though, to get living with each other out of the system'. Nonetheless, if she ever shared again, Natalie explained that she would be reluctant to move in with someone she knew: 'I just wouldn't want to spoil any friendships'. Relations with her mother have also improved since moving out, and they are in touch either by phone or in person several times a week:

> I get on like adults with me and my mum. I'm still the little girl with my dad, and always will be. But me and my mum are just much more level now, I think. Grown up a lot of a lot since I first moved out.

James aged 25, is a research engineer, and rents a three bedroom town house with two old university friends. James first left home at 18 to go to university. In his first year he lived in a hall of residence, where he met Huw, with whom he currently shares. Huw and James lived together in the same house for the next two years, sharing first with three sitting tenants, and then with three friends, at which point 'it became noisier and a bit livelier, not worrying so much about the people we didn't know so well'. In their fourth year, Huw and James moved back into halls, sharing a flat with five strangers, which was 'okay', but 'wasn't that great'. On graduating, James found work in Suffolk, and lived briefly in a hostel, before renting a shared house with two work mates. Whilst they socialized together at weekends, and threw several parties that acquired legendary status, James wasn't entirely comfortable living with people whom he didn't know well. Neither was he happy in his job, nor much enamoured with the location, so he began to look for a new position.

Within a year of graduating, he found work in the town where he had been a student, and moved back. Huw was still there, sharing a house with a mutual friend. James moved in, supposedly temporarily, but stayed for six months, until the landlord sold up. Huw and James then moved, with another old friend, to the house they currently share. Life here, he argued, is 'almost as homely as family life'. They have established a routine of sorts: occasional Sunday roasts and shared pizzas, certain television programmes that they all watch together, videos on Friday nights. On Wednesdays they sail together, and at the weekends they often go cycling together. On the subject of their friendship, Huw and James regard each other as 'closest friends'.

James has been seeing someone for just under two years, and thinks that his next move will probably be to cohabit. However,

> I don't know that I'm ready just yet. I mean I think I will be, I'm anticipating it...It's sort of the inevitable thing to happen next. But we'll move in together and see how that goes. Not expecting too much, maybe I might end up back in the same house again, I don't know. But I think it would be fun to live with her.

At the moment, they try to spend equal amounts of time in each other's houses, although this is difficult to achieve without upsetting the balance in their respective households:

> It's a potential source for conflict at the moment. Well potentially, because I'm very conscious, because there's more space in my house and I've got a double bed and she's just got a single bed. It's very tempting to stay at my house a lot of the time. That's not really fair on the others. But it's difficult to

keep it 50/50. Because on the one hand if I'm round her house, her house is smaller so I'm more likely to be noticed by her friends, whereas at this house we can disappear into my room.

On reflecting on the changes in his relationship with his family, James felt that he had become increasingly independent with each move. From fairly frequent contact when he first left home, he now rarely visits his parental home and 'I hardly seem to phone home at all'. Indeed, he talked of his decreasing sense of dependence on his parents, to the point of 'switching over to sort of dependence on friends rather than family'. Both Huw and his girlfriend are central players in this new form of dependency.

Carol is a 32 year old teacher. She shares with one other woman and two men, one of whom – Jed – owns the house. Carol first left home at 18 to go to a small college of higher education. She lived in a hall of residence with about 50 students, 'quite a little community in itself'. She made good friends in her first year, and in the second and third year she lived with five other women in a small, three bedroom terrace in a nearby town, two to a room: 'It was a little home, we were very close and did everything together'. Nonetheless, she was happy to move out when her course finished. On graduating, she moved back to the parental home for a while, which was hard work:

> My family's laid back and quite mellow and I never wanted to do anything particularly wild that they would be totally anti against...but you feel quite constrained, you feel constrained to eat meals at certain times. It doesn't matter if you're hungry or not, it's six o'clock so you're going to have your tea, and you know it's just sort of constraints like that.

She then moved to London to take up a job, and at her parents' insistence had initially lived in a women's hostel, sharing a room with a stranger: 'It was locked up at night and you couldn't have men there. So my dad thought it was a safe place to be'. A work mate then invited her to share his house, which she did for three and a half years, with other lodgers (including an old college friend) coming and going throughout that period. This was a really positive experience; he was a 'great guy', and she thoroughly enjoyed sharing with him. However, after four years in London, and two different jobs, Carol wanted a change and applied to train as a teacher. She left London and moved in with her boyfriend:

> And that was really crap. Well, it wasn't, but I think we realised that you know it wasn't going – the relationship wasn't really going to happen, but it was sort of an easy move.

The relationship ended after a year, and it was at this point that she moved into Jed's house with an old college friend, Chrissy. Jed was a friend of a friend, and a year older than Carol. He had bought a house with some friends when he first graduated, but the others had since moved out, leaving him alone in a four bedroom house. It was mutually convenient for Chrissy and Carol to move in, and Carol had now been there for six years. She felt very settled there, which she attributed to Jed's relaxed attitude:

> ...although it's his house, it doesn't feel like that. Feel quite welcomed into it. Sharing it, it's like *our* house...I think in general I felt quite comfortable in houses where I felt completely relaxed and where I felt it is like my house as well, and that was in London and here. I think when I moved into my boyfriend's house it felt very much like it was *his* house.

Carol also found it easier to move in with people she did not know well, as moving in with friends often brought with it certain expectations. Chrissy, for example, had clearly expected that they would cook together or go out together. It was often simpler, she felt, to 'share a house with a group of people that they're your friends because you moved in with them, but they weren't your friends before. For me that works really well.' Chrissy had eventually moved out in order to get married, and Carol said that after that she had felt 'even more comfortable' living there.

Carol and Jed get on extremely well and are privy to the details of each other's couple relationships, in Carol's case with a boyfriend living at some geographical distance, and in Jed's case with a boyfriend living locally. They joke about never moving out ('till we grow old together, that's what we think'), although both are aware that Carol may move out if her boyfriend relocates:

> My boyfriend and I are sort of happy at the moment. But he lives in the Midlands, I live down here, so that's an issue really. And it is an issue. But his family are down here, my family are down here and my mum's not very well, so I don't plan to move up there, but I think we are sort of at a stage where we would really quite happily move in together. So I don't really know what will happen... .

Carol is conscious that the relative lack of privacy in her house is sometimes a problem for her boyfriend when he visits, although she herself likes the 'buzz' of the house at weekends. Nonetheless, she also enjoys quieter weekends at his house, where he lives alone. At the end of the day, though, Carol is currently happy to be sharing. She enjoys the closeness of her fellow housemates, particularly Jed, and feels part of a supportive, caring community:

It feels like a really nice place to go back to. A really secure, safe place. It feels like people are interested. I think for me I never particularly wanted to go back to an empty house where it was just me. So it is, it's like a family in a way and that's lovely...I mean I like doing my own thing, it's fine when I'm in a relationship, but when I'm not in a relationship I'm very happy. Because I still think I've got a close relationship and a lot of support. And you know that if things are bad, whatever, I don't have to drive to somewhere, I don't have to pick up the phone, I can just chat to the people around. And it's the same for them.

Nathan aged 24, is a catering supervisor. He rents a three bedroom house with his younger brother and his friend Steve. Nathan lived with his mother and his brother until he was seventeen, but found his mother increasingly difficult to live with:

My mum is completely neurotic so I was forced to move out, really...I just couldn't get on with mum, so that's when I decided I better move on...I mean I know it was rocky with my mum, but it got worse as I got older because, obviously, I wanted to start doing my own thing and stuff.

One evening, he had simply packed his bags and moved in with his father in a neighbouring town. He stayed there for two years, with his brother in close pursuit, but living with their father was in many ways worse than living with their mother. They soon discovered, for example, that he was an alcoholic and a gambler: 'During that time I learned more about him than what I'd learned over the previous seventeen years'. Nathan had never felt close to his father during this period, and when his brother had moved in it had become 'a bit of a doss house':

So we stayed there for two years and discovered what the old man was like and that place never, ever felt like home. It was almost a stop gap. I would have liked it to be home, idealistically. Stayed there until I was 25 and dad would have been a wonderful guy but, you know, it's not always the way it is. Haven't actually seen him now for five years. Never want to see him again for the record.

His father eventually lost his job, and asked his sons to leave. Nathan initially returned to his mother's house, then moved into a friend's spare room, but soon decided to move in with his girlfriend, and 'played happy families for basically a couple of years'. His girlfriend was ten years his senior and had four children of her own, but 'that didn't make a blind bit of difference'. For the first year or so they were very happy together, particularly when they moved to a bigger house which they were able to make their own. After two years, though, his relationship 'hit the rocks' and he was forced to move back to his mother's house: 'Nightmarish time. I really didn't want to go back. I had to put my leg – what's the expression, tail between my legs or something'? His mother was charging him £45 a week board, which Nathan felt was too much: 'I could pay for a bedsit for 45 quid and not have a neurotic mother chasing me up all the time'.

At this point, his friend Steve was also looking for a place to live, so they decided to look together, and eventually found their current house. However, Nathan started seeing his ex-partner again, and for the first six months spent more time at her house than at his own, so he sub-let his room in order to move in officially with his girlfriend. Unfortunately, the relationship soon folded again, leaving him homeless and forcing him to live at his workplace for a couple of months:

> And I also had to go back to my mum's for about three weeks because I didn't want to outstay my welcome at work and destroy the relationship I had with my boss...So went back to my mum's for about three weeks, they finally kicked out Nina (his replacement in the shared house) and then I got back into my flat and it's been happy families ever since.

Nathan regards his current house very much as his home, even though he and his fellow residents have invested little in the purchase of 'home comforts' and consequently feel that they have a sense of freedom to 'up and leave at any point'. With hindsight, he feels that he has reversed a more usual pattern of household formation: 'Live life the wrong way round: married, settled down, then be a wild child and have fun'. He is now seeing a new girlfriend, but is insistent that he will not give up his flat: 'I still need that branch of independence there available to me'. Nonetheless, he admitted to a longer-term desire to live once again in a family setting, with a partner and children:

> That would be the ultimate goal to make that release from the flat sharing situation to the domestic situation of house sharing with a partner...(But) I'm scared, I'm scared that if I move in with someone, give up my flat and it goes sour after a year I could find myself in an awkward situation. Things may be different if I can financially look after myself and have the backing to be able to find somewhere to live again, but I don't want to go back to my mum's.

As for his parents, Nathan argued that relationships with friends were now much more important:

> ...they became, essentially, they became my family and friends...I was never close to my mum, so I try and avoid her. Obviously, effectively lost my dad as

a member of the family or anything like that. They did, they became my friends and stuff, family friends, it was my second home.

Discussion: Managing the Boundaries of Intimacy

All four of these case studies demonstrate the strong links that exist between housing and domestic transitions. In each account, housing decisions cannot easily be divorced from parallel considerations concerning the robustness of relationships with parents, friends and partners, and the consequences for those relationships of living together or apart. It is widely acknowledged, and confirmed within these four accounts, that relationships between young people and their parents tend to alter upon leaving home (Jones, 1995a), and not always for the better. However, whilst parents remain important to and well-loved by most of our respondents, they also become increasingly marginal to their accounts the older they become and the further they move away geographically. This is one reason why returning to the parental home can be so painful for many young people – even those who got on well with their parents as children and/or have maintained good relationships since leaving – as both parties are forced back into ways of relating to each other that will have been largely superceded by their experiences in the period since first leaving. For young people who have managed to renegotiate a relatively good relationship with their parents, the fear of jeopardizing that relationship can act as a strong disincentive to return, however desperate they might otherwise be. However, a return to the parental home is sometimes the only option available and, particularly for those with an already poor relationship, an enforced return can often prove disastrous.

Relationships with parents once having left home are also affected by further subtle differences contingent on with whom, if anyone, a young person lives. Across our sample we have found, for example, that parents have been more inclined to visit their child's own home when they have been living with a partner, or (to a lesser extent) alone, and have been less inclined to do so when they have been living in shared households. Carol, James and Natalie, in common with most of our respondents, usually have to travel to the parental home if they wish to see their parents. Whilst there may be practical reasons underpinning this, it nonetheless has consequences for the parent-child relationship: affecting, for example, the extent to which the child feels that their independence is acknowledged and respected by their parents. Most of our respondents feel that they revert to a position of dependency even on the briefest of visits home, whereas within their own home they feel much more in control. These sorts of considerations have implications for the degree to which parent-child relationships can feasibly move towards Giddens' ideal of the egalitarian pure relationship. Until a young person feels that their living arrangements receive the parental seal of approval, such equality is hard to achieve; and our research suggests that most parents do not regard shared households or one person households (unless owner-occupied) as 'proper' households.

Relationships with friends are also affected by a young person's specific living arrangements, particularly when they choose to live together. Living with friends undermines the more common practice of conducting friendships at a level above the territorial and social domain of the home. Contact with friends within the personal space of home is more usually marked by varying degrees of privacy maintenance and territoriality: for example, specific times will probably be set for arrival, departure times may be governed by a shared sense of an appropriate time for leaving, and certain spaces within the house are likely to be out of bounds to visitors (Allan, 1989; Adams and Allan, 1998). When friends live apart, this sense of being 'in place' or 'out of place' in a friend's house is also mediated by the presence of other occupants. Young people still living with their parents, for example, may rarely invite their friends back home for these very reasons.

Choosing to actually live with friends almost inevitably creates a distinction between an inner circle of household friends and an outer circle of non-household friends. As the case studies illustrate, living with friends in this way may sometimes test friendships to the point of destruction, but can also be the making of them. Similarly, strangers can quickly become close friends under the accelerated 'hothouse' conditions of shared living. Indeed, shared households may, for some young people, constitute a form of 'family of choice', akin to those identified in Weston and Week's work on the kinship networks of gay men and lesbians (Weeks et al., 1999; Weston, 1991). For many of our respondents, platonic friendships are clearly more important as a source of day-to-day support than parents, and possibly more so than partners: Carol certainly hints at this in her closing comments. Moreover, many of our respondents take great pride in the closeness of the relationships they have formed with their friends (both inside and outside the household), and derive a strong sense of independence from them.

The extent to which platonic friendships may conform to Giddens' model of the pure relationship will, of course, vary from case to case. Pure relationships based on equality, reciprocity and mutual self-disclosure may be easier to sustain between friends who live apart, given that 'a balance between autonomy and the sharing of feelings has to be obtained if personal closeness is not to be replaced by dependence' (Giddens, 1991, p.95). As we have seen, living in a shared household can place an extraordinary strain on even the closest of friendships, with the issue of privacy being a particular flashpoint. There is no doubt, though, that these friendships only work well (particularly amongst friends who live together) for as long as both parties benefit equally from the arrangement. Whilst the application of this principle to couple relationships may mark a change in attitude, this is hardly a new phenomenon in relation to friendship (Allan, 1996).

Despite some evidence in support of the increased importance of platonic friendship to single young people, it is generally accepted amongst our respondents that the eventual formation of couple households will nonetheless take priority over the maintenance of shared households with friends. In households where at least one person is in a steady relationship, for example, there is often a sense of trepidation concerning both the household's long term future and of not wanting to be left behind. This hints at our respondents' expectations that, in the longer term if not in the short term, couple relationships should legitimately be conducted within the private space of the (couple) home, with platonic friendships largely conducted outside of the home. However, with young people increasingly waiting until their late twenties – and often beyond – before choosing to form couple households, this expectation is not infrequently reversed: partners living *outside* the home, friends living *inside* the home. Moreover, couple relationships are increasingly conducted across the boundaries of at least two household spaces, often in the company of other young people in at least one of those spaces. Interestingly, notwithstanding my opening remarks about the problems of privileging couple households in models of domestic transitions, all four case studies are underpinned by a strong sense of linear progression towards the inevitability of such a household form. However, in common with the broader sample, they do not feel that cohabitation or marriage have in any sense been delayed in their lives, and neither do they have particularly high expectations of what it will be like to live with a partner. Rather, they are moving towards cohabitation very much at their own pace and, of those currently with partners, most are happy to live apart from them for the immediate future.

Nonetheless, it is also important to consider the impact of the vagaries of romantic love and desire on processes of household formation, and their potential for undermining even the best-laid plans. Love and romance, unlike sexuality and to a lesser extent desire, have generally been neglected by sociologists (Jackson, 1993; Jackson and Scott, 1997), yet they are arguably integral to a serious consideration of the factors that influence young adults' domestic and housing transitions. 'Being in love' and/or 'in lust', can often act as the spur to a radical and far-reaching change of direction in a young person's housing and domestic career. Some such moves appear to be quite rational and well thought out, but others can appear to be quite the opposite: irrational, unplanned and spur-of-the-moment. Nathan, for example, found himself returning to a doomed sexual relationship despite having finally sorted out his housing situation, whilst – as a postscript to her story – Natalie's boyfriend has now moved into her new flat, despite her protestations that she would not countenance such a move in the immediate future. A more extreme example is provided by another respondent, Amy, who first left her London home at 20 in order to move to the south coast to live with her new boyfriend, an arrangement which had only lasted for three months before their relationship broke down irretrievably. When interviewed, Amy had vowed never to repeat such a mistake (as she now saw it), yet six months later she had uprooted again in order to move to Durham with a new boyfriend.

Conclusion

In a period when normative scripts concerning leaving home and 'settling down' are in the process of being rewritten, single young people are becoming increasingly adept at negotiating intimate relationships both within and across a variety of domestic settings. Work mates may become best mates, strangers may become housemates; partners may be kept at a distance, friends may live together; family members may become friends, and friends may become 'like family'. Definitions of adulthood and independence shift accordingly, and are no longer dependent on the attainment of a new family of one's own, although this still remains a landmark experience for most young adults. Of course, not all young people negotiate their most intimate relationships from a position of strength, and those with restricted resources and few realistic alternatives available to them at any given time may feel that they are being *forced* into ways of relating to strangers, friends, parents and partners which are not of their choosing. Nonetheless, regardless of differential access to resources, the mapping of shifting constellations of relationships within broader networks of intimacy should be regarded as crucial to the task of tracking young people's housing and domestic transitions, inextricably linked to changes in their housing tenure and household type.

Acknowledgements

This research was funded by the Economic and Social Research Council (award number R000237033). I would like to thank Liz Kenyon, co-researcher on the project, for her invaluable help and support. I am, of course, indebted to all the young people who agreed to take part in the research. All names used are pseudonyms, and some details have been changed to protect anonymity.

References

Adams, R. and Allan, G. (1998), *Placing Friendship in Context*, Cambridge, Cambridge University Press.

Ahier, J. and Moore, R. (1999), 'Post-16 education, semi-independent youth and the privatisation of inter-age transfers: re-theorising youth transition', in *British Journal of Sociology of Education*, vol.20, no.4, pp.515-530.

Allan, G. (1989), 'Insiders and outsiders: Boundaries around the home', in Allan, G. and Crow, G. (eds.), *Home and Family: Creating the Domestic Sphere*, London, Macmillan.

Allan, G. (1996), *Kinship and Friendship in Modern Britain*, Oxford, Oxford University Press.

Beck, U. (1992), *Risk Society: Towards a New Modernity*, London, Sage.

Beck, U. and Beck-Gernscheim, E. (1995), *The Normal Chaos of Love*, Cambridge, Polity Press.

Bell, R. and Jones, J. (1999), *Independent Living: Income and Housing*, Leicester, Youth Work Press.

Berrington, A. and Murphy, M. (1994), 'Changes in the living arrangements of young adults in Britain during the 1980s', in *European Sociological Review*, vol.10, no.3, pp.235-57.

Berthoud, R. and Gershuny, J. (2000), *Seven Years in the Lives of British Families: Evidence of the Dynamics of Social Change from the British Household Panel Study*, Bristol, The Policy Press.

Du Bois-Reymond, M (1998), 'I don't want to commit myself yet': Young people's life concepts', in *Journal of Youth Studies*, vol.1, no.1, pp.63-79.

Bynner, J., Ferrie, E. and Shepherd, P. (1997), *Twenty-Something in the 1990s: Getting On, Getting By, Getting Nowhere*, Aldershot, Ashgate.

Coles, B. (1995), *Youth and Social Policy: Youth Citizenship and Young Careers*, London, UCL Press.

Ermisch, J. (2000), Personal Relationships and Marriage Expectations: Evidence from the 1998 British Household Panel Study, *ISER Working Papers*, Paper 2000-27, Colchester, University of Essex.

Ermisch, J., Di Salvo, P. and Joshi, H. (1995), 'Household formation and housing tenure decisions of young people', *Occasional Papers of the ESRC Research Centre on Micro-Social Change*, Occasional Paper 95, Colchester, University of Essex.

Furlong, A. and Cartmel, F. (1997), *Young People and Social Change*, Buckingham, Open University Press.

Giddens, A. (1991), *Modernity and Self-Identity: Self and Society in the Late Modern Age*, Cambridge, Polity Press.

Giddens, A. (1992), *The Transformation of Intimacy: Sexuality, Love and Eroticism in Modern Societies*, Cambridge, Polity Press.

Hall, R., Ogden, P. and Hill, C. (1997), 'The pattern and structure of one-person households in England and Wales and France', in *International Journal of Population Geography*, vol.3, pp.161-181.

Hall, R., Ogden, P. and Hill, C. (1999), 'Living alone: Evidence from England and Wales and France for the last two decades', in McRae, S. (ed.), *Changing Britain: Families and Households in the 1990s*, Oxford, Oxford University Press.

Heath, S. (1999), 'Young adults and household formation in the 1990s', in *British Journal of Sociology of Education*, vol.20, no.4, pp.545-561.

Heath, S. and Kenyon, E. (2001), 'Single young professionals and shared household living', in *Journal of Youth Studies*, vol.4, no.1, pp.83-100.

Holdsworth, C. (1999), 'Leaving home in Britain and Spain', in *European Sociological Review*, vol.16, no.2, pp.201-222.

Jackson, S. (1993), 'Even sociologists fall in love: An exploration in the sociology of emotions', in *Sociology*, vol.27, no.2, pp.201-220.

Jackson, S. and Scott, S. (1997), 'Gut reactions to matters of the heart: Reflections on rationality, irrationality and sexuality', in *Sociological Review*, vol.45, no.4, pp.551-575.

Jamieson, L. (1998), *Intimacy: Personal Relationships in Modern Society*, Cambridge, Polity Press.

Jamieson, L. (1999), '"Intimacy transformed? A critical look at the "pure relationship"', in *Sociology*, vol.33, no.3, pp.477-494.

Jamieson, L., Stewart, R., Li, Y., Anderson, M., Bechhofer, F. and McCrone, D. (2000), 'Single, twenty-something and seeking?' *Paper presented at the British Sociological Association Conference*, University of York, April 2000.

Jones, G. (1995a), *Leaving Home*, Buckingham, Open University Press.

Jones, G. (1995b), *Family Support for Young People*, London, Family Policy Studies Centre.

Kenyon, E. and Heath, S. (forthcoming), 'Choosing 'This Life': Narratives of choice amongst house sharers', in *Housing Studies*.

Kiernan, K. (1985), 'The departure of children: The timing of leaving home over the life cycle of parents and children', in *CPS Research Paper 85-3*, London, Centre for Population Studies.

McGlone, F., Park, A. and Roberts, C. (1999), 'Kinship and friendship: Attitudes and behaviour in Britain', in McRae, S. (ed.), *Changing Britain: Families and Households in the 1990s*, Oxford, Oxford University Press.

McRae, S. (1999), 'Introduction: Family and household change in Britain', in McRae, S. (ed.), *Changing Britain: Families and Households in the 1990s*, Oxford, Oxford University Press.

Morris, K. and Fuller, M. (1999), 'Heterosexual relationships of young women in a rural environment', in *British Journal of Sociology of Education*, vol.20, no.4, pp.531-543.

Scott, J. (1997), 'Changing households in Britain: Do families still matter?', in *Sociological Review*, vol.45, no.4, pp.591-620.

Scott, J. (1999), 'Family change: Revolution or backlash in attitudes?' in McRae, S. (ed.), *Changing Britain: Families and Households in the 1990s*, Oxford, Oxford University Press.

Weeks, J., Heaphy, B. and Donovan, C. (1999), 'Families of choice: Autonomy and mutuality in non-heterosexual relationships', in McRae, S. (ed.), *Changing Britain: Families and Households in the 1990s*, Oxford, Oxford University Press.

Weston, K. (1991), *Families We Choose: Lesbians, Gays, Kinship*, New York, Columbia University Press.

Wilkinson, H. (1994), *No Turning Back: Generations and the Genderquake*, London, Demos.

Wilkinson, H. and Mulgan, G. (1995), *Freedom's Children: Work, Relationships and Politics for 18-34 year olds in Britain Today*, London, Demos.

Chapter 9

Ignoring the Past: Under-Employment and Risk in Late Modernity

GARY POLLOCK

Introduction

Many researchers have traditionally focused their attention on the problem of youth unemployment. However, in recent years the issue of underemployment has emerged, in part because it is seen as a product of the wider changes associated with the movement to a Post-Fordist or a risk society. In this chapter I suggest that underemployment is indeed a common experience for many people of all ages today. However, data from the early twentieth century also points to the widespread experience of underemployment amongst the workforce. Such evidence therefore raises questions about the supposed novelty of current employment experiences. Such data also calls into question the alleged distinctiveness of risk society from earlier forms of modernity. It suggests in fact that underemployment is not unique to late modernity, rather it is a feature of a capitalist, market economy that must periodically reinvent itself.

Underemployment is significant as it represents the situation whereby young people are not given the opportunity to use their skills and credentials in the labour market. This wastage of talent is a cause for concern not least because early employment experiences can shape later careers and the wider transitions to adult life. Despite suggestions by some commentators that risk societies now offer new choices and opportunities for self-actualization the evidence of underemployment points to how long term historical processes still structure individual life chances. The evidence suggests that, despite the 'upskilling' of the workforce, underemployment has been a key structural feature of labour markets throughout much of the twentieth century. Consequently this raises important questions about current government policy (the so-called Third Way) which targets individuals (by developing human capital and promoting employability) rather more than it does the structural features of labour markets.

Contemporary debates on labour market structures have advanced swiftly since Doeringer and Piore's (1971) work on dual labour markets. We now have a more sophisticated understanding of the ways in which labour markets work at local levels, and how they can (dis)advantage different social groups. The work by Ashton and colleagues (Ashton and Field, 1976; Ashton, et al., 1982; Ashton, et al., 1990) applied this to youth labour markets to show the differing employment experiences of young people, particularly in relation to age, class and gender. More recently, labour market analysts have turned their attention towards the methods deployed to maintain or increase profit and efficiency levels. The techniques of 'just-in-time', 'outsourcing', 'flexible specialization', 'downsizing' and so on, have all altered the overall structure of organizations and impacted upon the conditions under which young and old people work. The 'underemployment' debate has emerged from this earlier research and theorizing and draws on segmentation theory which allows for a more complex analysis of supply and demand and how the labour market is influenced by a variety of processes linked to the individual, the family and the state.

While temporary and part-time employment are often perceived as being low-status and insecure (Payne and Payne, 1993) there is evidence that some people look for, enjoy and prefer temporary or flexible work as opposed to full-time permanent work albeit often within a framework of gendered employment and family structures (Crompton, 1996). Moreover, there is evidence that temporary jobs are only marginally less secure than permanent jobs (Korpi and Levin, 2001). It is thus important not to overplay the negative features of certain forms of underemployment where its existence is actually advantageous to the individual or family (or even the state). Nonetheless, it is important to examine the features of structures of underemployment in relation to some sort of 'ideal type' in relation to employment-based security, benefits, and conditions. A final qualification to this paper is in its location within a British context. It is more accurate to talk about different forms of capitalism rather than to characterize it as being universal, or homogeneous. Esping-Andersen's work shows clearly how capitalism is largely dependent upon contextual factors, in particular socio-political traditions (Esping-Andersen, 1990). Indeed it is the ability of capitalism to adapt and mutate into different forms that proves to be its enduring quality, as noted by Marx himself. What is characterized as being insecure below could easily be made more secure by government regulation thus demonstrating the importance of the embeddedness of economic relations in wider society.

Defining Underemployment

Though the following discussion is a general one it will nonetheless be apparent that the categories as described below correspond to labour market positions commonly experienced by many young workers.

Underemployment connotes a variety of employment experiences that can be contrasted with the ideal type of 'full employment'. It can relate to employment status, composite employment experiences, labour market sectors and contractual positions. Thus it is a classification of a variety of statuses and experiences such as flexible or insecure work (Heery and Salmon, 2000). Below is a schema that attempts to capture some of these salient features (adapted from Dex and McCulloch [1997]):

1. *'Non-standard' employment.* The experience of part-time employment and self-employment contrasted with full-time employment. The actual employment experience may not be negative, it may be desired, it can be associated with a decrease in employment rights, benefits and conditions of work.

2. *Insecure employment* due to the contract of employment or from the volatility of a particular industrial sector as types of industry (and thus labour markets and employment, e.g. hourly paid workers) contract and expand. Contractual insecurity reflects the temporary nature of paid employment. Hourly paid workers and annually contracted workers alike share the prospect of the end of the contract with no guarantee of renewal.

3. *Employment below one's capabilities* in terms of the amount of work undertaken, measured in hours, or the skill level of the work itself. The availability of employment and of suitable employment is not guaranteed in market economies, hence there are inevitable supply and demand mismatches as we see in some local labour markets.

4. *Movement in and out of employment.* This may be voluntary or involuntary. It is characterized by relatively short periods of employment and unemployment.

5. *Movement between different employment spells* through choice or necessity, possibly in the same sector, with the same conditions of work, or from one sector and status to another. For example a succession of annual contracts, or moving from a short contract job to self-employment, then a short period of unemployment.

To talk of an ideal type or standard employment experiences is problematic. What is ideal to a young woman may be far from ideal to a middle aged man. Rubery (1997) suggests labour market theories are deficient as they are unable to deal with a diverse workforce with diverse requirements and are often androcentric. Nevertheless 'non-standard' is generally used to describe forms of employment that are not full-time, have insecure or short contracts, and little if any employment protection. This definition fails to capture the positive features of non-standard employment, a point that must be remembered when examining the evidence. It is, however, important to articulate underemployment in terms of the status of the employment and not in relation to its positive or negative features at the individual, attitudinal level. This separation of positive and negative features as defined by the researcher and as defined by the individual is a necessary simplification for the sake of my argument. Future research will have to address this false division. Notwithstanding this problem, underemployment can thus be used as an adjective describing a specific job or spells of employment over time in contrast to a 'better' form of employment (or work).

By looking at longitudinal data it becomes possible to identify different categories of employment experience, from those who have continuous full-time employment to those who go into and out of employment, possibly experiencing self and/or part-time employment. This longitudinal definition of underemployment captures a lived experience more accurately than any other. This avoids an over-reliance on aggregated data which while reflecting structural changes in the labour market (important enough in itself), says nothing about how such changes are experienced at the individual level. This employment experience is very significant for young people as early labour market opportunities can influence other aspects of young people's lives as well as shape their more general transitions to adulthood (Banks et al., 1992).

Underemployment and Late Modern Society

Although various writers such as Beck (1992, 2000), Giddens (1991), Bauman (1998), Castells (1996), and Gorz (1999) have all examined the significance of waged employment in their research they suggest that the 'centrality of work' over the life-course may now be in decline. Hence the phenomena of unemployment and then 'underemployment' has become much more significant in recent research.

Many attempts have been made to capture the essence of late modern society. Has society changed significantly or is it simply that the outward manifestation of underlying structures and processes have changed? Has there been a change in form or simply a change in content? Can we accurately say that society at the turn of the century *is* significantly different from say thirty years ago? Commentators point to a number of new phenomena, such as the rise of information and communication technologies. It is not clear, however, to what extent we are looking at a cause of social change, or an effect of it. Are information technologies and engine of social change or are they artefacts of changing social needs (or changing requirements of advanced capitalism)? These questions are difficult to address adequately. However, by exploring employment and underemployment we can shed some light, not only on the experiences of contemporary youth but also on the wider questions of the emergence of risk society. Beck, in particular has been influential in exploring the emergence of late modern or risk society:

> The ongoing debate on the rise and fall of Fordist mass production, mass consumption and standardized full employment as well as the corresponding picture of a standardized society and political formula of Keynesianism, belong to the paradigm of the first modernity. In the second modernity, however, the risk regime prevails in every field: economy, society, polity. Here the appropriate distinction is…between the securities, certainties and loss of boundaries in the second modernity (Beck, 2000, p.69-70).

For Beck the second modernity (late modern society) is described as risk fraught, individualized and fragmented. He argues that the coherence and predictability that life once had has broken down and that we live in a melting pot where we are less sure what the future holds than our parents were. Moreover, we feel (or are encouraged to feel) that we are more individually responsible for ensuring that we are successful in life. Beck's thesis contains a broad mix of ideas, few of which can be said to be new, but together they capture elements of contemporary everyday life. His work addresses both macro, (for example the risk of environmental disaster) and micro issues such as the active construction of individual life biographies. While the Beck perspective is far reaching, touching upon a diverse range of issues in society, it provides a useful starting point for a critique of contemporary employment structures. Underemployment is seen as a constituent of the risk society. It is thus first necessary to clarify what is meant by the 'risk' discourse and explain which elements are of use in the study of employment. It is useful to start with a list of polar opposites from which the distinctiveness of the risk discourse can be outlined.

Table 9.1 Different dimensions of 'rational' and 'risk' societies

	'Rational' Society	'Risk' Society
Risk dimensions	certainty	uncertainty
	coherence	fragmentation
	predictability	unpredictability
Moral dimensions	stultifying	liberating
	unproductive	productive
Political dimensions	ideological	anti-ideological
	utopian	distopian
	socialism	capitalism
Sociological dimensions	modern	post-modern
	constraint	choice
	individualization	collectivism

Table 9.1 shows an oversimplified set of dichotomies, it tries to capture the spirit of the transition from modernity to risk society. There is no single 'risk' position though it can be understood as various departures from traditional sociological perspectives. Different dimensions are identified in order to separate out the descriptive from the analytic and normative. On the left hand side we can see various elements associated with what has been described as the 'project of modernity'. Through the belief that rational planning could improve society by the reduction in poverty and such like, national welfare, health and education systems were set up. The twentieth century, more than any other before it, witnessed large-scale interventions by governments in the pursuit of equality. Class in particular but also gender and ethnicity became important categories by which inequalities were understood. These efforts remain intact in the shape of welfare regimes throughout Western Europe. On the right hand side are listed the features of a society that is moving beyond the rationality of modernity away from the certainties and optimism of Beck's 'first modernity'.

Risk may be regarded positively or negatively. The moral/political dimensions from table 9.1 indicate such possibilities. When viewed positively in relation to its liberating and productive qualities it relates to political individualism and thus a version of liberalism that celebrates the supposed individuality of people. The ability to realize ones desires, express ones beliefs and cultivate ones individual identity is made real. This new risk society is thus offering people the chance to realize their own unique ambitions. Here a generational difference can be identified whereby young workers are less interested in the 'job-for-life' or extended career than their parents were. The more fragmented nature of employment biographies of many young professionals is regarded positively by these young people (Sennet, 1998).

Viewed negatively the risk society is one in which there has been a breakdown in a range of supporting structures which hold peoples lives together. There has been a fragmentation of institutions which contributes to a growing uncertainty of the future and is a source of disorder. Traditional patterns of life are threatened, and social 'evils' such as unemployment and irregular employment spiral upwards.

Both versions are extreme versions of perceived changes in society. While they may contain elements of truths, they both fail to recognize continuities with the past and over emphasize discontinuities. It is tempting to portray contemporary life as somehow unique with its own set of distinctive problems but to do so is to ignore important findings from the past. The evidence from recent surveys, as I discuss in the next section, suggests that it is possible to view underemployment as a new phenomenon. However, as I show later, we only have to look at the inter-war period to illustrate how it has a much longer history.

Evidence for the Existence of Contemporary Underemployment

A variety of contemporary survey data based on aggregate employment statistics suggests that underemployment types 1 and 2 (non-standard and insecure employment as discussed above) have increased over time, partly as a result of the changing structure of the labour market. As I go onto show individual level data also illustrates how other forms of underemployment have also increased in recent years.

1. Non-Standard Employment

The economic restructuring of the 1970s impacted upon the overall shape of the labour market. The initial shock waves led to a reduction in the level of those in employment and a rise in unemployment (figure 9.1). The sharp rise in unemployment during the early 1980s and its subsequent downwards trend is clearly apparent. This is matched by upwards trends in both part-time and self-employment. Hence, while it is possible to argue that there is evidence that unemployment is finally being brought under control, this does not mark a corresponding increase in full-time employment. We are witnessing a structural shift in the labour market whereby self-employment and part-time employment are becoming ever more prevalent.

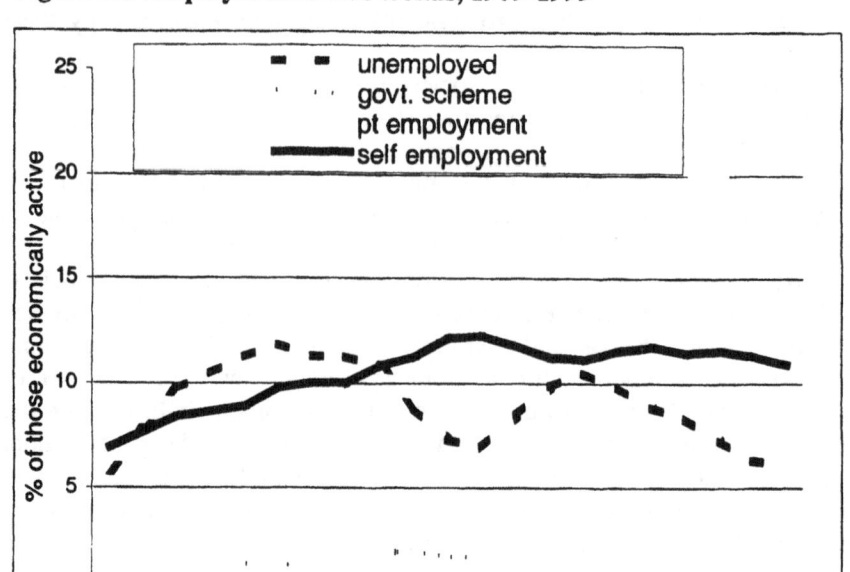

Figure 9.1 Employment status trends, 1979-1999*

*From Labour Force Survey Historical Supplement (1999). No data for 1980 and 1982

2. Insecure Employment

Table 9.2 demonstrates the increasing importance of temporary contracts in the labour market. While data is limited, there is a clear trend showing that this form of employment is increasing and that these increases are largely the result of the growth of this type of contract in the service sector. While there is no evidence of a systematic policy of reducing core staff in preference for those on temporary contracts (Philpott, 1999) the upwards trend nonetheless indicates that employers are gaining from having lower overheads associated with this insecure status. While these gains are to a large extent short-term, allowing the employer to expand and contract their workforce as demand fluctuates as exists in seasonal jobs, the long-term implications are less clear. In the long term, employers are likely to suffer from having to devote resources to periodic recruitment drives, staff loyalty and commitment is likely to be low with corresponding effects in the quality of work done and perhaps also rates of absenteeism and sickness.

Table 9.2 Trends in temporary employment*

Year	% on temp contract	% of temp employees in service sector
1992	4.2	76.9
1993	4.4	78.8
1994	4.9	80.8
1995	5.3	79.0
1996	5.4	80.0
1997	5.8	80.4

*From Labour Force Survey Historical Supplement (1999)

The increasing importance of non-standard/insecure employment is graphically shown by Dex and McCulloch:

> ...the climate of deregulation in the labour market over the 1980s...has created an environment in which the low skilled sector and more vulnerable workers can be exploited (Dex and McCulloch, 1997, p.185).

Their work shows that this is an international phenomenon, and one effecting both men and women, albeit women to a far greater extent. They are in no doubt of the negative consequences of these developments upon young people.

3. Being Employed Below One's Capabilities

This is a difficult concept to operationalize. What is needed is a measure that shows that a person's qualifications exceed that required to do a particular job. To do accurately this would require an in-depth analysis of qualifications and employment at the individual level, classifying a person as suitably matched, over extended or under extended. This would require an elaborate methodology beyond the scope of this paper, the beginnings of which have been attempted elsewhere (Pollock, 1998). For our purpose here, qualifications were examined alongside the occupational classification of employment at the age of 30 for members of a nationally representative survey. This work showed significant increases in the level of qualifications being attained as well as significant changes in the relationship between qualification and occupation over time. Briefly, it was found that for both men and women the growth in the numbers of people receiving qualifications (and becoming better qualified) was far in advance of any 'upgrading' that could be seen in the jobs being done by the time the respondent was aged thirty. While this finding requires a more refined measure, it appears as Batenburg and de Witte (2000) found in Holland, that the workforce is better qualified than is required by the work. Far from there being a 'skills gap' as employers are keen to argue, the workforce is crying out for jobs that will require the education and training they have acquired.

4. and 5. Moving Between Various Employment States

The last two forms of underemployment refer to experiences over time rather than aggregate changes in the structure of the labour market. Moving in and out of employment and moving between a variety of employment states is evidence of employment instability. While it has always been the case that women and young people have experienced a more varied employment history than men, and older people respectively, there is evidence that such variation is on the increase. Using an examination of individual employment histories it is becoming apparent that people born in the last thirty years are experiencing more varied employment histories than those born earlier. This is true for men as well as women and thus shows a more general trend. The following table summarizes the findings of a project examining the employment histories of men and women, during the first part of their employment histories in Britain during the 1980s (Pollock et al., 2000). Thirteen different categories of experience are identified (described as clusters because of the statistical process used).

Table 9.3 Cluster membership broken down by sex and birth cohort

	Male		Female	
Cluster	1953-62	1963+	1953-62	1963+
1: Much non-employment, short periods of other states, three or four different statuses, likely employed by the time of survey	3	4	11	6
2: Mostly full-time employed. short periods in other states	71	47	35	37
3: Mainly self-employment some time in other states	14	4	4	2
4: Non-employed with one or two short periods in other states	2	8	4	10
5: Half of the time in full-time employment, the other half in non-employment	4	24	5	20
6: First three years in part-time, second three in full-time	*	1	3	1
7: First three years in self-employment, second three in full-time employment	1	1	1	*
8: Beginning in full-time employment, then a gap of nine months, then part-time employment	*	1	2	5
9: Beginning in full-time employment and then moving into non-employment	1	2	3	4
10: Mainly in part-time employment, short periods in some other states	1	1	22	5
11: Half of time in part-time employment, the other half in non-employment	*	3	4	7
12: First three years in full-time employment the second three in self-employment	3	3	1	2
13: First three years in non-employment, second three in part-time employment	0	*	7	1
	100%	100%	100%	100%
N	560	525	605	611

*= less than 0.5%

Table 9.3 provides evidence that employment experiences are becoming more fragmented. Cluster 2 represents mainly continuous full-time employment which shows that over time for men there is a significant decline in this type of experience. To some extent this (and all other findings from table 9.3) are partly cohort effects in that as one gets older one's experiences change due to movement to a different life-stage. It does however, seem that the younger cohort are far more likely to be in cluster 4 and 5, where there are regular periods of unemployment. For women the pattern is different, with similar levels of continuous full-time employment for young and old cohorts alike. Indeed, the decreasing security of employment for men could be a reflection of the increased economic activity of women. Despite this, non-employment experiences (clusters 4 and 5) also appear to be on the increase.

While it is difficult to draw absolute conclusions from table 9.3, it is important to examine how a person experiences a range of employment episodes over time. For example the table suggests that there are clear differences between the two birth cohorts, notably over time there is an increasingly fragmented employment experience for both men and women, though more so for men than women.

Employment and Underemployment in Capitalist Economies

The evidence above demonstrates that there is an emergent phenomenon of underemployment since the 1970s and that this is related to the trajectory of late modern society. It does not, however, show that this sort of experience is new, far from it. Indeed, the features of employment relations and experiences of employment from the inter-war period show it is possible to contest the 'newness' of notions of underemployment. As the change in employment relations is also a key element of the risk discourse such evidence also therefore raises more general questions about the emergence of a risk society. There are contemporary forms of underemployment that are new, as one would expect given technical advances, but that to a large degree the risk discourse in relation to employment experiences is one of 'new wine in old bottles'. Underemployment is a significant development with many negative consequences for young people particularly in relation to career development, employee rights and the impact these have more generally on transitions to adulthood. However, the focus on 'risky employment' as a contemporary development promotes an historical amnesia that prevents a more sophisticated long-term analysis of employment trends.

Both employers and employees are exposed to risks – this is simply an inevitable feature of a competitive market environment. Yet capitalism has existed for a long time so why has risk and underemployment only now become a major topic of debate and research? It does indeed seem paradoxical that it is only recently, under *late* capitalism that the crisis of underemployment becomes manifest. The answer lies in an anomaly. This anomaly is that of the post war period. This period, which lasted up until the early 1970s, witnessed labour shortages, increasing affluence, increasing employment rights and increasing welfare entitlements. Unemployment levels were low and could be argued to be little more than one would expect in conditions of full-employment. It was not unusual for young people to switch jobs frequently if they did not like the work or the employer for they knew that they would easily find another job (West and Newton, 1983). This was a far cry from Marx's 'reserve army of labour' thesis, in fact quite the opposite. The situation changed with the onset of the oil crisis in the early 1970s and the subsequent world recession. Since then there has been a gradual decline in the demand for labour, particularly in the manufacturing sector partly as a result of the globalizing influences mentioned above and the subsequent restructuring and relocation of much manufacturing industry. While the rise in the service sector meant that unemployment did not take off immediately, it was perhaps inevitable that even this sector would not be immune to change, this time brought on by advances in information technologies. It is then no surprise that there is discontinuity with the recent past and that, when compared to the boom years in the 50s and 60s, employment structures are more risky for the employee and balanced in favour of the employer. It is thus worth going further back to examine employment experiences before the war-for the evidence suggests there are very real similarities between then and now.

Prior to the Second World War it should be remembered that welfare provision in Britain was minimal, there had not yet been a majority left-wing government, and the power of workers expressed through trades unions was weak. Employment in itself was no guarantee of security with wages often so low as to be considered barely enough for subsistence. Unemployment fluctuated and many found themselves in and out of work on a regular basis (Burnett, 1994). The general strike of 1926 and the Jarrow Crusade for jobs both failed to stir governments into remedying the insecurity experienced by workers. International markets were already influencing local labour markets in Britain. For example cheap labour in Japan forced Lancashire textile companies into producing specialized high priced materials during the 1920's and 30's as they could no longer compete in the basic textiles market (Jewkes and Winterbottom, 1933).

Young employees were generally the first to be made redundant as their older counterparts were regarded as more useful due to their longevity in the company. As Stovel et al. show (1996), the semi/unskilled worker does not generally follow a career path – they have a succession of jobs in a less coherent sequence. The precariousness of the unskilled worker has always rested upon the availability of jobs. In terms of life-time employment experiences there are clear class differences. The notion of 'career' is generally a middle class one, followed by those in professional occupations or top level apprenticeships leading to skilled work.

Increasing Choice in Risk Societies?

When one examines biography, risk theorists argue that there is a greater focus upon a person constructing their own life biography/life project today than in previous generations. This is an important consideration given the stress made above on life-time processes rather than aggregate descriptions. While most people in employment do experience stability, the evidence above shows that we need to pay close attention to unstable or insecure experiences. The risk discourse contains assumptions as to the ways in which people are faced with choice about there biographies:

1. There are a greater number of choices to be made than before.
2. That these *are* choices and not simply the façade of choice.
3. That people in the past had fewer choices to make...and fewer possibilities to be socially mobile.
4. As a result of 1-3, that a young persons social origin is not a good predictor of their adult social status.

The key term here is individualization and one which is often a euphemism for what is often described as agency (at least agency at the individual level). Risk theorists are thus arguing that there is now a greater scope for agency, or choice, than existed in the past. And the corollary, that those structural constraints are less powerful than before. Thus to a large extent the risk society is argued as being the society where agency triumphs over structure. At this point it is necessary to establish what these individualized choices are. In relation to a young person leaving full time education in Britain (1. post-16 qualifications, 2. post-16 training schemes, 3. employment possibilities), there can be no doubt that there has been an explosion of the different possibilities open to young people. These increased possibilities, often inaccurately described as 'choices', exist in all three of the above whereas previously, few if any choices needed to be made by young people leaving school. The question is, how far the choices that need to be made offer prospects of real opportunities? This fundamental point was made long ago (Roberts, 1968). To some extent, that there are choices to be made is simply an artefact of the fragmentation of education and employment into a variety of forms and little to do with real choice. This fragmentation of forms was described as a feature of modernity long ago in Berman's vivid description of the needs of capitalism to periodically renew itself (Berman, 1983). It can be accepted that a greater number of choices have to be made, and that therefore to some extent one can be said to be individually responsible for certain pathways in one's own biography, and it can also be accepted that many of these choices are ones that were not available to young people of previous generations. There are arguably an increasing number of individualizing processes; ways in which we are 'forced' to actively construct our own lives. To what extent can these choices said to contain differing elements of risk so that to follow one route may be more hazardous than to follow another? How far are these risks different from the risks that the young people of the past faced going into the mining industry or manufacturing in the 60s and 70s, and who have subsequently faced redundancy or 'reskilling'? The young people of today make choices and the young people of past generations had fewer choices to make. The fragmentation of education and employment does mean that choices exist where they never did in the past but these choices are not ones which in themselves empower the chooser. This paradox has been described as the 'epistemological fallacy' of individualization (Furlong and Cartmel, 1997). Social barriers remain as powerful as ever with class still a good predictor of education, gender differences in pay, and so on such that we can understand the present condition as 'structured individualization' (Roberts et al., 1994) whereby we are unwise to depart from traditional sociological categories in our analysis of society.

Conclusion

Young people today are forced to negotiate their way through an ever more fragmented education system and labour market. While unemployment is no longer as prevalent as in the early 1990s, there has been a rise in various forms of underemployment which may inhibit young people's employment futures. The rise in underemployment has resulted from both economic restructuring and new management techniques. Attempts, by Beck in particular, to theorize the trajectory of contemporary Western society have utilized underemployment as evidence of global processes which have led to a society that is characterized by risk at both macro and micro levels. A key feature of Beck's work has been to argue that contemporary society is qualitatively different to that of 30 years ago to the extent that we can consider these two eras as different 'paradigms'. The risk discourse has thus proved to be influential in characterizing contemporary society without invoking a 'grand narrative'. Despite this it is not clear that when applied to an analysis of changing employment structures it enhances our understanding of the current situation. By identifying the period between 1950 and the early 1970s as anomalous in providing conditions of full-employment it becomes clear that labour market conditions that existed before this time and since are quite similar. To some extent the past has been ignored in the construction of contemporary theory. The specific experiences of young people today are very different to those of 30, 50 or 70 years ago but there are continuities that seem to have been neglected by many contemporary commentators.

Acknowledgements

Thanks to Phil Mole for comments on an earlier draft of this chapter.

References

Ashton, D. N. and Field, D. (1976), *Young Workers*, London, Hutchinson.
Ashton, D. N., Maguire, M. and Garland V. (1982), *Youth in the Labour Market*, Research Paper No.34, London, Department of Employment.
Banks, M. et al. (1992), *Careers and Identities*, Milton Keynes, Open University Press.
Batenburg, R. and de Witte, M. (2001), 'Underemployment in the Netherlands: How the Dutch "Polder Model" failed to close the education-jobs gap', in *Work, Employment and Society*, vol.15, no.1, pp.73-94.
Bauman, Z. (1998), *Work, Consumerism and the New Poor*, Buckingham, Open University Press.
Beck, U. (1992), *The Risk Society*, London, Sage.
Beck, U. (2000), *The Brave New World of Work*, Cambridge, Polity
Berman, M. (1983), *All That is Solid Melts Into Air, The Experience of Modernity*, London, Verso.
Burnett, J. (1994), *Idle Hands: The Experience of Unemployment 1790-1990*, London, Routledge.
Castells, M. (1996), *The Rise of the Network Society*, Oxford, Blackwells.
Crompton, R. (1996), 'Paid employment and the changing system of gender relations', in *Sociology*, vol.30, no.3, pp.427-445.
Dex, S. and McCulloch, A. (1997), *Flexible Employment: The Future of Britain's Jobs*, London, Routledge.
Doeringer, P.B. and Piore, M.J. (1971) *Internal Labour Markets and Manpower Analysis*, Lexington, Heath.
Esping-Andersen, G. (1990), *The Three Worlds of Welfare Capitalism*, Cambridge, Polity.
Furlong, A. and Cartmel, F. (1997), *Young People and Social Change: Individualization and Risk in Late Modernity*, Buckingham, Open University Press.
Giddens, A. (1991), *Modernity and Self-Identity: Self and Society in the Late Modern Age*, Cambridge, Polity.
Gorz, A. (1999), *Work: Beyond the Wage Based Society*, Cambridge, Polity.
Heery, E. and Salmon, J. (eds.) (2000), *The Insecure Workforce*, London, Routledge.
Jewkes, J. and Winterbottom, A. (1933), *Juvenile Unemployment*, London, Allen and Unwin.

Korpi, T. and Levin, H. (2001), 'Precarious footing: temporary employment as a stepping stone out of unemployment in Sweden', in *Work, Employment and Society*, vol.15, no.1, pp 127-148.

Labour Force Survey (1999), *Seasonally Adjusted Historical Supplement 1992-1999*, United Kingdom, Office of National Statistics.

Payne, J. and Payne, C. (1993), 'Unemployment and peripheral work', in *Work, Employment and Society*, vol.7, no.4, pp.513-534.

Peck, J. (1996), *Work Place: The Social Regulation of Labour Markets*, London, The Guilford Press.

Philpott, J. (1999), 'Temporary jobs, constant opportunity? flexibility, fairness and the role of employment agencies', in *Economic Report*, vol.14, no.3.

Pollock, G. (1998), 'Qualifications and employment in Britain: a longitudinal analysis', in Thomas Lange (ed.), *Understanding the School to Work Transition: An International Perspective*, New York, Nova Science Publishers.

Pollock, G., Antcliff, V. and Ralphs, R. (2001), 'Work orders: analysing employment histories using sequence data', forthcoming, in *Social Research Methodology, Theory and Practice*.

Roberts, K. (1968), 'The entry into employment: an approach towards a general theory', in *Sociological Review*, vol.16, pp.165-184.

Roberts, K., Clark, S. and Wallace, C. (1994), 'Flexibility and individualism: a comparison of transitions into employment in England and Germany', in *Sociology*, vol.28, no.1.

Rubery, J. (1997), 'What do women want from full-employment', in Philpott, J. (ed.), *Working for full-employment*, London, Routledge.

Sennet, R. (1998), *The Corrosion of Character*, London, W. W. Norton and Company.

Stovel, K., Savage, M. and Bearman, P. (1996), 'Ascription into achievement: models of career systems at Lloyds Bank, 1890-1970', in *American Journal of Sociology*, vol.102, no.2.

West, M. and Newton, P. (1983), *The Transition from School to Work*, London, Croom Helm.

Wynne, D. (1998), *Leisure, Lifestyle and the New Middle-Class*, London, Routledge.

Index

active Citizenship 5, 121
adulthood as the norm 107
adventure education 23, 27
alternative careers 10, 109

bail hostels 28-30
Beck, U. 1-9, 26, 36-8, 43, 61, 105, 138, 163, 173
Bennett, A. 7, 41, 44, 48, 54, 78, 84
bricolage 89

Cartmel, F. 8, 11, 13, 26, 43, 58, 101, 122, 138, 173
Centre for Contemporary Cultural Studies (CCCS) 41, 62, 77
Cieslik, M. 5, 10, 14
club cultures 41, 74-5, 85
cohabitation 101, 112, 139, 154
communitarianism 120
Csikszentmihalyi, M. 36
cultural flows 11, 81-3, 90
culturalization 11

detraditionalization 3-5, 122
Douglas, M. 2

education 5-12, 25, 46, 60, 77, 101, 117-120
employability 6, 120-121, 127, 159
employment
    full 161, 171
    part-time 160, 165
    self 161, 165
    under 159-173

flexible specialization 160
Foucault M. 11
Furlong, A. 8, 11, 13, 26, 43, 58, 101, 122, 138, 173

Giddens, A. 2-4, 14, 26, 35-8, 43, 56, 120, 138, 154, 162
global club cultures 75
globalization 10-13, 80, 93-4, 122

human capital 159

illicit drugs 41-6, 49-54
individualization 7-12, 26, 66, 108, 112, 122-3, 172-3
interpretative communities 78

learning society 127

MacDonald, R. 1, 8, 42, 59, 65, 101, 113, 121
management of risk 28, 31
Miles, S. 7, 12, 32, 41, 44, 48, 58-60, 80

neo-tribes 12
new deal 6, 16, 117-8, 120-132
normalization 42, 52-3, 93

ontological insecurity 4, 14
outward bound 25

personal development 24
Pollock, G. 9, 122, 167
post fordist 91, 159
post modernity 7, 43, 46, 79
post structuralist 11
postsubculturalists 79

rave 85
reflexive modernization 103, 107
reflexiveness 3
risk 2-4, 12, 22-4, 26, 58-62, 93, 103, 117, 125, 138, 159-163
risk society 2-4, 12-16, 70-2, 95, 117, 125, 159, 163, 170
risk-taking 24, 36-7
Roberts, K. 8-11, 25-6, 55, 66, 122, 172-3

self-identity 26, 33-8
sexuality 10, 102, 109, 155
social exclusion unit 119
structure-Agency 12

Structured individualization 133, 173
subcultural Theory 11

third way 1, 4, 13, 117, 120, 125, 132, 159
transformation of intimacy 138, 140
transgressive identities 10
tribus 79
trust 3, 7, 22, 35-8, 143

unemployment 60, 105, 117, 132, 159, 165
upskilling 139

welfare to work 118

workfare 121

Youth
   cultures 7-15, 41, 54, 63-4, 76-80, 94, 117
   crime 6
   employment 60
   identities 11, 44
   labour market 160
   lifestyles 14, 41, 65-71,
   research 1, 7, 11, 15-17, 43, 59, 100, 109-112,
   subculture 11, 63, 77
   transitions 7-10, 43, 64, 100-103, 118-123
   unemployment 61, 117-119, 159